W9-BBH-365

A SHEARWATER BOOK

A

NATURAL

HISTORY

OF

NATURE

WRITING

1995

A
Natural
History
of
Nature
Writing

FRANK STEWART

ISLAND PRESS / Shearwater Books
Washington, D.C. / Covelo, California

A Shearwater Book
published by Island Press

Shearwater Books is a trademark of
The Center for Resource Economics.

Library of Congress Cataloging-in-Publication Data

Stewart, Frank, 1946–
    A natural history of nature writing / Frank Stewart.
    p.   cm.
    Includes bibliographical references and index.
    ISBN 1-55963-278-X (cloth). — ISBN 1-55963-279-8 (pbk.)
    1. American prose literature—History and criticism.   2. Natural
history—United States—Historiography.   3. Nature in literature.
I. Title.
PS163.S74   1995
810.9'36—dc20   94-29330
                                                              CIP

Printed on recycled, acid-free paper

Manufactured in the United States of America

10 9 8 7 6 5 4 3 2 1

For my mother and father,

for Cal and Paloma,

and for Chloe

ACKNOWLEDGMENTS

My thanks foremost to Howard Boyer, whose encouragement, love of nature writing, and good judgment from the beginning have been of immeasurable help in completing this book. I thank Pat Matsueda for patiently and expertly reading drafts and suggesting ways to compress a complex history; Tom Farber for, among other gifts, a writer's friendship; and Kathy Matsueda for proofreading and technical assistance. Ann Hawthorne provided keen, superb copyediting, for which I am most grateful.

Finally, I can hardly begin to thank Lisa Erb, because of whom, as Thoreau said, "I have never got over my surprise that I should have been born into the most estimable place in all the world, and in the very nick of time."

CONTENTS

A

NATURAL

HISTORY

OF

NATURE

WRITING

PROLOGUE

In a recent letter, the poet Nick Bozanic reminded me that in medieval times there was a favorite torture cabinet called, in English, "the little ease." The box was constructed in such a way that, inside it, the imprisoned victim could neither stand up nor lie down. Instead, his agony was to be always uncomfortably in between. Over time the hapless victim's inability to straighten himself out caused him untold discomfort and, eventually, a spirit-breaking agony and, finally, madness.

In the unhappy genius of this box is a metaphor for most Americans' relation to what we call Nature. The lack of ease, the "disease," in our culture is that we can neither quite stand among nor quite lie down peacefully with our fellow creatures. We feel neither entirely one with them nor entirely separate.

Nature writers have become increasingly important to us because they struggle, in memorable language, to resolve the deep issue of this in-betweenness, a resolution crucial to the physical and spiritual survival of our world. From their own direct experiences they are aware of the limits of both objectivity and subjectivity in giving accurate accounts of nature that will grip our emotional as well as rational understanding. They pursue this understanding with an avidity for fact accessible only through the scientific method and with a passion for metaphors, patterns, feelings, and self-awareness accessible only through poetry and art. In this way, they seek to make our minds and our hearts whole again. When we look at nature, they believe, we are looking mainly at ourselves. They make us aware of a kind of knowing that is potential in us but that we are apt to ignore or suppress, as though half-asleep. There are many parts to our cognitive selves, they believe, and few of us are attentive enough to the most luminous facets of our being.

Nature writers show us that our in-betweenness can be both harmful and good and they make us conscious of the potential conflict. Although they do not hesitate to express their fears, they are in some fundamental way optimistic. Like Henry David Thoreau, whose work is the model for their form of literary expression, in the midst of their doubts they are moved by the joyous, wild, and dazzling beauty in the world. Its factualness. Its tangibleness. And that joy leads them to explore whether we can achieve a conjunction with nature in the future as profound as our disjunction has been in the recent past.

Nature writing is the pursuit of the seeable and the unseeable. It is an attempt to give voice to "the corn and the grass and the atmosphere writing," as Thoreau asserted, to speak for what cannot speak. It is also an attempt to transform us in a way that seems impossible but is essential if we are to realize, in a biologically diverse world, a future that is moral and compassionate.

Not everyone who has been called a "nature writer" has been pleased with the designation. Edward Abbey, for example, was uncomfortable with the name when he thought it pinioned the wings he tried to give his work or corralled him into being something he was not. Two of the characters in his *Desert Solitaire* discuss the human propensity for labeling things and attempt to determine whether naming is always necessary.

"Why call them anything at all?" asks Bob Waterman, turning to his friend Ranger Abbey. The two are building a cook fire in the desert sundown near southern Utah's Elaterite Butte, smoking cigars, and looking toward the horizon at a formation of as-yet-unnamed sandstone spires and mesas. Through these geologic forms glowing in the last light of day, a tributary of the Colorado River has cut a deep labyrinth of canyons called The Maze. The canyon walls cast serpentine patterns of dark and light on the land.

"Why not let them alone?" Waterman asks again.

Abbey, although he has just moments before been thinking of various high-flown names for the spires, agrees. "The itch for naming things is almost as bad as the itch for possessing things," he concedes. And yet, he quickly maintains, "if we don't name them somebody else surely will."

"Then," says Waterman, certain that naming the geologic formations is pointless, "let the shame be on their heads."

Abbey vacillates. He turns to Waterman again. "Rilke said that things don't truly exist until the poet gives them names," he asserts.

"Who was Rilke?" asks Waterman.

"Rainer Maria Rilke was a German poet who lived off countesses."

"I thought so; that explains it."

Ranger Abbey sees the logic of Waterman's response but is still unable to let the problem go. "Through naming comes knowing," he urges. "We grasp an object, mentally, by giving it a name—hension, prehension, apprehension. And thus through language create a whole world, corresponding to the other world out there. Or we trust that it corresponds. Or perhaps, like a German poet, we cease to care, becoming more concerned with the naming than with the things named; the former becomes more real than the latter. And so in the end the world is lost again. No, the world remains—those unique, particular, incorrigibly individual junipers and sandstone monoliths—and it is we who are lost. Again. Round and round, through the endless labyrinth of thought—the maze."

"Amazing," says Waterman, going to sleep.

———————

Barry Lopez, one of the leading living practitioners of the nature-writing form, has also occasionally balked at the name. In a 1990 interview in *Bloomsbury Review* he suggested that sometimes the label tends to be confining and reductive, that it fails to convey the essence of what essayists like himself are about. "The way I understand the world is through natural history, geography, and anthropology." But Lopez is concerned with more than these subjects. "These disciplines are my metaphors," he explained; he uses them to take the reader into other issues, including the issue of how we are to find a just and dignified relationship with one another and the place where we live.

Gary Nabhan, a conservation scientist in Arizona, is another who emphasizes the importance of nature writing as a window onto our humanity and an aid to understanding the "otherness" of the nonhuman world. Nature writing, Nabhan asserts in his recent anthology *Counting Sheep*, is not only an attempt to record habitats and creatures in order to make them vivid in the minds of readers but also a way to demonstrate respect for the experiences of lives that are not our own, whether human or nonhuman. Such respect goes to the heart of our humanity. Nature writers, Nabhan states, "keep our tendencies toward ethnocentrism and anthropocentrism from becoming all-consuming. Without them, our society would become incapable of reading the signs that we have irreparably damaged our life-support system."

It is not surprising that essayists engaged in such a complex task might chafe at being assigned to what might sound like a minor, rather simplistic genre. But what to call their enterprise will be less worrisome, I think, as readers learn more about what distinguishes their work from other kinds of essays. Perhaps another term will be invented. For now, though, the name "nature writing" does their work injustice only if it designates no more than a vague appreciation for nature, pastoral sentimentality, or purely subjective musings.

I use the term in this book to suggest far more than handbooks and trail guides, travelogues and private jottings—although these forms, too, deserve their place in the spectrum. Nabhan characterizes nature writing's higher ambition as "the combining of the two cultures of humanistic art and technical science into a seamless view of culture and nature interacting." And he makes a plea for openness. "The result may take the form of beautifully detailed notes from a scientist who has fallen into 'the naturalist's trance' that biologist E. O. Wilson so aptly described. Or it may sound like a story shaped by a novelist, an ethnographic sketch roughed out by an anthropologist, or a quirky feature forged by a gonzo journalist."

Whatever forms it takes, nature writing at its best is a literary art as rigorous as natural science, with a similar allegiance to verifiable fact. As literary artists, nature writers interpret and vivify their observations through aesthetic language. More important, they are mindful of the role that storytelling and dramatic narration play in our psychic and cultural well-being. This awareness makes their best writing as expressive, as rigorous, and as carefully structured as a novel or a poem.

Whether scientists or poets, nature writers make us aware that neither biology nor imagination by itself can illuminate the call of the last American timber wolf, the tossing meadow grasses in a mountain rainstorm, the strangely shining organisms that cruise the deep oceans, or the sweet tumbling notes of a thrush. But both disciplines, working together, may give us a new, more powerful lens of perception. "And that is the way I would like to suggest the fiery circle of science and humanities could be closed and creativity in the two branches of learning might converge," E. O. Wilson observed in Edward Lueders' collection of dialogues, *Writing Natural History*, "through natural history and nature writing of the kind that may well be emerging into its twenty-first-century form."

My purpose in the following pages is not to take the reader far into the maze of naming and defining that Ranger Abbey and his friend

Bob Waterman warned about. For that, the reader is encouraged to
follow those scholars who over the past half-century have mulled
over the taxonomy of nature writing and its possible subspecies.
In particular, Philip H. Hicks, Joseph Wood Krutch, and, more recently, John Hildebidle and Peter Fritzell have opened our minds
to fresh perspectives.

Although these scholars have their differences, all of them regard Henry David Thoreau as the originator of nature writing in
America. Thoreau wanted not only to see nature accurately but
also to see "the nature of nature," an enterprise that involves embracing the knowledge of humanists, poets, and artists. Joseph
Wood Krutch noted that Thoreau's work is "not 'about' plants or
animals or birds"; rather, "it is about his relation with them; one
may almost say about 'himself in connection with nature.'" Observing nature, Thoreau knew, was an activity inseparable from
observing himself—scrutinizing not only his mind as it perceived
the world but also his language, which he understood to be one of
the most powerful instruments of perception. Thoreau forged a
new kind of prose to help him see, combining scientific modes of
discourse with a personal voice and subtle narrative intentions.

In *Walden*, as in much of his other work, Thoreau pursued
scientific discoveries, but his project was equally philosophical
and psychological. His writing was also aesthetic, ethical, and
spiritual, and this breadth is part of what made Thoreau's work
distinctive, laying the groundwork for a kind of American essay
striving to view the natural world in all its physical and cognitive
fullness.

Holding the very modern belief that knowing perceived phenomena requires knowing the perceiver, Thoreau was at times intensely self-conscious, self-reflexive, self-parodying, and contradictory. He loved to turn a proposition on its head to display it
from a new perspective, to explore a pun, a joke, or a metaphor
not only for fun but for a revelation about language and outlook
that could be got only by taking intellectual and spiritual risks.

He drew on the methods of empirical natural history while he plumbed what it means to be alive. Thoreau explored the notions of freedom, independence, and responsibility. He excluded no rhetorical form to get to the truth. As a result his work is replete with paradox, figurative language mixed with scientific fact, autobiography mixed with self-invention, and a melding of literary narratives that include travel, adventure, autobiography, biology, geology, and art history.

Not all nature writers share Thoreau's formal and stylistic idiosyncrasies, of course. But understanding Thoreau's place in the forefront of nature writing helps us to see the general outlines of a tradition—or, rather, a conversation—that is broad and inclusive, wide enough to contain the writing of botanists and entomologists, bee farmers and beef ranchers, explorers and novelists, physicians and literary critics, whether they are on safari in Africa, sitting on a barstool in Tucson, or gazing into the night from a high-rise in Manhattan. Their unifying characteristic is that, in the words of essayist Edward Hoagland, they "combine rhapsody with science and connect science with rhapsody."

This book tells the stories of some of those who over the last 150 years have contributed in especially important ways to this literary conversation called nature writing. Some of the best in that tradition are writing now, in midcareer, reshaping the form through vigorous experimentation and ever-greater inclusiveness, with increasingly cultural approaches and voices, and diverse definitions of nature. My focus is not these living writers, but instead the "natural history" of their work. I have mentioned some of them in the bibliography as a guide for interested readers.

All but one of the writers included here are Americans. That exception is Gilbert White (1720–1793). White has long been the model for what many people still associate with nature writing. Certainly, those who wrote about nature and landscape immediately after White, including Thoreau, were measured, in style and content, in accuracy and in humility, against the gentle curate of

Selborne. We can better understand Thoreau and those after him by seeing how Thoreau deliberately differentiated himself from White.

Henry David Thoreau (1817–1862) is the touchstone throughout. Thoreau's writing continues to reveal its subtlety and relevance year after year as readers look more and more closely into his life and work. His enterprise was continued in each of the major authors who followed him, as each discovered in reaction or emulation his or her own ways to clarify, articulate, and express humanity's relation to the rest of the planet.

John Burroughs (1837–1921) heightened people's awareness of the small and familiar natural creatures at their doorsteps. He transformed them into subjects that a broad cross-section of readers could care deeply for and sympathize with. His enormously popular writing prepared millions of Americans, especially young ones, to see the natural world as worthy of preservation for its intrinsic interest alone, but also for its relation to the divine. And he elevated the nature essay into a much-loved and respected literary form.

John Muir (1813–1914), Burroughs' contemporary, avoided the well-worn Eastern landscapes and instead took his readers into the trackless mountains of California, celebrating the wilderness of the Far West as few before him had—the violent storms and the high glaciered peaks along with the small grasses and wildflowers. Muir insisted on a respect for the rights of all creation. He explored the spiritual need for freedom and solitude, then out of social responsibility threw himself into a bitter public debate at a national level.

In the middle of the twentieth century Aldo Leopold (1887–1948) wrote a single, deeply felt book that motivated readers to reexamine the range of creatures that ought to arouse their ethical concern. He extended our sense of moral responsibility to include animals and plants, the entire biota of what he called The Land;

and he argued persuasively for the importance of aesthetics to a complete understanding of ecology.

Rachel Carson (1907–1964) raised the consciousness of the nation through her respect for life in the sea and her awareness of how entwined the human and nonhuman worlds have become. Using a blend of science and storytelling, she revealed how disruptions caused by human intervention in the environment can have catastrophic effects throughout the Earth's living systems.

Most recently, Edward Abbey (1927–1989) demonstrated that the rape and destruction of the West are still going on. His language liberated nature writing from an overly serious style and repetitious formulas. He took risks with the narrative voice and explored the contradictions and connections between private freedom and wilderness. Like many of his predecessors, he charted new boundaries of ecological responsibility; unlike most of them, he tied these boundaries closely to political action. At the same time, his humor, expansive love, and storytelling gifts carried his wakeup call to a wide and appreciative audience.

These and other nature writers have made the world larger and richer by giving us ways of seeing with our hearts and imaginations as well as with our eyes. As Thoreau often said, "we have not seen a thing until we have felt it." Through their literary art they have made us feel not only the beauty and divinity of the natural world but also a new sense of community, and thereby a greater sense of our responsibility to all of creation—the living world— the human and the nonhuman.

Chapter One

A HOUND, A BAY HORSE,

AND A TURTLEDOVE

One of the most famous and most written-about passages in *Walden* is also one of the most puzzling. It appears in the first chapter, "Economy," where it stumped readers in Thoreau's own time and remains a riddle for many today.

Thoreau wrote: "I long ago lost a hound, a bay horse, and a turtledove, and am still on their trail. Many are the travelers I have spoken concerning them, describing their tracks and what calls they answered to. I have met one or two who had heard the hound, and the tramp of the horse, and even seen the dove disappear behind a cloud, and they seemed as anxious to recover them as if they had lost them themselves."

Commentators have offered many explanations for the parable of the lost creatures. John Burroughs, at the turn of the century, suggested that Thoreau was talking about some essence of nature that he was reluctant to name. Francis H. Allen, an early editor of *Walden* and of Thoreau's journals, thought that he was creating a metaphor for the vague desires residing within all of us for the spiritual aspects of nature. Henry Seidel Canby, Thoreau's early biographer, saw the passage as a quest for a spiritual reality behind and beyond nature.[1] William Howarth speculates that the hound, the bay horse, and the dove were metaphors for "the losses all men must endure." He suggests that Thoreau may have been thinking of the Hindu transmigration of souls, about which he had recently been reading.[2] Other writers have interpreted the passage as a coded reference to certain friendships in Thoreau's life, to unrequited love affairs, to his dead older brother, to an alleged homosexual encounter, and to any number of other things.[3]

Although some of these explanations are far-fetched, their authors were right in believing that Thoreau loved metaphors and parables. He enjoyed producing twists upon a subject through analogical reasoning, examining phenomena this way and that, viewing them from every perspective, including linguistic ones. At the same time, much of what he had to say interpreted the materials of his own life. In his journal in May 1853, just before his thirty-sixth birthday, Thoreau wrote, "Some incidents in my life have seemed far more allegorical than actual; they were so significant that they plainly served no other use . . . they have been like myths or passages in a myth."[4]

In addition to what the parable of the three lost animals might have meant to him in terms of his own tragedies, hopes, and disappointments—and it clearly refers to some essence that he felt moving through nature—there is another way to understand Thoreau's hound, bay horse, and dove, one that may illuminate the method of his nature writing and the way that nature writers after him have also looked at the world.

In the paragraph before the passage about the three lost animals, Thoreau wrote, "If I should attempt to tell how I have desired to spend my life in years past, it would probably surprise those of my readers who are somewhat acquainted with its actual history; it would certainly astonish those who know nothing about it . . . You will pardon some obscurities, for there are more secrets in my trade than in most men's, and yet not voluntarily kept, but inseparable from its very nature. I will gladly tell all that I know about it, and never paint 'No Admittance' on my gate."

Taking Thoreau's words literally—something we must do as often as we take them figuratively and playfully—we can infer that his parable refers not only to *what* he sought in nature and what he might have missed, but also to the *methods* of his enterprise—how he went about hearing an essence in the vocalizing wind, in snowstorms and torrents, and how he sought discoveries on forest paths and on his saunterings across the woodlots of his neighbors. In writing *Walden*, and by carefully preserving the forty-seven manuscript volumes of his journal, spanning twenty-four years and comprising two million words, it appears that Thoreau meant to hold back no secrets in the accounts he faithfully kept of the red huckleberry, the sand cherry, the white grape, and the yellow violet. His fellow townspeople may have had no faith in his work, but he would not place a "No Admittance" sign on it—although to pass through his gate requires of the guest more tolerance for surprise than many have been prepared to endure.

Before considering the three parts of his method as revealed in Thoreau's parable, we should note several general aspects of his trade that are also mentioned there. One of these is that the three animals are pursued out of doors, out in the world, "in any weather, at any hour of the day or night," as Thoreau himself put it in *Walden*, so that he might find them at "the meeting of two eternities, the past and future, which is precisely the present moment." At this meeting point of so many contrary figures, Thoreau spent his life "trying to hear what was in the wind, to hear and carry it express!" And if he missed it on the lower pathways, he was willing to climb, if necessary, so that he might stand "at other times watching from the observatory of some cliff or tree, to telegraph any new arrival; or waiting at evening on the hill-tops for the sky to fall, that I might catch something, though I never caught much, and that, manna-wise, would dissolve again in the sun."

Above all, Thoreau desired to record events as a firsthand witness. This quality alone differentiated him from a good many natural scientists of his age, as much as it set him apart from the dreamers and "sublimo-slipshod" poets, as he called them, who, he felt, had very little real nature in their verse. He did not wish to learn "by inference and deduction and the application of mathematics to philosophy, but by direct intercourse and sympathy" with the facts of the natural world as he found them.[5] By wanting to front nature directly, he separated himself not only from philosophers in their studies but also from literary men in their libraries.

For Thoreau to practice his trade as he wished, being in the field was not only a practical requirement but a moral necessity. He noted in his journal in 1851, "How vain it is to sit down to write when you have not stood up to live! Methinks that the moment my legs begin to move, my thoughts begin to flow, as if I had given vent to the stream at the lower end and consequently new fountains flowed into it at the upper." Writing based only on book learning was likely to miss the point, he said. "Only while we are in action is the circulation perfect. The writing which consists with habitual sitting is mechanical, wooden, dull to read."[6]

Another important aspect of this writing enterprise, as revealed in his riddle, was that it somehow involved a commitment to his neighbors, who, although they often misunderstood him, were willing to lead him to his best thoughts, even when they did not know it. This may seem surprising, given Thoreau's reputation as a recluse. But we should remember that according to the narrator himself, *Walden*, though allegedly composed "alone, in the woods, a mile from any neighbor," would not have come about at all "if very particular inquiries had not been made by my townsmen concerning my mode of life."

In the first paragraph of the chapter in *Walden* titled "The Village," Thoreau wrote, "Every day or two I strolled to the village to hear some of the gossip which is incessantly going on there, circulating either from mouth to mouth, or from newspaper to newspaper, and which, taken in homeopathic doses, was really as refreshing in its way as the rustle of leaves and the peeping of frogs.

As I walked to the woods to see the birds and squirrels, so I walked in the village to see the men and boys." Similarly, early in his journal writing, Thoreau wondered, "What if a man were earnestly and wisely to set about recollecting and preserving the thoughts which he has had! How many perchance are now irrecoverable!" But they might not be lost if one might "call in his neighbors to aid him."[7] Two months earlier he had confided to his journal, "I wonder that I ever get five miles on my way, the walk is so crowded with events and phenomena. How many questions there are which I have not put to the inhabitants!"[8]

In his journal Thoreau tells a story of a certain wild azalea bush that he found in the local woods with the help of a reluctant neighbor. Despite his daily wanderings, Thoreau had never seen this conspicuously beautiful flower in Concord until one day his sister, Sophia, brought the blossom home on a single stem. Sophia had got it from Mrs. Brooks, who had got a sprig from her son George, who had got a bunch from Thoreau's neighbor George Melvin. Having traced its source this far, and after inquiring of others who had obtained similar sprigs from Melvin within the past few days, Thoreau went to Melvin's house. He discovered the young man in the early afternoon shade by the backdoor, still nursing a hangover. Wasting no time, he abruptly asked Melvin where he had found the bloom he had given Mrs. Brooks' son.

Perhaps because it was so rare for anyone to find a plant that Thoreau had not seen, Melvin teasingly decided not to tell his naturalist neighbor where he had found the blazing pink flowers he called "red honeysuckle." "Well, you better tell me where it is," Thoreau pressed him. "I'm a botanist and ought to know." When this assertion of authority had no effect, Thoreau tried another ploy. He told Melvin that his nose was as keen as a hound's, and that once he had crossed the river, where he suspected the azalea was, he would be able to smell the flower's sweet fragrance from half a mile away. And so he would find it anyway, and Melvin would get none of the credit for it.

Thus persuaded, Melvin called his dog, and the three crossed the brook, made their way through the woods, and found the beautiful shrub of rosy-pink blooms growing in the shade of a large stand of trees like laurel. As a good botanist, Thoreau described the plant precisely in his journal. But he also noted the implications to the community of what he was seeing. When "a rare and beautiful flower which we never saw, perhaps never heard of, for which therefore there was no place in our thoughts, may at length be found in our immediate neighborhood," he wrote, "the limits of the actual" are proved to be but "a thin and undulating drapery," and "no more fixed and rigid than the elasticity of our imaginations."[9] Thoreau would find other rare plants, creatures, and phenomena, but this one came to him by way of George Melvin, not by his own efforts, and in his journal he gave that neighbor credit—hangover notwithstanding—for his sweet discovery.

What, then, might Thoreau's passage about the hound, bay horse, and dove tell us about his method of seeing and writing about nature—about his trade secrets?

In the chapter "Winter Animals" in *Walden*, Thoreau tells a story about hounds. A pack of them, hunting on their own for a fox, found his cabin and "would pass my door, and circle round my house, and yelp and hound without regarding me, as if afflicted by a species of madness, so that nothing could divert them from the pursuit . . . Thus they circle until they fall upon the recent trail of a fox, for a wise hound will forsake every thing for this." These hounds kept their noses close to the ground, focused on the minute data there, the local details, as had Melvin's dog on the trail of the wild azaleas. Like the best of their kind, they were "empirical" and "objective"; they were in pursuit of facts and would not be turned aside until they had found their fox.

Thoreau admired the hounds' "species of madness" because he could be just as single-minded. In the chapter called "Higher Laws," he wrote that, once or twice when he lived at the pond, "I found myself ranging the woods, like a half-starved hound, with a strange abandonment, seeking some kind of venison which I might devour, and no morsel could have been too savage for me."

But of course there is more than one kind of hound. Before publishing *Walden*, Thoreau remarked in his journal on a passage from William Gilpin, the English traveler and art theorist, who mentioned the old practice of "lawing" or "expedition." These forest terms referred to cutting out the sole of a dog's foot or removing two of its claws in order to hobble it so that the dog was unable to overtake and kill deer in forests that belonged to the king. Gilpin had written that only greyhounds that had been "lawed" were allowed within ten miles of certain woods. "It reminds me of the majority of human hounds that tread the forest paths of this world," Thoreau commented; "they go slightly limping in their gait, as if disqualified by a cruel fate to overtake the nobler game of the forest, their natural quarry. Most men are such dogs. Ever and anon starting a quarry, with perfect scent, which, from this cruel maiming and disqualification of the fates, he is incapable of coming up with. Does not the noble dog shed tears?"

Thoreau's hounds, his determined pursuers of fact, then, are of several sorts. Besides those whose natures bestow on them a species of madness, with an instinct for savage prey of woodchuck and fox, there is a "noble" hound able to locate a swifter quarry and to overtake it. And he himself, Thoreau noted, had been yet another kind of hound at times for the people of Concord. As he wrote in "Economy," just after presenting the metaphor of the lost hound, bay horse, and dove, "I have looked after the wild stock of the town, which give a faithful herdsman a good deal of trouble by leaping fences; and I have had an eye to the unfrequented nooks and corners of the farm."

Although Thoreau was always preoccupied with being outdoors, with the nourishment of visions that come from traveling abroad and observing closely, he was also concerned with the scale at which he should be observing in order to see most accurately. He was concerned with not being confined by too close an observation, lest he see nothing at all of essence. As Thoreau's biographer Robert Richardson notes of this period in his life, just as he undertook yet another total reshaping of *Walden*, Thoreau began "growing more afraid of subsiding into trivial detail," of losing himself in close observation. Thoreau saw the necessity for a balance between fact and idea, detail and ideal. "I fear that the character of my knowledge is from year to year becoming more distinct and scientific," Thoreau wrote; "that, in exchange for views as wide as heaven's cope, I am being narrowed down to the field of the microscope. I see details, not wholes nor the shadow of the whole. I count some parts, and say, 'I know.'"[10]

During these months Thoreau read more and more widely— travel books as well as natural history—looking closely for a way to harmonize the outward movement of the mind with the inward, in order to make what he called the "marriage of the soul with Nature that makes the intellect fruitful, that gives birth to imagination." Richardson notes that Cato's *rem tene verba sequentur* could well have been Thoreau's motto: Grasp the thing; words will follow.[11] The danger that lay in the method of the hound, it was clear to Thoreau, was that although the hound—like the taxonomist and the species hunter—could grasp a thing well enough, the hound's perspective involved too much concern with detail, and perhaps lost something vital thereby. Thoreau wished to know accurately the close at hand; he was a practical man who could design machines to make pencils, and he made a living as a skilled surveyor. But he wished also to travel beyond and through what was nearby to a more general observation, to relationships, and to synthesis. "My practicalness is not to be trusted to the last," Thoreau said to his journal. "To be sure, I go upon my legs for the most part, but, being hard-pushed and dogged by a superficial common sense which is bound to near objects by beaten paths, I am off the handle, as the phrase is,—I begin to be transcendental and show where my heart is."[12]

All during July of 1851, the year he turned thirty-four, Thoreau was eager for his heart to be allowed far afield, where it wanted to wander. To break out of old habits he began to write in the afternoon instead of in the morning. "When we may so easily, it behooves us to break up this custom of sitting in the house, for it is but a custom, and I am not sure that it has the sanction of common sense," he wrote. "Is the literary man to live always or chiefly sitting in a chamber through which nature enters by a window only? What is the use of the summer?"[13]

Thus it seems that the second of the figures in his parable, the bay horse, involved, as Thoreau put it time after time, "wandering toward the more distant boundaries of a wider pasture" and thereby approaching, in some measure, a more adequate truth, less tangible than the hound's and less savage, perhaps, but no less participative in the world. Unlike the hound, the bay horse will leap across open fields in order to graze a wider area, to range across gullies and divisions in the landscape, places that the hounds, in their determined quest for the fox, never discover.

In a long essay that he began to shape during this period, later titled "Walking," Thoreau praised the virtues of sauntering into the countryside, not with some practical goal in mind such as taking exercise or reaching some specific destination, but for no other reason than to abandon the roads and lose one's way in the woods. "I am a good horse to travel," he says of his brand of walking, "but not from choice a roadster."

Thoreau's identification with the horse is a central image in this most pivotal and representative of his essays. "Walking" contains his most famous apothegm—"in Wildness is the preservation of the World"—which has become the cornerstone of the modern conservation ethic. An important part of what Thoreau meant about wildness in this essay is suggested by the horse—a creature wild by nature, but whose wildness is not like that of, say, the tiger, which lives far from mankind. The horse may have a "high use" in the company of humans. The horse is a creature that might carry pilgrims on their quests to the Holy Land. A horse's in-betweenness, its double nature, both wild and useful to man, is "but a faint symbol of the awful ferity with which good men and lovers meet," Thoreau said.

"I rejoice that horses and steers have to be broken before they can be made the slaves of men," he wrote later in the essay, "and that men themselves have some wild oats still to sow before they become submissive members of society. Undoubtedly, all men are not equally fit subjects for civilization; and because the majority, like dogs and sheep, are tame by inherited disposition, this is no reason why the others should have their natures broken that they may be reduced to the same level."

The bay horse for all its in-betweenness keeps close to the Earth, usefully attached to the land, no matter how wild the horse's nature. Its practicalness appealed to Thoreau, but there was also a part of him that wanted to take wing, to break free of his usefulness. And this is the third part of the nature writer's trade as Thoreau may have been explaining it.

Many kinds of birds take flight in *Walden*, just as there are many kinds of hounds and horses, and it would be incorrect and reductive to say that Thoreau discussed any of these creatures only to make an analogy to the writer's imagination. Still, Thoreau's explicit quest was to discover how his self, his language, and nature, all three, might in the words of critic William C. Johnson, Jr., be "mutually informing 'works' groping for expression," and "that meaning, as it manifests itself in time and form, reveals the nature of life as the interpretive enterprise."[14]

The dove in Thoreau's parable—at least in its soaring—might be compared to the hawk that he described in his journal and later in *Walden*. "Circling and ever circling, you cannot divine which way it will incline . . . It rises higher above where I stand, and I see with beautiful distinctness its wings against the sky,—primaries and secondaries, and the rich tracery of the outline of the latter (?), its inner wings, or wing-linings, within the outer,—like a great moth seen against the sky. A will-o'-the-wind."[15] The hawk appears in the chapter of *Walden* called "The Beanfield," in which Thoreau notes how the bird reveals the "kindredship" of earth and sky, wing and water, world and mind. Seeing the bird soar above the pond he wrote, "The hawk is aerial brother of the wave which he sails over and surveys, those his perfect air-inflated wings answering to the elemental unfledged pinions of the sea. Or sometimes I watched a pair of hen-hawks circling high in the sky, alternately soaring and descending, approaching and leaving one another, as if they were the embodiment of my own thoughts."

Soaring and descending, approaching and leaving one another, lost and found, Thoreau's hound, bay horse, and turtledove all travel together; they are all in an essential way kin to one another and to Thoreau and his way of seeing and understanding nature. They remind us of another of Thoreau's three-part descriptions of the writer, one which I will return to again: "A writer, a man writing, is the scribe of all nature; he is the corn and the grass and the atmosphere writing. It is always essential that we love to do what we are doing, do it with heart."[16]

Over the years, Thoreau has been misunderstood most often by those who would reduce him to some fraction of his calling or to some fraction of what he meant. He has been called a poor naturalist, a poor imitation of Emerson, a poor sensualist, a half-hearted pantheist. For the most part such characterizations have resulted from an incomplete understanding of Thoreau's process of perpetually seeking a truth in nature and a way to render it that would betray neither nature nor language. As he told Emerson in a youthful letter, "in writing conversation should be folded many times thick. It is the height of art that on the first perusal plain common sense should appear—on the second severe truth—and on a third beauty—and having these warrants for its depth and reality, we may then enjoy the beauty forever more."[17] Thoreau here was remarking in yet another context how a subject should be pursued, then folded at least three ways. After such folding, the truth that emerges will not be a simple certainty, any more than the parable of the hound, the bay horse, and the turtle-dove will be unraveled into merely an analogy for nature writing. "We Yankees are not so far from right, who answer one question by asking another," Thoreau asserted in an early journal entry. "Yes and No are lies. A true answer will not aim to establish anything, but rather to set all well afloat."[18]

Our own time, self-consciously cognizant of how unstable received truths may be, has understood Thoreau better than his own, particularly his riddling paradoxes and his enormous ambition to give pursuit to the intangible within nature and ourselves. And this may be because we have come to need him even more than earlier generations did. He speaks profoundly to the modern urgency to see the world whole again—to see it as phenomenal and mysterious while understanding it factually; to comprehend nature while including ourselves within it; to empathize with a myriad of human and nonhuman perspectives. As Johnson says, "Thoreau demands that we read not only with empirical eyes, but with eyes that see through surfaces so that intuition can inform the logic of intellect. We are challenged to rediscover that what we see and measure depends on what we look for and how we look. If the world, especially the world of nature, is largely mysterious, then we will need an especially sensitive instrument to know it . . . To track the hound, horse, and dove becomes another metaphor for the arduous unlocking of secrets, textual and existential, in the reintegrative quest for whatever wholeness is possible in one life, one reading."[19] I would add that this "arduous unlocking" can be successful only if it is fueled by a passion for life, a love for the world. In Thoreau's case, as in that of many nature writers, this passion has its foundation in diligent study and observation.

It is no accident that the first chapter of *Walden* is called "Economy." Thoreau knew well that the word derives in part from the Greek *oikos*, meaning *home*. His project was to make all of nature, including human nature, *eco*-nomical and *eco*-logical once again; that is, to make it a household in which all of life might dwell together. In Thoreau we recognize the urgency to reintegrate our fragmented selves and our fragmented world. And to do this we must, like hound, horse, and dove, become lost in the world and found again, to see with new eyes, to go in search of new possibilities for what matters in us and in nature, and to make the world home again.

Thoreau's paradoxical, relational way of seeing and writing, using the factual world of nature observed firsthand as his subject, but restored to its metaphorical and even mythical implications, has made him the model for an enterprise called, for better or worse, nature writing. Many writers who have come after Thoreau have found their kinship with one another through a kinship with him; the best of them—including those who, like Thoreau, might be "agreeably disappointed" with any label given them—have progressively refined and extended this particular type of conversation. Before considering them, however, it may be helpful to look at Thoreau's most influential predecessor, the gentle English naturalist named Gilbert White.

Chapter Two

TIMOTHY THE TORTOISE

When Rebecca Snookes died at age eighty-six in March 1780, her nephew Gilbert White was sincerely grieved. Ever since he was a child, White had been visiting his father's sister almost yearly. The visits turned into holidays as he got older. Members of the family would meet at and enjoy Aunt Rebecca's well-stocked Sussex household, renew friendships there, and celebrate an ever-enlarging clan of nieces and nephews, brothers and sisters, uncles and aunts.

But for all the sadness that the entire family felt over the elderly aunt's passing, the occasion was not without some good news for White. Aunt Rebecca left her nephew sole possession of a hefty old tortoise named Timothy that she had kept in her garden for nearly forty years.

Since his boyhood, White had carefully observed Timothy's behavior: what the old reptile ate, how often he fed, and the way he buried himself each year in hibernation. Everything about Timothy intrigued White. But of all the tortoise's behaviors, most striking was his ability to recognize Aunt Rebecca whenever she came into the garden; he hobbled toward her with "awkward alacrity," although Timothy paid no attention at all to strangers. In other respects, too, Timothy had a delicate, discerning nature. White observed, for instance, that although the tortoise had a shell so strong that he might be run over by a loaded cart without damage, at the first sign of rain Timothy would shuffle away like "a lady dressed in all her best attire" and hide his head in a corner of the garden wall until the sprinkle was over.[1]

Timothy was still in deep hibernation when Aunt Rebecca died, so White had to dig the tortoise out of his underground nest. He loaded the hissing creature into a box filled with dirt, placed him on the seat of his carriage, and trundled him eighty miles over rough roads to Selborne, White's home parish. Once released into the enclosed garden, Timothy dragged himself twice around the borders, sniffed the air, then stoically reburied himself in the leaves and earth to finish his winter sleep.

Gilbert White was born in Selborne in 1720. His father, John, married a woman with sufficient family money to allow him to retire as a barrister and move to the country, establishing a household that included his wife's parents. Gilbert was the first of eleven children who arrived in rapid succession. Several years after he was born, the expanding family moved into a rambling little country house called, after the previous owner, "the late Wake's," thereafter shortened to the Wakes. White loved this home and contrived to spend most of his adult life there. He eventually inherited it and slowly enlarged it until his death.

White's cheerful, tenderhearted temperament as an adult suggests a happy childhood. At age twenty he entered Oriel College, Oxford, where he read the classics, wrote poetry, and enjoyed riding, hunting birds, playing cards, and going to parties with his fellow undergraduates. However, since his large family had only modest means, he also kept careful records of his expenses. After graduating, White was elected a Fellow of the college, took a master's degree, was made a deacon, and within five years became an ordained priest. But he was not ambitious. More than a well-paying appointment he seems to have wanted to stay close to home. He took temporary curacies close to Selborne until age forty-one, when he settled into the curacy in a village two miles away. For the next twenty-three years he discharged his duties there while living at the Wakes. When the incumbent curate of Selborne died, Gilbert replaced him, remaining in this post until his own death at age seventy-two.

As the village curate, White presided over births, baptisms, and funerals and delivered occasional sermons. But his parish was small, and these duties left him ample time to pursue his lifelong interest in local animals and plants. Even as a boy White had kept records of birds and plants in and around his neighborhood, fascinated by what he called "natural knowledge" and "the life and conversation of animals." As an adult, White collected his daily observations in a formal journal that he maintained for twenty-six years, almost to the day of his death. He transcribed the best of these observations into the scrupulously restrained but magically affecting prose of his personal letters. Eventually White collected these letters, with extensive revision and reshaping, into a modest book published by his brother and called simply *The Natural History and Antiquities of Selborne.*

A small, prim, and courteous man, White was apparently well liked by his parishioners, who often saw him poking into hedges, hunting for birds' eggs, and spying on swifts and wood larks. He never married, but neither was he alone. His nephews and nieces—who at one point numbered sixty-two—gathered frequently with their friends and parents, and with White's friends and their children at the Wakes. There White entertained them with dances, games, hikes along the countryside paths, and inventive amusements that included experiments on Timothy.

During one of these large gatherings a young woman named Hester, the daughter of White's close college friend John Mulso, was so taken with Timothy that she wrote a long poem to the tortoise and read it to the guests. It tells us much about White's empathy with Timothy that White soon afterward forwarded a letter to the young woman allegedly written by Timothy himself. Addressed "From Timothy the Tortoise to Miss Hecky Mulso from the border under the fruit wall," it began with an apology: "It is my wish to answer you in your own way, but I never could make a verse in my life, so you must be contented with plain prose." In that plain prose, Timothy told Hecky Mulso his life story, as well as he knew it.[2]

"Know then that I am an American," the tortoise wrote, "and was born in the year 1734 in the Province of Virginia in the midst of a Savanna that lay between a large tobacco plantation and a creek of the sea. Here I spent my youthful days among my relations with much satisfaction, and saw around me many venerable kinsmen . . . Happy should I have been in the enjoyment of my native climate and the society of my friends had not a sea-boy, who was wandering about to see what he could pick up, surprised me as I was sunning myself under a bush; and whipping me into his wallet, carried me aboard his ship."

Timothy then described his kidnapping to England, being sold to Aunt Rebecca's husband for half a crown, and a giddy forty-mile horseback ride in a sack. The lady of the house treated him well, but Timothy recalled that when she died he was dug out of his winter retreat and whisked off to Selborne in White's carriage. "I was sore shaken by this expedition, which was the worst journey I ever experienced."

Timothy complained further about his experiences at the hands of his curious new master. Gilbert's experiments in the company of the nephews and nieces taxed him more than anything Aunt Rebecca had done to him. "For you must know that my master is what they call a *naturalist*, and much visited by people of that turn, who often put on whimsical experiments, such as feeling my pulse, putting me in a tub of water to try if I can swim, etc.; and twice in the year I was carried to the grocer's to be weighed, that it may be seen how much I am wasted during the months of my abstinence, and how much I gain by feasting in the summer. Upon these occasions I am placed in the scale on my back, where I sprawl about to the great diversion of the shopkeeper's children."

Timothy then confessed how desperately he wished to be with creatures of his own kind—especially each spring when the mating urge came upon him. "It was in the month of May last that I resolved to elope from my place of confinement," he wrote to Hecky, recounting his most recent attempt at escape, "for my fancy had represented to me that probably many agreeable tortoises of both sexes might inhabit the heights of Baker's Hill or the extensive plains of the neighbouring meadow." Timothy had watched for his opportunity, found the wicket open, and "escaped into the sainfoin, which began to be in bloom, and thence into the beans. I was missing eight days," he boasted.

But Timothy had found no other tortoises in the beans and woods outside the garden gate. Hungry and homesick, he at last surrendered himself to his keepers.

Timothy ended his letter with a plea for sympathy from Hecky Mulso. "Suppose you were to be kidnapped away *tomorrow,* in the bloom of your life," he wrote, "to a land of Tortoises, and were never to see again for fifty years a human face!!! Think on this, dear lady, and pity your sorrowful Reptile, Timothy."

These plaints notwithstanding, Timothy was well cared for and loved by White for the rest of his master's life. And White continued to sympathize with the tortoise's urge to mate. "Pitiable seems the condition of this poor embarrassed reptile," he wrote, "to be cased in a suit of ponderous armour, which he cannot lay aside." Each spring he would see Timothy walking "on tiptoe" and "stirring by five in the morning," apparently intent on "sexual attachments," understandable behavior for a creature "said to be a whole month in performing one feat of copulation" (although of course White never saw Timothy engaged in that feat).[3]

White himself was also deliberate and "most assiduous." Not until he was forty-nine did he begin to think about writing a book of natural history. The eminent zoologist Daines Barrington, with whom he had been corresponding, suggested that he produce "an account of the animals in your neighbourhood." Realizing the scale of such an undertaking, White was dubious. "Your partiality towards my small abilities persuades you, I fear, that I am able to do more than is in my power," he wrote Barrington. "For it is no small undertaking for a man, unsupported & alone, to enter upon a natural history from his own remarks." If a person wanted to be truly accurate in his reports, White continued, he would make "but slow progress: & all that one could collect in many years would go into a very narrow compass."[4]

The task seemed daunting to White for at least two other reasons. The first was that he was determined to write only about phenomena he could verify with his own eyes or through reliable witnesses, which would make the work go even more slowly. And second, White was not interested in writing merely a list of descriptions. If anything, he would write the "life & manners of animals [which] are the best part of Nat: history."[5]

The letter from Timothy to Hecky Mulso demonstrates White's unusual compassion for the lowly reptile plodding through his lettuce patch. His empathy is even more unusual given that in White's time most people, following Descartes' reasoning, considered animals to be rather like mechanical contrivances, insensitive to pain and suffering, much less to subtler feelings. Science and religion were in agreement on this rigid separation of the human race from the nonhuman in terms of a capacity for feeling; both agreed that animals possessed no soul or indwelling spirit. One of the curiosities about animals in the Age of Reason was their ability to simulate the appearance of great fear, painful suffering, maternal love, and other emotions, when everyone believed they were incapable of these responses. The fact that White seriously considered an alternative view of the natural world, at once scientific but also sympathetic to and moderately respectful of the rights and emotional lives of nonhuman entities, placed him at the beginning of a revolutionary movement in science and ethics.[6] For all its restraint and emphasis on accuracy, the book White eventually wrote shows him filled with the same empathy for the behavior of cuckoos and field mice, horses and deer, snakes and eels living throughout his parish. Few naturalists before him had had such enthusiasm for what we would now call behavioral ecology—a firsthand description of animals seen not as specimens, but as possessors of a life in the world separate from that of humans.[7] When Timothy implored Hecky Mulso to imagine being a tortoise, White implied that the lives of animals may be richer than humans imagine—and that humans may affect those lives for good or ill.

Gradually, as White considered the suggestion that he write a natural history, it occurred to him that if he restricted his focus to his own neighborhood he might indeed be able to contribute something worthwhile to science. A narrow focus might have its own virtues: "For, as no man can alone investigate all the works of nature, these partial writers may, each in their department, be more accurate in their discoveries, and freer from errors, than more general writers; and so by degrees may pave the road to a correct universal natural history."[8]

Over the next eighteen years White stalked the twin eggs of the nightjar, opened the nests of swifts, and gently probed the burrows of mole crickets with pieces of straw. Meanwhile, his enthusiastic and supportive friend John Mulso pleaded with White to complete the manuscript and send it to the printers before they both died of old age. But White's book, like his observations of nature, was not to be rushed. Not until age sixty-eight did White produce *The Natural History of Selborne*. It became one of the most published books in the English language, and certainly the most beloved and influential British nature book of all time. Comprising 110 letters to zoologists Thomas Pennant and Daines Barrington, the book had a wide influence on other writers, including Charles Darwin and Henry Thoreau, and it continues to be a model for what many people think of as literary natural history: a book of rural observations of ordinary plants and creatures in the countryside, written in unpretentious and economical language and expressing an idyllic affection for the author's home region.

White followed a tradition of rural writing that reached back to the *Idylls* of Theocritus and the *Eclogues* and *Georgics* of Virgil, to Varro and Columella. Using these models, White touched on more than the creatures that were his main focus. He also portrayed the rural folk of Selborne. They included the gypsies who migrated through the countryside and who apparently preferred, even in bitter rainstorms, to sleep on the exposed ground; and a poor idiot boy who gleefully sucked honey by the handful from the bodies of bees and overturned hives for what he called "bee-wine." And it was with Virgil in mind, according to Virginia Woolf, that White described the farmers' wives dipping rushes into animal fat to make their rough candles.[9]

From this pastoral tradition, White created a new model of the amateur scientist: a field naturalist at home in his immediate surroundings and eager to learn all there was to know about a relatively small neighborhood, what we would now call its ecology. "The Author of the following Letters takes the liberty, with all proper deference, of laying before the public his idea of *parochial history*, which, he thinks, ought to consist of natural productions and occurrences as well as antiquities," White wrote in the opening paragraph of *Selborne*. "He is also of the opinion that if stationary men would pay some attention to the districts on which they reside, and would publish their thoughts respecting the objects that surround them, from such materials might be drawn the most complete country-histories." White was criticizing the common practice of his time. Most natural history then was done indoors. It consisted of comparing anatomical variations among animals and bird corpses gathered by others, whose primary tools were rifles and bird shot, and of comparing plants that had been dried and pressed, often with resultant loss of their living color and shape.

White, in contrast, was, as he described himself, "an out-door naturalist," one who took his observations from the subject itself and not from the writings of others. "Faunists, as you observe, are too apt to acquiesce in bare descriptions, and a few synonyms," he wrote in *Selborne*. "The reason is plain; because all that may be done at home in a man's study, but the investigation of the life and conversation of animals, is a concern of much more trouble and difficulty, and is not to be attained but by the active and inquisitive, and by those that reside much in the country."[10] White preferred to know the creatures around him alive and as they existed interrelated in their complex environment.

Concerning much that he heard and read, White also maintained a consistent skepticism that distinguished him from even the most prominent natural scientists of his day. The faults of most science, White wrote, were "the comparing one animal to the other by memory" and the trusting of the conjectures by "ingenious" writers who lacked firsthand knowledge but who nevertheless speculated in order to advance a theory.[11]

White's emphasis on direct observation of the natural world over extended periods and in varying seasons gave *Selborne* its distinctive form and sensibility. Despite White's concern that his book be graceful and readable, no matter how long it took to write, many modern readers upon their first encounter find it almost too exacting, artless, somewhat fragmentary, a little redundant, scrupulous in detail but random in organization. John Burroughs noted, "There is indeed something a little disappointing in White's book when one takes it up for the first time, with his mind full of its great fame. It is not seasoned quite up to the modern taste. White is content that the facts of nature should be just as they are. When I myself first looked into his book, many years ago, I found nothing that attracted me, and so passed it by."[12]

But although *Selborne* appears to be merely a group of letters joined roughly by chronology, John Hildebidle sees in it a methodical progression from observation to investigation to generalization.[13] The opening nine letters of the book introduce the region of Selborne systematically and elegantly. Virginia Woolf remarked on their being the carefully crafted device they are: "no novelist could have given us more briefly and completely all that we need to know before the story begins."[14] The book begins in earnest with the tenth letter, which White edited and revised along with the rest of the letters to fit into an overall plan.

The first third of the book, following these introductory letters, consists largely of reports, some of them terse and seemingly random, of the calls, migrations, nesting, and feeding of birds and other animals. Framed as letters to Thomas Pennant, each presents small details, freshly seen and vivid, sometimes stripped to the minimum, but revealing months and years of painstaking observation.

"Nightingales, when their young first come abroad, and are helpless, make a plaintive and a jarring noise: and also a snapping or cracking, pursuing people along the hedges as they walk: these last sounds seem intended for menace and defiance.

"The grasshopper-lark chirps all night in the height of summer.

"Swans turn white the second year, and breed the third.

"Weasels prey on moles, as appears by their being sometimes caught in mole-traps.

"Sparrow-hawks sometimes breed in old crow's nests, and the kestrel in churches and ruins.

"There are supposed to be two sorts of eels in the island of Ely. The threads sometimes discovered in eels are perhaps their young: the generation of eels is very dark and mysterious."[15]

With such apparently random observations, such as the sighting of an unfamiliar peregrine falcon or the shooting of an osprey as it sat on the handle of a plow, White conveys a sense of daily jottings on a wide range of occurrences, as well as a sense of anticipation that something even more marvelous is just about to be discovered, beyond the accumulation of facts.

In the next part of the book, his letters to Daines Barrington, White begins to categorize his facts and to speculate. His syntax and style become more varied and the observations more generalized. By the latter part of the book the letters again take the form of short essays on single animals, swifts, martins, and other creatures. And so the book is rounded off with letters that resemble the first group.

By shaping his letters into book form, compressing and modifying the original texts when necessary, using some of the novelistic devices of his time to produce a nonfiction work, White not only unified *Selborne* but also inaugurated self-consciously *literary* natural history. Darwin would later do the same thing in *Voyage of the Beagle*, creating an account "in the *form* of a journal," as he said, but with the appearance of being merely raw data.[16] And as White set out deliberately to craft his observations into a finished, unified account, he also created an ingenuous narrator, not entirely unlike the persona of Timothy, confessing to his confusions, admitting when he had been deceived, scrupulously dedicated to following a clue to its end and to imparting what the animals had taught him.[17] Although the narrator is undoubtedly much like Gilbert White in his daily life, the voice is literary, and the personality and sympathies in the voice distinguish White's book from objective, scientific writing. White's readers over the years have come to love *Selborne* because of that gentle and likable narrator, not merely, or principally, because of his facts.

White's extensive journal conveys a picture of a man constantly busy, frequently surrounded by friends and relatives, faithfully tending to parishioners, cultivating his garden, planting trees, and experimenting with crops and fertilizers. He exchanged seeds with friends in other parts of Britain and corresponded about bird migration with distant acquaintances. And during all this busyness and modest concern about his book, White also made original contributions to natural history. He was the first to identify the lesser whitethroat, the harvest mouse, and the noctule bat. He was the first to distinguish, chiefly by song, three species of leaf warblers. He noted the importance of sexual characteristics in birds and mammals. He anticipated theories of territoriality among birds, and his speculations on earthworms probably inspired Darwin's late work on the subject. His interests ranged across zoology, botany, geology, meteorology, and human history, observing individual species against the background of the environment they inhabited.[18]

Despite his care, however, White's observations and conclusions were not always accurate. Perhaps the best example concerns Timothy, who died a year after White. Since Timothy had never laid an egg, White always assumed that the tortoise was a male, but an autopsy revealed otherwise. White's reticent boarder had kept other secrets from her naturalist master as well: she was not American, but Algerian; and although after White's death a brief campaign was undertaken to make of her a new species, to be named after her master, she was not new after all, but plain *Testudo ibera*.

Timothy's shell is preserved in the British Museum of Natural History. A sign attached to her venerable carapace reads in part, "died in Selborne in 1794, after an existence of about 54 years in England . . . formerly in the possession of the Rev. Gilbert White."

The summer wind was cold during White's final illness, which came over him rapidly; just two weeks earlier, he had presided over the funeral of a young girl. In his will he requested that his burial be "as plain and private as possible" and that his casket be carried by six honest laborers, "men such as have bred up large families," who were to be paid ten shillings each for their trouble. All this was done. The body was placed lovingly but unpretentiously in the churchyard of his parish, where the spot was marked with a small stone. Engraved on the stone were only his initials and the date of his death, June 26, 1793.

In the decade that followed, the success of *The Natural History of Selborne* was also very modest. But by the time Darwin was a young schoolboy, in 1820, avid naturalists knew the book well. In 1818 *Blackwood's Magazine* had reported that natural history, "at one point so much neglected in this island, has now become a general study. The man of business, as well as the philosopher, takes an interest even in the delight of this delightful branch of knowledge." And in 1831 *Blackwood's* announced that "the works of genuine naturalists, such as White's *Selborne* . . . are selling by thousands, and will continue to sell to the tens of thousands."[19] Historian David Elliston Allen suggests the reason for White's belated recognition: "It was not till the late 1820s that a new, no-nonsense, mainly middle-class audience eventually emerged, able to discern the one great quality in White that has helped to bring this book such prominent renown: his gift of empathy, his ability to infuse deep feeling into what he described and recorded so carefully and soberly."[20]

Allen asserts that White was "perhaps the first writer in Britain to display this much more modern gift, and for that reason alone *Selborne* is of special historical significance. White's preference for patient observation, in an age when most people stopped merely to collect, is, similarly, far in advance of its time. But over and above even these there still remains that one ingredient without which no work attains the status of an irresistible classic: somehow, it enshrines a portion of our necessary collective mythology. [James Russell] Lowell came very close to the truth in calling *Selborne* 'the journal of Adam in Paradise.' For it is, surely, the testament of Static Man: at peace with the world and with himself, content with deepening his knowledge of his one small corner of the earth, a being suspended in a perfect mental balance. Selborne is the secret, private parish inside each one of us. We must be thank-

ful it was revealed so very early—and with such seemingly un-
studied simplicity and grace."[21]

By about 1830, what has been called "the cult of Gilbert White"
had spread throughout England and reached America. Among the
steady stream of pilgrims—scientists, poets, and ordinary citizens—who traveled to Selborne to pay homage to the source of
White's Arcadian and ecological dream were Charles Darwin,
James Russell Lowell, and John Burroughs. According to Donald
Worster, "The rise of the natural history essay in the latter half of
the nineteenth century [in America] was an essential legacy of the
Selborne cult. It was more than a scientific-literary genre of writing, modeled after White's pioneering achievement. A constant
theme of the nature essayists was the search for a lost pastoral haven, for a home in an inhospitable and threatening world." Soon a
kind of nature writing arose in which, as Worster says, "natural
history was the vehicle that brought readers to the quiet peace of
hay barns, orchards, and mountain valleys. These virtuosi of the
nature essay were among the best selling writers of their age."[22]

Meanwhile, before this shift occurred, Henry Thoreau was
working through the implications of his own response to nature,
in a small village with some similarities to Gilbert White's Selborne. The glacial meadows and scrub-oak woods, the sandy
plains and meandering streams gave Thoreau the opportunities to
saunter and observe the workings of nature far enough from the
city to avoid the chaos of industrialism, but near enough to the
highway to feel the changes that were coming. Many of these
changes were astride the "Iron Horse," whose rails cut through the
Walden woods, linking Concord with Boston, and whose screams
brought punctuality even to the farmers in the remote countryside.

Gilbert White's *Natural History of Selborne* was one of Thoreau's
favorite books and was well known to others in his circle. When

Thoreau got around to answering an invitation to join the Association for the Advancement of Science in 1853 (an invitation he declined because, he said, he would not be able to attend the meetings), he stated, "I am an observer of nature generally, and the character of my observations, as far as they are scientific, may be inferred from the fact that I am especially attracted by such books of science as White's *Selborne* and Humboldt's 'Aspects of Nature.' "[23]

When Evert Duyckinck asked Nathaniel Hawthorne in 1845 whom he might include in a new series of American books being published by Wiley & Putnam, Hawthorne suggested Thoreau but added, "The only way, however, in which he could ever approach the popular mind, would be by writing a book of simple observations of nature, somewhat in the vein of White's History of Selborne." In a letter written in 1856, Thoreau's friend Thomas Chomondeley urged him to "try a history. How if you could write the sweet, beautiful history of Massachusetts? . . . Or take Concord . . . Take the spirit of Walton and a spice of White." Edward Jones lamented Thoreau's apparent failure as an author at the time of his death by saying, "It was hoped that he would write a history of Concord, like White's Natural History of Selborne."[24]

Thoreau's biographer Robert Richardson notes some of the similarities between Thoreau and White.[25] Like Thoreau, White traveled very little and spent virtually his entire life in a single landscape. White says in his natural history, "Men that undertake only one district are much more likely to advance general knowledge than those that grasp at more than they can possibly be acquainted with: every kingdom, every province, should have its own *monographer*."[26] This emphasis on the small details of a single region was of course attractive to Thoreau. "I cannot but regard it as a kindness in those who have the steering of me that, by the want of pecuniary wealth, I have been nailed down to this my native region so long and steadily, and made to study and love this spot more and more," he wrote. "What would signify in comparison a thin and diffused love and knowledge of the whole earth instead, got by wandering?"[27]

But in reading *Selborne*, Thoreau felt that White's observations conveyed little sense of the author as a person, beyond certain sympathies. In contrast, Thoreau believed that in order to know the thing observed, we must also know the observer. As Richardson notes, Thoreau was conscious of the need to balance subjective with objective knowledge and to be skeptical about attaining either.[28] In this respect Thoreau was much more modern, as a scientist and as a poet, than Gilbert White. "I am not interested in mere phenomena," Thoreau wrote in his journal, "though it were the explosion of a planet, only as it may have lain in the experience of a human being." The next month he added, "There is no such thing as pure objective observation. Your observation, to be interesting, i.e. to be significant, must be subjective. The sum of what the writer of whatever class has to report is simply some human experience, whether he be poet or philosopher or man of science. The man of most science is the man most alive, whose life is the greatest event. Senses that take cognizance of outward things merely are of no avail. It matters not where or how far you travel, the further commonly the worse,— but how much alive you are."[29]

Thoreau was distinguishing himself from Gilbert White even as he learned from him. Thoreau continued in this passage: "All that a man has to say or do that can possibly concern mankind, is in some shape or other to tell the story of his love,—to sing; and, if he is fortunate and keeps alive, he will be forever in love. This alone is to be alive to the extremities." Both men "loved," but Thoreau's love was far more complicated, in a literary sense, than Gilbert White's. Moreover, while White admired the tidy economy of nature, the neat hedgerows and carefully tilled fields, Thoreau was equally enamored of nature's excesses and its exuberance. Toward the end of his life he wrote, "How rich and lavish must be the system which can afford to let so many moons burn all the day as well as the night, though no man stands in need of their light! There is none of that kind of economy in Nature that husbands its stock, but she supplies inexhaustible means to the most frugal methods." And shortly before he died he wrote in the same vein, "I love . . . the inexhaustible vitality in Nature."[30] S. A. Jones, a disciple of Thoreau, wrote to A. W. Hosmer in 1891, "White's 'Selborne' shows how fitly Channing called Thoreau the Poet-naturalist. White is a naturalist; Thoreau is the naturalist *plus* the poet, and crowning these is the moralist."[31]

Other differences between White and Thoreau help us to understand the latter's extraordinary contribution to the literary form he was pioneering, a form that would incorporate the methods and language of natural history. Among the first is one pointed out by John Hildebidle. White was interested primarily in explanation; his response to the unexplainable was to seek out the most reasonable explanation and to reject wild speculation. Thoreau, in contrast, although he always stayed close to facts, was on the lookout for the marvelous, the mythic, and the unexplainable—the poetry in a situation and in a fact. Thoreau, though a true naturalist, also wanted to take an original stand, to unsettle and not to reassure, to confuse and thereby to wake up his reader.[32] Ultimately, he must have been impatient with White's narrator—the ingenuous curate of the British countryside—and in *Walden* set about creating a narrator of a fundamentally different sort: highly individualistic, unpredictable, unsympathetic with his neighbors' complacency, possibly unreliable, prone to wordplay, and in love with parables. As Thoreau wrote at the end of *Walden,* "It is a ridiculous demand which England and America make, that you shall speak so that they can understand you. Neither men nor toadstools grow so. As if it were important and there were not enough to understand you without them . . . I desire to speak somewhere *without* bounds; like a man in a waking moment, to men in their waking moments."[33]

This off-putting voice, individualistic, direct, bordering on ar-

rogance, has been a discouragement to some readers of *Walden*—
a "naturalist" and a "scientist" who seems to prefer mystery to clarity, to being out of bounds with his neighbors rather than civil and
affable. But if we read all of Thoreau, particularly his journals, we
can understand how much this voice in *Walden* was a literary one.
While using a method that depended solely on facts, Thoreau as-
pired to more. "Facts should only be as the frame to my pictures,"
he wrote in his journal. "They should be material to the mythology
which I am writing; not facts to assist men to make money, farmers
to farm profitably, in any common sense; facts to tell who I am, and
where I have been or what I have thought . . . I would so state facts
that they shall be significant, shall be myths or mythologic. Facts
which the mind perceived, thoughts which the body thought—
with these I deal. I, too, cherish vague and misty forms, the vaguest
when the cloud at which I gaze is dissipated quite and naught but
the skyey depths are seen." Thoreau's method was to accumulate
facts and then to "associate" and juxtapose: "Having by chance recorded a few disconnected thoughts and then brought them into
juxtaposition, they suggest a whole new field in which it was possible to labor and to think. Thought begat thought."[34]

Thoreau's nature writing, rather than merely emphasizing the
native creatures of the region, the responses of the inhabitants, or
the sympathies of the narrator, conferred authenticity on the *relations* among fact, phenomena, and observer. "I think the man of
science makes this mistake, and the mass of men along with him,"
Thoreau wrote in his journal, "that you should coolly give your attention to the phenomenon which excites you as something independent of you, and not as it is related to you."[35] For him, the objective independence of nature was an irrefutable reality to be
steadily observed. But phenomenological experiences—senses
and imagination together—were also legitimate subjects of the
naturalist. They are the realities that inextricably bond the human
and nonhuman world, heart and glimmering fact.

In its enterprise to associate and juxtapose imagination, mind, and matter, Thoreau's writing was more subtle and ambitious than Gilbert White's—and, we might even say, more reverent. Moreover, Thoreau's writing called for the participation of his readers—his neighbors—in a way that makes his writing particularly modern. He urged each of them to allow him his ambiguities and to accept his oxymorons, puns, and contradictions as challenges "to find and pursue *his own way*." He urged his readers to become lost in order to rediscover themselves, to become wide awake for the renewed exertion of intellect that leads to the poetic and divine life.

An old man who came upon Thoreau's cabin beside Walden Pond shortly after it was built regarded it pleasantly as having been constructed for the convenience of fishermen. Thoreau, more than once in *Walden,* demonstrated that, as the occupant of the cabin, he was indeed a fisherman, but of a peculiar sort. Sometimes, he wrote in *Walden*'s chapter called "The Ponds," he would go fishing at night, and, lying back in his boat, after a while he would feel a tugging on his line as he began to dream. The vibration would make him stir and would bring him back to the solid world again—or at least to the solid world of his little boat. As hand over hand he slowly raised a nocturnal fish from the depths of the pond, it seemed to him as if "I might next cast my line upward into the air, as well as downward into this element which was scarcely more dense. Thus I caught two fishes as it were on one hook."

In this image, as throughout *Walden*, Thoreau suggested that his project was to unify two worlds and to hold them on a single line stretching back to himself. Such a difficult task made his writing a continual "project," ongoing, groping toward an almost unsayable condition involving the reader as well as the author.[36]

Such imaginative, aesthetic, and even mystical qualities in Thoreau expanded nature writing, making it a way of seeing the world not only with empirical eyes but with heart and mind, intuition and logic combined. Gilbert White opened the door to this consciousness, and Thoreau propelled nature writing through it, using factualness as the guiding principle to a luminous and revelatory understanding of the natural world.

Chapter Three

THE POUT'S NEST AND

THE PAINTER'S EYE

On November 26, 1858, Henry David Thoreau took
his rowboat onto Walden Pond, as he often did whenever the
weather permitted. Like all the ponds close by—Hubbard's,
Goose, and Little Goose—Walden was unusually low this season.
Thoreau observed that despite the cold, the sweet-ferns along the
banks still held their green. The fallen oak leaves lay like bright,
crisp quilts in the muddy shallows. Evergreens had withered and
turned reddish, he noted in his journal, but the buds of the high-
blueberry bushes were expanding into small red leaves. Partially
frozen, partially wet, the ground was sugared with a light snow,
turning the landscape white and shimmering.

Alone, Thoreau searched for a pout's nest he had seen the previous spring. It had been underwater then, but today he found it
stranded in the mud, exposed by the receding waterline of the
pond. Leaving his boat on the bank, he bent down and dismantled
the nest's frozen roof to peer inside. Tiny frogs and hundreds of
pollywogs, along with a few small fish and minnows, struggled
in the icy bottom of the muddy cavity. From all the tracks about,
Thoreau speculated that otter, mink, and foxes had waded into

the shallows and fed on the minnows. The little fish had an especially odd coloration, he noted, "exceedingly pretty," like fabulous
coins. Collecting some in a jar, he took the most interesting of
them home.

During the evening Thoreau looked again at the colorful minnows and was surprised at what he saw. The next day he eagerly
walked back to the pond for more. To his growing astonishment,
he realized that hardly a mile from the middle of Concord, in
waters familiar to every local fisherman, he had discovered a species of striped bream never before recorded. "Very pale golden like
a perch, or more bluish," distinctly shaped with a single dorsal fin
of spiny rays, he wrote in his journal.

Thoreau could scarcely believe he had found a new creature so
close to home. "I cannot but see still in my mind's eye those little
striped breams poised in Walden's glaucous water," he wrote excitedly several days later. Elated by his discovery, he presented
specimens to the Boston Society of Natural History, whose library
he often used for reference, and the society's biologists confirmed
his conclusion. Soon afterward the story of Thoreau's new bream
appeared as an item of interest in the local newspapers.

The naturalist in Thoreau was justifiably satisfied at his discovery, but almost immediately another side of him began to search
for a larger meaning to his findings. "What is the amount of my discovery to me?" he asked. And at once he concluded, "it is not that
I have got one in a bottle, that it has got a name in a book."[1] Nature's
disclosure of something new at his very doorstep invoked a further, deeper mystery about the surrounding land, about expectations, and about patient observation. And this larger meaning was
the discovery's real importance to Thoreau. The water of Walden
Pond, which had seemed so familiar just a few days before, now
seemed a place where under everyone's nose things wholly unac-
counted for were still occurring. "How wild it makes the pond and
township to find a new fish in it!" he wrote. "I can only poise my

thought there by its side and try to think like a bream for a moment." To find this new inhabitant was like discovering that "a poet
or an anchorite" had been living in the village undetected for centuries and now revealed himself.[2]

In terms of its importance to science, Thoreau knew, his discovery might be as abstract as a name added to a list. Moreover, to
his dismay, a dead specimen in a jar of alcohol was as good to the
natural historians of his day as a living creature, and more conve-
niently tidy for having been removed from its surroundings. However, he probed for a more comprehensive understanding of this
phenomenon.

In *Nature*, a book Thoreau knew well and had read twenty years
before, Emerson had asserted that "every natural fact is a symbol
of some spiritual fact." But by the time Thoreau discovered the
new species of bream, he was forty-one and was no more satisfied
with abstracting the natural world into spiritual symbols, as Emerson advocated, than with abstracting it into the terms of science or
aesthetics. What distinguished Thoreau from Emerson—and the
reason Thoreau was so much more of a nature writer than his more
philosophical neighbor—was his reluctance to leave nature behind and to see the world from only one perspective, subordi-
nating all others. Thoreau would never allow the astonishing,
sentient world to become merely glyphic.[3] He had written in his
journal several years before, "Let me not be in haste to detect the
universal law; let me see more clearly a particular instance of it!"[4]
Science gave Thoreau discipline and terminology; poetic vision
gave him the freedom to make conceptual leaps and uncover analogies in structures and relationships; and spiritual vision gave him
sturdiness, as well as moral and ethical insights. It was the combination of all these modes of understanding that enabled Thoreau to see nature as comprehensively and penetratingly as he did.

The majority of his countrymen, Thoreau felt, too often allowed their vision to narrow. Their aesthetic vision, in particular,
withered away the older they got. More and more the imagination

was devalued as a useful instrument for understanding and replaced with either pragmatism or scientism. "How was it when the
youth first discovered fishes?" he wrote as he pondered his new
species of bream. "Was it the number of their fin-rays or their arrangement, or the place of the fish in some system that made the
boy dream of them? Is it these things that interest mankind in the
fish, the inhabitant of the water? No, but a faint recognition of a living contemporary, a provoking mystery. One boy thinks of fishes
and goes a-fishing from the same motive that his brother searches
the poets for rare lines. It is the poetry of fishes which is their chief
use; their flesh is their lowest use. The beauty of the fish, that is
what it is best worth the while to measure. Its place in our systems
is of comparatively little importance. Generally the boy loses some
of his perception and his interest in the fish; he degenerates into a
fisherman or an ichthyologist."[5]

Much of Thoreau's contribution to literary natural history derives, as H. Daniel Peck observes, from his creation of "a new mode
of apprehension that mediates between science and art, between
'naturalism' and 'poetry.' Characteristically he drifts back and
forth between these poles . . . yet all the while seeking a space of
consciousness that lies integrally apart from them and that balances the claims of outer and inner life."[6]

Peck notes Thoreau's extraordinary patience in seeking this
consciousness, that he did not expect to come quickly or easily to
any revelations. When Thoreau died, only three years after that
autumn day on which he discovered the new bream, his greatest
work lay in voluminous unpublished notebooks and charts, an experiment in apprehension and perception that included indirect
as well as direct modes of seeing. Like naturalists before him such
as Gilbert White and Charles Darwin, he recorded minute phenomena observed firsthand; but also, like the poet Emily Dickinson, thirteen years his junior, he pursued shadows as well as light,
echoes and silences as well as solid objects, "seeing with the side of

the eye," as he called it in language reminiscent of Dickinson, or hearing "with the side of the ear."[7]

Thoreau's quest for an adequate method of perception, a seeing that would be "relational" while being grounded in what he actually saw, required the discerning skill of the taxonomist combined with the innocence and analogy-making of the poet. He needed an attentiveness that could be learned only over many years, practiced until it became a daily habit and experienced as part of the writer's own life.[8] The perception that he brought to his writing not only balanced modes of seeing—scientific and poetic—but produced a synthesizing way to conduct one's life. "See not with the eye of science, which is barren, nor of youthful poetry, which is impotent," he wrote in his journal. "But taste the world and digest it."[9]

While a student Thoreau had read Emerson's assertion in *Nature* that "the eye is the best of artists . . . And as the eye is the best composer, so light is the first of painters." In conversation with Emerson, he had undoubtedly heard the older man refer to the imagination as "a very high sort of seeing, which does not come by study, but by the intellect being where and what it sees."[10] In his twenties Thoreau wrote in his journal, "The eye has many qualities which belong to God more than man. It is his lightning which flashes in it."[11]

This was the period of American travel, exploration, and expansion on an epic scale. Fascinated by the breadth and diversity of North America and the world, Thoreau avidly read the accounts of Lewis and Clark, Parkman, Kalm, Frémont, Catlin, Michaux, and Darwin, among others. Soon after finishing their studies, many of his classmates from Harvard sailed on explorations into the far Pacific, and members of Emerson's circle were publishing books on their own travels. Margaret Fuller's *Summer on the Lakes* (along with Goethe's *Italian Journey*) probably influenced Thoreau's first book, *A Week on the Concord and Merrimack Rivers*, not the last of his literal and metaphorical accounts of travel—a metaphor that fascinated him and recurs constantly in his writings.

Nevertheless, so confident was Thoreau in the concentrated power of the eye that in his early journals he asserted, "How much virtue there is in simply seeing!" And he added, "The woman who sits in the house and *sees* is a match for a stirring captain. Those still, piercing eyes, as faithfully exercised on their talent, will keep her even with Alexander or Shakespeare."[12]

If, as Thoreau was ready to claim at age twenty-three, "We are as much as we see," his progress as a writer and artist would be measured in large part by how well he could learn to *look*, and then by how fully he could learn to express what he saw, to put his "vision" into vivid and powerful language. "As you *see*, so at length will you *say*," he wrote to himself. "When facts are seen superficially, they are seen as they lie in relation to certain institutions, perchance. But I would have them expressed as more deeply seen, with deeper references; so that the hearer or reader cannot recognize them or apprehend their significance from the platform of common life, but it will be necessary that he be in a sense translated in order to understand them; when the truth respecting his things shall naturally exhale from a man like the odor of the muskrat from the coat of the trapper."[13]

Thoreau's work, then, is a search for the "deeply seen." But what the eyes see is related not only to who we are but also to what system (or "institution") the eye has been conditioned to believe in. Moreover, simply to look hard at an object, he knew, is to see it neither accurately nor deeply. In fact, to look too closely at an object can be to overlook it. "I must walk more with free senses," he wrote. "It is as bad to *study* stars and clouds as flowers and stones. I must let my senses wander as my thought, my eyes see without looking. . . Be not preoccupied with looking. Go not to the object; let it come to you . . . What I need is not to look at all, but a true sauntering of the eye."[14]

At age forty Thoreau remarked in his journal how inadequately most writers described nature, how inadequate was their language. The "mealy-mouthed enthusiasm of the lover of nature" seemed no better than the cool and inexpressive language of science. Thoreau had found in reading Linnaeus a system for seeing botanical details, a system that allowed him to discover distinctions that otherwise would have been missed. But he continued to search for a system for seeing aesthetically, as, for example, a visual artist would see: a system attuned on the one hand to the facts of natural history—to the number of fin-rays in the striped bream and their arrangements—and on the other hand to the natural world's aesthetic mystery and delight, its heroism and darkness. Whatever system he might find, it had to embrace the physical reality in each sensuous curve of the snow flea's eye and the muskrat's claw, while allowing a meaning to the imagination and a relation to the divine.[15] It is not surprising that drawing and painting were among the systems that most interested him throughout his life.

The fall of 1858, when Thoreau discovered the new species of bream, must have been exceptionally brilliant, and his eyes were particularly acute that season on account of his intense search for a language to render nature's beauty. For many years he had wanted to write what he called "a memorial of October." He filled his journal with the colors of spangled leaves and evening clouds. He compared the luminous atmospheric blue reflected on a white house beside the river to the "transcendent blue" of wildflowers, and the intricately painted feathers of jays and loons to the delicate tints on the skin of a salamander—so many unnamed subtle shades and hues. "In describing the richly spotted leaves," he wrote, "how often we find ourselves using ineffectually words which merely indicate faintly our good intentions, giving them in our despair a terminal twist toward our mark,—such as reddish, yellowish, purplish, etc. We cannot make a hue of words, for they are not to be compounded like colors, and hence we are obliged to use such ineffectual expressions as reddish brown, etc. They need to be ground together."[16]

Thoreau elaborated on the impossibility of describing "the infinite variety of hues, tints, and shades, for the language affords no names for them, and we must apply the same term monotonously to twenty different things. When the tints are the same they differ so much in purity and delicacy that language, to describe them truly, would have not only to be greatly enriched, but as it were dyed to the same colors herself, and speak to the eye as well as to the ear."[17]

The year before Thoreau's discovery of the new bream, he had been reading widely in aesthetic theory, particularly John Ruskin's *Elements of Drawing*, which discussed sketching from nature, color, and composition. Ruskin admonished the artist in much the same terms as Gilbert White had the natural historian: pay attention to what is in front of the eye; note it accurately in the moment, in detail, and do not rely on memory to reconstruct what has been seen. "The perception of solid form is entirely a matter of experience. We *see* nothing but flat colours," Ruskin wrote elsewhere. "The whole technical power of painting depends on our recovery of what may be called *the innocence of the eye*: that is to say, of a sort of childish perception of these flat stains of colour, merely as such, without consciousness of what they signify,—as a blind man would see them if suddenly gifted with sight."[18]

There was much for Thoreau to like in Ruskin concerning seeing, not only because of Ruskin's stress on accuracy but also because of his allowance for the obscure and invisible. Years earlier Thoreau had noted in his journal the disadvantage of too much detail in writing about landscape—a fault to which even excellent writers were prone. "They express themselves with too great fullness and detail," he complained. "They give the most faithful, natural, and lifelike account of their sensations, mental and physical, but they lack moderation and sententiousness."[19] In Ruskin, however, he found a corrective instruction that would have seemed paradoxical to almost anyone but himself: "Try to draw a bank of grass with all its blades; or a bush with all its leaves; and you will soon begin to understand under what a universal law of obscurity we live, and perceive that all *distinct* drawing must be *bad* drawing, and that nothing can be right till it is unintelligible."[20] Such instruction surely reminded Thoreau of his own words in *A Week on the Concord and Merrimack Rivers*: "The most stupendous scenery ceases to be sublime when it becomes distinct, or in other words limited, and the imagination is no longer encouraged to exaggerate it."

Thoreau applied this paradoxical observation to creative prose. "I should like to meet the great and serene sentence, which does not reveal itself,—only that it is great,—which I may never with my utmost intelligence pierce through and beyond (more than the earth itself), which no intelligence can understand," he wrote in *A Week*. "There should be a kind of life and palpitation to it; under its rind a kind of blood should circulate forever, communicating freshness to its countenance."[21] Similarly, *Walden* concluded: "I do not suppose that I have attained to obscurity, but I should be proud if no more fatal fault were found with my pages on this score than was found with the Walden ice."

For Ruskin, the sense of mystery and obscurity did not derive from some inherent inadequacy of the human eye. Instead, like Thoreau, he considered it a numinous, positive quality at the heart of the natural world and of existence. Ruskin's third "law" of landscape drawing, for example, emphasized respect for the way in which mystery participates in the true character of plants, rocks, clouds, and waves. In this powerful, cloaking mystery, he saw a kinship between natural objects and human nature. Just as there is "a perpetual lesson in every serrated point and shining vein which escape or deceive our sight among the forest leaves, how little we may hope to discern clearly, or judge justly, the rents and veins of the human heart; how much of all that is round us, in men's actions or spirits, which we at first think we understand, a closer and more loving watchfulness would show to be full of mystery, never to be either fathomed or withdrawn."[22]

Thoreau did not concur with all of Ruskin's opinions regarding the relation of nature to spirit. He strongly disliked Ruskin's tendency to look at nature through art rather than the other way around. He often found *too much art* in Ruskin, and not enough of the out-of-doors, not "Nature as Nature, but as Turner painted her." And he dismissed Ruskin's conventional moralizing, the imposition of a Christian conscience on nature's non-Christian truths, and his inclination to transform nature into mere symbols or correspondences—the tendency he also disliked in Emerson.[23]

Thoreau nevertheless found Ruskin instructive for training the eye with regard to color and detail, and for conveying a sense of the pictorial qualities in the landscape. As he recorded the colors he saw on Poplar Hill in October, he attempted, in words, what Ruskin had urged the artist to accomplish with paint. "Now, methinks, the autumnal tints are brightest in our streets and in the woods generally," he wrote in his journal. "In the streets, the *young* sugar maples make the most show. The street is never more splendid. As I look up the street from the Mill-Dam, they look like painted screens standing before the houses to celebrate a gala-day. One half of each tree glows with a delicate scarlet. But only one of the large maples on the Common is yet on fire. The butternuts on the street are with, or a little later than, the walnuts. The three-horned acacias have turned (one half) a peculiarly bright and delicate yellow, peculiar also for the smallness of the leaf. Asparagus-beds are a soft mass of yellow and green. Buttonwoods have no bright colors, but are a brownish yellowish green, somewhat curled and crisp and looking the worse for the wear. Stand where half a dozen large elms droop over a house. It is as if you stood within a ripe pumpkin rind, and you feel as mellow as if you were the pulp."[24]

Thoreau revised these notes along with the ones he had made

the previous fall into a lecture on the season's colors, which he delivered several times to the Concord Lyceum. He planned to turn his lecture into an extended work to be called "The Fall of the Leaf," but in the months that followed he put his notes aside in favor of even larger projects. Not until he lay on his deathbed did he return to them. In order to raise money for his family, Thoreau readied four major essays for publication in less than two months. "Autumnal Tints," the first of these, appeared in print in the fall of 1862, five months after his death.[25]

Like so much of Thoreau's work, "Autumnal Tints" is ultimately about phenomena, about the relational meaning of science and imagination, and about preparing the eye to see the world as a whole. "There is just as much beauty visible to us in the landscape as we are prepared to appreciate—not a grain more," Thoreau wrote in this wonderful essay. "It requires different intentions of the eye and of the mind to attend to different departments of knowledge! How differently the poet and the naturalist look at objects!"[26]

In "Autumnal Tints," the eye of the scientist and the eye of the poet do not inhibit each other because Thoreau prepared himself to see outer and inner experiences as dependent upon each other for meaning. The observer must cultivate his or her vision just as the farmer cultivates his field, he wrote,[27] but, unhappily, most people cultivate their minds neither as naturalists nor poets. And so, "the greater part of the phenomena of Nature are for this reason concealed from us all our lives."

When nature is concealed from us, Thoreau said, we are most certainly asleep to the present moment, which is all we can know of heaven. While he revised "Autumnal Tints," his body weakening rapidly from tuberculosis and respiratory stress, he recalled how many seasons he too had been asleep—despite all the precise natural history he had seen and recorded—until his eyes at last opened to beauty. "I had walked over those Great Fields so many Augusts, and never yet distinctly recognized these purple companions that I had there. I had brushed against them and trodden on them, forsooth; and now, at last, they, as it were, rose up and blessed me. Beauty and true wealth are always thus cheap and despised. Heaven might be defined as the place which men avoid."

Ruskin was not the first art theorist that Thoreau read as he looked for a language of the eye—especially a language for color and composition—and for a way to comprehend the aesthetics of a landscape systematically. In the spring of 1852, about six years before reading *The Elements of Drawing*, Thoreau came upon the works of William Gilpin in the Harvard College Library. Gilpin, the well-known English travel writer, artist, and art theorist, had died in 1804, but his theories on landscape painting and aesthetics were just beginning to have their widest influence on American art. Gilpin's system for apprehending and appreciating landscapes reinforced certain ideas Thoreau had already formed; moreover, Gilpin had elaborated his ideas into a detailed study "examining the face of a country by the rules of picturesque beauty."[28] Ruskin helped Thoreau with a language for color, hue, and atmosphere; Gilpin showed him how the larger components of the landscape could be defined aesthetically, and confirmed that wilderness was a necessary and desirable element in nature and art.

In the same year that he read Gilpin's works, Thoreau also read Linnaeus' *Philosophia Botanica*. These two sets of readings, in concert, are emblematic of Thoreau's search for a way to combine natural history with science and art, reason with imagination. They are also emblematic of Thoreau's desire to account for the problems of perspective and scale—the relation of the large environment to individual objects and species.[29]

Gilpin, though fundamentally an artist, was also a natural historian. In addition, he was interested as much in the social history and archaeology of the regions he visited as he was in the trees, birds, and fauna.[30] Like his contemporary and fellow Hampshire clergyman Gilbert White, he kept a naturalist journal for more than twenty years, recording, among other things, the daily

weather and changes in the seasons.[31] He corresponded with eminent scientists and had his *Remarks on Forest Scenery* and other
works checked for accuracy by a prominent Fellow of the Royal
Society. He became such a skilled naturalist and writer on nature
that his discussions of certain trees were considered models of botanical observation for well over a century after his death.[32]

Like Thoreau, Gilpin pursued writing and drawing to produce
not merely descriptions of nature but what Thoreau often called
"critical accounts." Gilpin's concern was "to guide those who wish
to look more carefully upon real nature, to observe it with more
critical, intelligent appreciation."[33] Toward this end, he champi-
oned a kind of landscape that was not "beautiful" in the era's popular sense—that is, "elegant," "smooth," and "domesticated"—
but rather what he called "picturesque." Along with certain writers
who came after him—such as Uvedale Price and Payne Knight—
Gilpin made the word "picturesque" more than an artistic term; it
came to stand for a revolutionary way of regarding the natural
world and natural scenery.[34] Gilpin's method trained his readers to
recognize aesthetic elements in settings previously considered
coarse and repulsive, to seek out desolate and unpopulated areas,
to prefer the stark and rugged to the domestic. Gilpin's reforma-
tion of sensibility generated enthusiasm for the untamed aspects
of human nature and engendered as much respect for imagination
as a means of perceiving the world as was accorded reason.[35]

Gilpin's taste for informal natural settings contrasted dramatically with the prevailing eighteenth-century preference for artificial and formal gardens. Formal gardens of his time were characterized by straight lines and topiary; sometimes even the birds in
the trees were artificial. After Gilpin successfully promoted the
picturesque, many formal English gardens were dismantled and
replaced with gardens containing gnarled, lightning-blasted trees
and broken walls. Gilpin also introduced an even more revolutionary idea: that a person might abandon the garden altogether in
favor of traveling into the wilder parts of the countryside to find

dramatically beautiful places in the natural world unaltered by human interference. *Remarks on Forest Scenery*, the first book by Gilpin that Thoreau read, asserted: "the wild and rough parts of nature produce the strongest effects on the imagination; and we may add, they are the only objects in landscape, which please the picturesque eye."[36]

The picturesque thus became an attitude, a form of social enlightenment. Emerson was later to write, "Our hunting for the picturesque is inseparable from our protest against false society."[37] To acquire this attitude, according to scholar Carl Paul Barbier, a person's eye had to be trained. Once this was accomplished by a systematic reading of Gilpin, the eye would be awakened to the landscape as a composition of starkly beautiful elements, and the person would become a seeker, "anticipating, finding, examining, comparing, recording, and re-creating" the picturesque in nature, whether in an actual sketch or in contemplation.[38]

Thoreau was fascinated by Gilpin's stress on training the eye to see patterns, colors, and surfaces that the untrained did not, and on training the senses. In his journal he wrote, "What Gilpin says about copses, glens, etc., suggests that the different places to which the walker resorts may be profitably classified and suggests many things to be said. Gilpin prefers the continuous song of the insects in the shade of a copse to the buzzing vagrant fly in the glare of day. He says the pools in the forest must receive their black hue from clearness. I suppose he means they may have a muddy bottom or covered with dark dead leaves, but the water above must be clear to reflect the trees."[39]

Ultimately, Thoreau kept his distance from Gilpin, refusing to be overly influenced by the ideas that swayed many American artists and idealists. He criticized Gilpin, just as he would Ruskin, for not realizing that the landscape was valuable for more than aesthetic reasons, for omitting something essential in the human relationship with nature. "The perception of beauty is a moral test," he wrote in his journal as he read Gilpin.[40]

But through Gilpin, Thoreau found a language for expressing the way in which color is affected by atmosphere, time of day, surrounding hues, the sharpness or fatigue of the viewer's eye, and the training of the viewer's mind. He came to understand the way in which certain features in nature draw our attention, and cause us to miss seeing others. He understood the effects of distances and reflections. In short, by studying Gilpin, Thoreau continued to develop the disciplined eye of the artist and a systematic way of studying perception.

Thoreau's written landscapes became as powerful and original as the bright landscape paintings of his American contemporaries Thomas Cole, Frederick Church, and others of the "luminist" school, many of whom were also influenced by Gilpin. But Thoreau had something that most visual artists did not: a grounding in science. A colorist and a scientist at once, he demonstrated in his writing how the whole person could be given expression through natural history—a literary form previously underused and regarded as minor. Robert Richardson calls this ability Thoreau's "synthesizing genius," and concludes, "One reason Thoreau's view of nature remains so attractive is that it sees nature as force, energy, and process *and* as landscape, view, scene, or picture."[41]

Thoreau's journal offers extensive proof of the difficulty of such a radical synthesizing of intellect and feeling. At times, he confronted sentimentality and extravagant subjectivity. At other times, he feared he was becoming too much of a scientist. In the later journals, his scientific observations dominated his writing; he read Darwin's work enthusiastically as soon as it was published, and he was reading the new discoveries in genetics at the same time he was pushing himself to complete a book-length research project on the dispersion of seeds. That work, in the words of botanist Gary Nabhan, anticipated "issues in plant population biology and coevolution that did not become fully articulated in evolutionary ecology until the early 1970s."[42] It is a measure of

Thoreau's absorption in scientific study that he made these leaps in learning and application.

But shortly before his death, Thoreau's search for a comprehensive way of seeing—his desire for a "true and absolute account of things—of the evening & the morning & all the phenomena between them"—brought him back to the conviction that beauty had a "high use" that must always be part of a true account.[43] He praised the glory of the fall colors in "Autumnal Tints" for no other reason than that they "address our taste for beauty alone." In his journal he affirmed, "It is only when we forget all our learning that we begin to know. I do not get nearer by a hair's breadth to any natural object so long as I presume that I have an introduction to it from some learned man. To conceive of it with a total apprehension I must for the thousandth time approach it as something totally strange. If you would make acquaintance with the ferns you must forget your botany. You must get rid of what is commonly called knowledge of them. Not a single scientific term or distinction is the least to the purpose, for you would fain perceive something, and you must approach the object totally unprejudiced. You must be aware that *no thing* is what you have taken it to be."

And he asked, "In what book is this world and its beauty described? Who has plotted the steps toward the discovery of beauty? You have got to be in a different state from common. Your greatest success will be simply to perceive that such things are, and you will have no communication to make to the Royal Society. If it were required to know the position of the fruit-dots or the character of the indusium, nothing could be easier than to ascertain it; but if it is required that you be affected by ferns, that they amount to anything, signify anything, to you, that they be another sacred scripture and revelation to you, helping to redeem your life, this end is not so surely accomplished."[44]

It is Thoreau's genius that he was affected by the ferns, saw them, and painted them with replete and accurate language. In his posthumously published essay "Walking," he lamented, "We have to be told that the Greeks called the world *Kosmos*, Beauty, or Order, but we do not see clearly why they did so, and we esteem it at best only a curious philological fact."[45] Through the form of nature writing that he perfected, Thoreau meant to demonstrate the reasons beauty and order are the true names of this world.

Chapter Four

THE LABOR OF THE BEES

Some historians have maintained that after his brother, John, died in his arms when Thoreau was just twenty-four, his love for the forest grew deeper and his tolerance for society diminished. Even before that tragic death, however, Thoreau in a dark mood had written, "In society you will not find health, but in nature . . . Society is always diseased and the best is the sickest. There is no scent in it so wholesome as that of the pines, nor any fragrance so penetrating and restorative as that of everlasting in high pastures."[1]

As he was writing *Walden*, society and nature, sickness and health, preoccupied Thoreau as metaphors. At times he felt that perhaps more than any of his contemporaries, he existed in a state between the two, a state both wild and civilized, solitary and convivial, self-assured and self-doubting. Like Walden Pond, situated between the sky and the wooded earth, at one time blue and at another green, his perceptions would partake of the color of each.

The poet is continually watching the self, Thoreau wrote in his journal, "as the astronomer watches the aspects of the heavens." In his life's work, he was striving for "a meteorological journal of the mind."[2] Thoreau's questioning of both interior and exterior nature seems so modern to us now because, as Edward Hoagland has observed, "most freewheeling essay-writing in America on any subject derives from him, and that's because he was exact, tactile, and practical in what he said."[3] Thoreau established an American nature writing that was in search of the language to unite the worlds of fact and rhapsody. The literature that followed him closely would be hard-headed, free of sentimentality and affectation, individualistic and contradictory, as mistrustful of society as of the self, and rooted in a specific locality while striving toward comprehensive truths. But nature writing in a popular, best-selling form would take a different turn before writers and readers returned to his example.

Thoreau's individualism and distrust of institutions could not help but be a challenge to the materialism of his neighbors and of what he called the "trivial and bustling 19th century." Thoreau opposed in particular mid-nineteenth-century industrialism and the way it increasingly took men and women off the land and forced them into sprawling gray cities. Industrialism, Thoreau saw— especially just before and during the Civil War—accelerated the plunder of the landscape, the extinction of large mammals, the destruction of rivers and streams, and environmental waste on a continental scale.

In 1864, two years after Thoreau's death, a brilliant, self-taught scholar named George Perkins Marsh published an extraordinary ecological study titled *Man and Nature; or, Physical Geography as Modified by Human Action*, which forcefully described in factual language the impact of this uncontrolled industrialism on America. In his farsighted book Marsh argued that the interrelatedness of "animal and vegetable life is too complicated a problem for human intelligence to solve," but that humans continue to commit irreparable crimes against the environment as if there would be no consequences. "The ravages committed by man subvert the relations and destroy the balance which nature had established," Marsh asserted, "and she avenges herself upon the intruder by letting loose her destructive energies."[4]

Marsh's radical viewpoint contradicted the prevailing religious

and cultural assumption that, because of man's God-given dominion over nature, human actions could only improve the land, and
that if damage were done to the environment, it would be rapidly
healed by natural processes. Marsh, however, counterargued that
"of all organic beings, man alone is to be regarded as essentially a
destructive power, and that he wields energies to resist which, nature—that nature whom all material life and all inorganic substance obey—is wholly impotent." In consequence, "the earth is
fast becoming an unfit home for its noblest inhabitant, and another era of equal human crime and human improvidence, and of
like duration with that through which traces of that crime and that
improvidence extend, would reduce it to such a condition of impoverished productiveness, of shattered surface, of climatic ex-
cess, as to threaten the deprivation, barbarism, and perhaps even
extinction of the species."[5]

Marsh did not oppose science or mechanization per se. Indeed,
he foresaw a time when great, beneficial technologies would dominate the planet. But like Thoreau, he was horrified by the "prof-
ligate waste" that ripped up forests, destroyed the topsoil, and
turned pasture into swamp. "No one before Marsh had realized the
basic importance of conservation and the nature of its extraordinary and complex patterns," according to Hans Huth, "and no one
had ever presented overwhelming facts" of the kind Marsh articulated in *Man and Nature* and in the book's second edition, *The
Earth as Modified by Human Action*, published ten years later.[6]

Marsh made a compelling argument for establishing public
parks and wilderness preserves: "It is desirable that some large and
easily accessible regions of American soil should remain as far as
possible in its primitive condition, at once a museum for the instruction of the students, a garden for the recreation of the lovers
of nature, and an asylum where indigenous trees . . . plants . . .
beasts may dwell and perpetuate their kind."[7] At the same time,
Marsh called for "wise use" of public resources, so that nature's
utilitarian value would be neither locked up in parks nor squan-

dered. And this pragmatism in Marsh conformed with a slowly growing trend in America during and after Reconstruction—to make government and industry accountable for environmental degradation without restricting the technological progress of the industrial age.

Although Thoreau's work almost certainly influenced Marsh in many regards, foreshadowing its call for wilderness reserves, for example, Thoreau's thorniness in print, his paradoxes, and his caustic rejection of the platitudes of his day concerning economics, politics, and nature helped to prevent his work from being widely read. The rise of the popular natural history essay and the eventual rejection of genteel sensibility in the late nineteenth century—a belief in social Darwinism and in a benign, divinely fated progress, led by professional scientists in their laboratories—came about not because of Thoreau but because the more Americans saw the devastation of forests and wildlife hitherto considered inexhaustible, the more nostalgic they began to feel for what historian Donald Worster has called "a lost pastoral haven." Unlike Thoreau's work, popular nature writing through the turn of the century by and large avoided attacking the excesses of the Gilded Age and concentrated instead on escapism.[8]

After the Civil War, American readers began to want "the literature of rest and delight," stories set in peaceful, idyllic scenes from which flowed "streams of healing for the discomforts of civilizations."[9] And because readers found little that was restful in Thoreau, his reputation—meager as it was at the time of his death—declined even as nature writing of a more popular sort began to proliferate. Reviewed in the press, his work was called "eccentric," "idiosyncratic," and "morbid."[10]

Several years after Thoreau's death, James Russell Lowell wrote a devastating analysis of Thoreau in the *North American Review*.[11] Thoreau had offended Lowell in 1858 when Thoreau objected to an unauthorized editorial change in one of his essays. In his article

Lowell satirized Thoreau as a weak imitator of Emerson, calling him one of the "pistillate plants kindled to fruitage by the Emersonian pollen," then charged him with excessive egotism and with attempting to disguise his character weaknesses as virtues. "He discovered nothing," Lowell wrote, and yet "he thought everything a discovery of his own, from moonlight to the planting of acorns and nuts by squirrels." Lowell accused Thoreau of being humorless and of having an "unhealthy mind" that made "his whole life a search for the doctor." In his widely read essay, Lowell battered home the notion that Thoreau had been nothing more than a misanthrope, a man who had staged a sentimental fraud at Walden Pond with his mock shanty-life.

Lowell's smug assessment was reprinted in *My Study Window* in 1871, by which time he had become one of the most influential literary critics in America. His opinion poisoned Thoreau's reputation for many years—Thoreau's biographer Walter Harding suggests several decades.[12] It may even exert an influence today. Certainly, during the decades of Lowell's greatest reputation, very little was published to change the public's opinion of Thoreau's achievement.

Meanwhile, by the turn of the century nature enthusiasm had spread among the new middle class, and Americans in great numbers embraced nature study with an energy matched only by their devastation of forests, damming of rivers, mining of land, extermination of large mammals, and pollution of cities. And while American industry voraciously exploited the country's natural resources, businessmen and politicians awakened to the public-relations benefits of being photographed camping in the national parks with naturalists and otherwise appearing to support environmental causes. This wave of nature sentiment—propelled largely by nostalgia, dissociated from Thoreau's subjectivity and social criticism, and devoted to the pastoral countryside—offered its audience a consoling rather than astringent view of nature and of humankind's relation to it. Most of these new nature writers were not averse to moralizing—as Thoreau was often accused of doing—but the reader and society were seldom the targets.

The most popular nature writer in the half-century following Thoreau's death—the one who set the tone for this new kind of nature writing and raised it to the level of literature—was John Burroughs. His well-crafted essays and affectionate books on the gentler creatures of the natural world established the standard for an enormously popular and optimistic form of the nature essay in America.

John Burroughs was born in upstate New York in 1837, the seventh of ten children. His father, a hard-working farmer and strict Baptist, expected John and his brothers to become farmers like himself. All of them did except John (although he returned to profitable fruit farming later in his life). Distrustful of books and schooling, Burroughs' father tried to thwart John's attempts to get an education beyond what the local schoolhouse provided, and he begrudged him even that much learning.

But from an early age Burroughs had become intoxicated with reading. By his own force of will, despite long hours laboring on his father's farm, he acquired enough education by age seventeen to leave home and become a rural teacher. A tall, thin boy, shy and awkward but with a strong back and handsome face, Burroughs boarded with the families of his students and spent his free time reading, writing in his notebook, and saving his meager earnings for tuition for more schooling. Three years into this itinerant, impoverished life, he courted and married the dark-haired, devoutly prim daughter of a local farmer. Ursula was a year older than Burroughs and unused to poverty, to her husband's dreamy ambitions, and to what she regarded as his "unwholesome" physical desires. But mismatched as they turned out to be, the two remained together until Ursula's death sixty years later.

A year before his marriage, Burroughs discovered the essays of

Emerson and, he said later, by reading them found his calling as a writer. Emerson's essays gave Burroughs a sense of the religious in nature, free of the doctrinaire fundamentalism Burroughs detested in his father's dogmatism. He read "Nature," "The Divinity School Address," and other essays "in a state of ecstasy. I got him in my blood," Burroughs wrote; Emerson "colored my whole intellectual outlook."[13]

Not long after falling under that spell, Burroughs' own Emerson-like essays began to appear in small literary magazines in New York and elsewhere. One in particular, titled "Expression," demonstrated the depth of his adulation for the older man. Burroughs sent it to James Russell Lowell, then editor of the *Atlantic Monthly*. Lowell suspected plagiarism but nevertheless accepted it and published it several months later. When the essay appeared in the *Atlantic Monthly* anonymously (as most articles in that journal did), it was so much like Emerson in style and sentiment that everyone who read it assumed it had been written by the great transcendentalist. In subsequent letters to the *Atlantic*, readers praised "Emerson's" newest essay.

Burroughs, seeing his idolatry on public display, was horrified. Twenty-three years old, an impoverished teacher in a small town having been mistaken in print for the sage of Concord, Burroughs vowed always from then on to write in his own voice and only about things that he knew, even though these things at the time amounted to no more than the farms, hills, and wildlife of the Catskills and the Hudson River Valley. Over his lifetime Burroughs would travel widely, often in grand style, and eventually what he knew firsthand would come to encompass much. But it was always to this region and its rural familiarity that he returned, both in person and in his writing.

During this period, while still a young schoolteacher, Burroughs encountered in a library Audubon's masterfully produced study *The Birds of America*. Although he had grown up delighting in birds, the beauty of this sumptuous work inspired Burroughs to take up ornithology with new seriousness. More importantly, like Emerson's essays, the book ignited in Burroughs an intense desire to write. He felt rising inside himself the ambition to convey in graceful prose the affection for wildlife that Audubon had rendered in paint. Beginning his study with the forested Catskills and surrounding farms of his rural home, Burroughs determined to turn his love for nature into literature.

His ambitions were high, but at age twenty-six Burroughs was so desperately poor that he and Ursula could barely afford to rent a house to live in. For years, Ursula roomed on and off with her family while John boarded around with the families of his students. Often traveling far from home in order to take teaching jobs, he returned to his father-in-law's home to find Ursula's bedroom uncomfortably close to her father's, an arrangement that strained his marriage even further.

Burroughs tried his hand at a number of other occupations. The strong-willed Ursula urged him to go to New York City and become a businessman. He even tried a scheme to sell buckles. But all his attempts at employment other than teaching failed. Ursula's dissatisfaction with their poverty, her displeasure at his paltry salary and at his unremunerative scribbling—his foolish masquerading as a writer, as she called it—led to frequent quarrels and more than once to separations. In a daring attempt to break free of his indebtedness, the frustrated and unhappy twenty-six-year-old Burroughs abruptly quit his most recent teaching position in the autumn of 1863 and traveled to Washington, D.C., leaving Ursula behind to live off her relatives and fend off creditors until he could find a job to support her.

Burroughs had no prospects when he left, but he was determined to make a change for the better. In the city as winter came on, he slept on a borrowed cot and worked, when he could find any employment, at menial labor. He was heartsick and lonely for Ursula. But to his good fortune, in Washington Burroughs very soon met an extraordinary older writer who would take his mind off his poverty. In the months and years to come, this man—a writer as complicated and out of bounds in his own way as Thoreau, but fatherly, gentle, and gregarious, as Thoreau would not have been—would take young Burroughs under his wing and change his life. The writer was Walt Whitman.

From their first walks together, the poet encouraged Burroughs' literary dreams and in particular nurtured his belief that he could make something wonderful out of his two loves: nature and writing. Their friendship may account for some of the best qualities in Burroughs' early essays on wildlife. Out of affection for the older man and his work, over the years Burroughs wrote scores of laudatory essays about Whitman, wrote and published at his own expense the first book ever written about him, and remained one of his most eloquent defenders against a scandalized public. In Whitman's old age, Burroughs saw to his friend's comfort whenever he could, raised money for his welfare, and was one of the pallbearers at his funeral.

When Burroughs met Walt Whitman in Washington, Thoreau had been dead a year and a half. Six years earlier, Thoreau had met Whitman through Bronson Alcott, and it is worth recalling that meeting in order to compare Burroughs with Thoreau.[14]

During the fall before he met Whitman, Thoreau had taken a job surveying a Fourierist commune that had folded near Perth Amboy, New Jersey. While he surveyed, subdividing the failed socialist community into lots for resale, Thoreau read some of his lectures as evening entertainment for the new suburban land owners. The surveying finished, Thoreau and Alcott traveled to New York for a few days, visiting among others Horace Greeley, the founder of the *New York Tribune*. Alcott and Thoreau roomed together for a day at Dr. Russel T. Trall's Water Cure and Hydropathic Medical College, then on Sunday went to Brooklyn to hear Henry Ward Beecher deliver a sermon at Plymouth Church.

Beecher was considered the most eloquent orator of his time; as a result, every space in the church was packed to overflowing. By all accounts, Beecher's lofty style and eloquence swept away most of the congregation, including Alcott. Thoreau, in contrast, fidgeted throughout the sermon, wincing at Beecher's overly dramatic delivery.

After the sermon Thoreau and Alcott went to find the notorious poet whom Alcott had met earlier in the year. Alcott had found Whitman "an extraordinary person, full of brute power, certainly of genius and audacity" and, though two years younger, "as hard to tame as Thoreau."[15] He looked forward eagerly to seeing the two together.

Whitman was not at home that Sunday, but when Alcott and Thoreau returned the next morning, the poet was there to greet them. He took them upstairs to the attic room he shared with Eddie, his retarded, epileptic brother. The living conditions looked a little rough to Alcott. The bed the brothers shared seemed not to have been made in a long time, and the chamberpot needed to be emptied.[16]

Thoreau was thirty-nine at the time and had published *Walden* just two years before. The book had been well reviewed but sold only modestly (it would not sell more than 2,000 copies in Thoreau's lifetime). Whitman's *Leaves of Grass*, first published a year after *Walden*, had also sold very few copies. But having received a glowing letter from Emerson concerning the book—the kind of letter Thoreau would have been grateful for but did not receive—Whitman had quickly ordered the printing of a second edition, with Emerson's praise quoted in gold leaf on the spine. The new edition had just come off press, and Whitman gave Thoreau an inscribed copy to take home to Concord.

During the two-hour meeting, Alcott did his best to bait Whitman and Thoreau. But, as he wrote later, "each seemed planted fast in reserves . . . like two beasts, each wondering what the other would do, whether to snap or run." Alcott may well have exaggerated the encounter. "Whether Thoreau was meditating the possibility of Walt's stealing away his 'out-of-doors' for some sinister ends, poetic or pecuniary, I could not well divine, nor whether Walt suspected or not that he had here, for once, and the first time, found his match and more at smelling out 'all Nature,' a sagacity potent, penetrating and peerless as his own, if indeed not more piercing and profound, finer and more formidable."

Despite Alcott's efforts, apparently only a few direct exchanges occurred between the two writers. Thoreau, in a letter to a friend a month later, remembered saying, "in answer to him as representing America, that I did not think much of America or of politics, and so on, which may have been somewhat of a damper to him."[17] Thoreau never felt himself to be close to the masses, whereas Whitman, though polite and gentle in responding to his guest, could speak of little else, other than himself and his own poetry, all of which were more or less bound up together in his mind and in his conversation. It was not that Thoreau disdained the common man. When it came to the American populace and to America in the abstract, however, he felt "that my connections with and obligations to society are still very slight and transient."[18] Not surprisingly, then, Thoreau, small-statured, tough and spare as the trunk of a young oak, was initially suspicious and guarded with this large, loquacious man for whom the entire human community and his own large ego were intertwined.

But Thoreau's suspicions did not extend to Whitman's poetry. He had already read the first edition of Leaves of Grass and thought enough of it to send a copy to an acquaintance. Back in Concord with the newly printed second edition in hand, Thoreau wrote to his friend Harrison Blake that Whitman's book had done him more good than any reading he had done for a long time. "We ought to rejoice greatly in him," Thoreau wrote. "He occasionally suggests something a little more than human."[19]

For his part, Whitman later recalled that during their meeting Thoreau had heatedly defended Leaves of Grass against its critics, of whom there were many.[20] Following Thoreau's death six years later, when Thoreau's reputation was low, Whitman described him as "one of the native forces—stands for a fact, a movement, an upheaval: Thoreau belongs to America, to the transcendental, to the protesters . . . he was a force—he looms up bigger and bigger: his dying does not seem to have hurt him a bit." And, Whitman added, "One thing about Thoreau keeps him very near to me: I refer to his lawlessness—his dissent—his going his own absolute road let hell blaze all it chooses."[21]

Burroughs was twenty-six, Whitman forty-four when they met in 1863. Because most people considered his poetry profane and obscene—the New York *Criterion* called it "a mass of stupid filth"—Whitman had recently been fired from his job as a clerk in the Bureau of Indian Affairs by Lincoln's Secretary of the Interior, James Harlan, who set out to purge the department of "all such persons, as disregard in their conduct, habits and associations the rules of decorum & propriety prescribed by a Christian Civilization." Harlan purged about eighty employees, including all the women in the department "on the grounds that their presence there might be injurious to . . . the 'morals' of the men." Under this directive he also purged Whitman.[22] Harlan had seen a copy of the third edition of *Leaves of Grass* in Whitman's office and declared he would rather resign his own post than stand to have Whitman remain within his department. The firing troubled Whitman's friends— who were outraged on his behalf—more than it did the poet, and shortly after his firing they secured him a new government job, as a clerk in the office of the Attorney General.

Burroughs, meanwhile, had arrived in the war-shocked city of Washington virtually destitute. The dusty, unpaved streets were crowded with tens of thousands of wounded and dying soldiers, their number exceeding the city's normal peacetime population. So many were sick and dying that they bunked even in the halls of the Capital Building and in the East Room of the White House. The war casualties occupied churches, taverns, and private homes, and they passed along the streets in slow processions of huge horse-drawn ambulances.

Burroughs' first job, which he found unbearable, involved digging mass graves for the burial of black Union soldiers. It was a heart-wrenching task, and not until midwinter of 1864 did he find another job, as a clerk in a government office. Landing his new position made Burroughs sleepless with joy. Released at last from his grim duties and from poverty, he could send for Ursula. And on top of all this he had Walt Whitman as a friend.[23]

Burroughs had idolized Whitman for some years before they were introduced by a young acquaintance of Burroughs who had moved to Washington. Burroughs and his friends had read Whitman's poems in the New York press, and the year before Burroughs relocated to Washington he had bought a copy of Leaves of Grass. Soon after he met the older man Burroughs wrote, "If that is not the face of a poet, then it is the face of a god."[24] Whitman seemed to him larger than life and full of health, "like a great wild buffalo with much hair."[25] To Whitman, Burroughs' face was "like a field of wheat," so innocent and raw did he seem. Whitman called him "Jack."[26]

Almost as soon as they became acquainted, Whitman began to take Burroughs on visits of mercy to wounded soldiers. Burroughs' admiration for Whitman only increased through witnessing these acts of humanity, and the two saw each other more and more frequently. When Ursula eventually joined Burroughs in Washington, the three breakfasted together daily in Burroughs' small rented house behind the Capitol. Ursula did the cooking, and the bachelor poet, who lived squalidly after spending most of his money buying gifts for sick and dying soldiers, talked and ate heartily, and charmed even the pragmatic Ursula.

Three years after moving to Washington, Burroughs finished his first extended piece of writing, a biographical study titled Notes on Walt Whitman as Poet and Person, which he published himself. Whitman seems to have composed some of the work, looking over

Burroughs' shoulder, adding insights and enhancing the analysis. The book had no commercial appeal at all. "Not fifty copies have been disposed of, which is proof, I think, that the book has something in it," Burroughs wrote to a friend six months after publication. But Burroughs was satisfied. He stacked the unsold copies in his living room, where Ursula found them an affront to her fastidious housekeeping and further proof that her husband's scribbling was a profitless waste of effort.[27]

As the two men became closer friends, Whitman took a warm interest in Burroughs' treks along Rock Creek and into the woods around Washington. Whitman had a profound interest in nature, and he listened well to the younger man's enthusiastic stories and observations about birds and wildlife. In the summer of 1865 Burroughs' passion embraced the hermit thrush. He told Whitman that the bird's song was "the finest sound in nature . . . perhaps more of an evening than a morning hymn . . . the voice of that calm, sweet solemnity one attains to in his best moments." Whitman jotted down what Burroughs said. "Sings oftener after sundown . . . is very secluded . . . likes shaded, dark places," he wrote in one of his notebooks. "His song is a hymn . . . in swamps—is very shy . . . never sings near the farm houses—never in the settlement—is the bird of the solemn primal woods & of Nature pure & holy."[28]

From these notes Whitman developed a portrait of the hermit thrush for his great elegy to Lincoln, "When Lilacs Last in the Dooryard Bloom'd." There Whitman evoked memories of the dead president in the voice of the bird's plaintive song:

Solitary the thrush,
The hermit withdrawn to himself, avoiding the settlements,
Sings by himself a song.

Song of the bleeding throat . . .

Burroughs' modest nature essays soon began appearing in popular journals, including such important and influential ones as

Atlantic Monthly, Putnam's, and *Scribner's.* He began to have something of a following, and in the fall of 1870, when Burroughs was thirty-three, the Boston publishers Hurd and Houghton asked him if he would consider collecting his essays into a book. Published the following year, *Wake-Robin* owed much, including the title, to Whitman's editing and guidance.[29] William Dean Howells, reviewing the book in *Atlantic Monthly,* said, "the dusk and cool and quiet of the forest seem to wrap the reader . . . It is sort of a summer vacation to turn the pages . . . Mr. Burroughs adds a strain of genuine poetry which makes his papers unusually delightful, while he has more humor than generally falls to the ornithological tribe."[30]

Much of this charming book is about common birds, such as the partridge. "Whir! whir! whir! and a brood of half-grown partridges start up like an explosion, a few paces from me, and scattering, disappear in the bushes on all sides," Burroughs wrote excitedly. "Let me sit down here behind the screen of ferns and briars, and hear this wild hen of the woods call together her brood. At what an early age the partridge flies! Nature seems to concentrate her energies on the wing, making the safety of the bird a point to be looked after first; and while the body is covered with down, and no signs of feathers are visible, the wing-quills sprout and unfold, and in an incredibly short time the young make fair headway in flying."

Burroughs' loving notice of these common creatures reminded his readers of Gilbert White, but with more figurative language, more tenderness, and more subjectivity. "When Nature made the bluebird she wished to propitiate both the sky and the earth," Burroughs began a chapter, "so she gave him the color of the one on his back and the hue of the other on his breast, and ordained that his appearance in spring should denote that the strife and war between these two elements was at an end. Here is the peace-harbinger; in him the celestial and terrestrial strike hands and are fast friends. He means the furrow and he means the warmth; he means all the soft, wooing influences of the spring on the one hand, and the retreating footsteps of winter on the other."

Later in his career, Burroughs differentiated himself from both Gilbert White and Thoreau. "There is really little or no resemblance between us," he wrote. "Thoreau's aim is mainly ethical, as much so as Emerson's is. The aim of White of Selbourne [sic] was mainly scientific. My own aim, so far as I have any, is entirely artistic. I care little for the merely scientific aspects of things, and nothing for the ethical. I will not preach one word. I will have a pure result, or nothing. I paint the bird, or the trout, or the scene, for its own sake."[31]

In writing his first book on nature, Burroughs had learned much through his friendship with Whitman about the craft of writing, but he had learned even more about the larger use to which an interest in natural history might be put. During those early talks with Whitman, he wrote in his journal, "I was trying to express to him how, by some wonderful indirection, I was helped by my knowledge of the birds, the animals—cows, and common objects." Whitman responded to Burroughs' passion supportively, saying that a close study of even insects would reveal insights greater than those of theology. Whitman's point was much like Thoreau's: that a fact, no matter how small, in the hands of a great writer might blossom into a truth. "There are so many ways by which Nature may be come at," the twenty-eight-year-old Burroughs continued in his journal, trying to catch the essence of a particular conversation with Whitman. "So many sides to her, whether by bird, or insect, or flower, by hunting, or science— when one thing is really known, you can no longer be deceived; you possess a key, a standard; you effect an entrance, and everything else links on and follows."[32]

Whitman confirmed all that Burroughs had dared to think about natural history as a subject. At the same time, he warned his friend that to render nature well, the nature writer had to be as inspired as the poet. On the basis of this counsel Burroughs dared to

reason that in the right hands natural history could actually be poetry if treated as vision and not merely as science. "So far as he had
observed," Burroughs wrote, again referring to his conversations
with Whitman, the authorities on natural history "have been mere
explorers, and have gone no farther than they could see; have
caught no hints or clues by which large and important inferences
can be drawn." Burroughs called these conversations "grand, glorious talk," and he became determined to reach the high goals for
his writing that Whitman urged him to believe attainable.[33] With
Whitman's guidance, he told a friend, he was setting out to "liber-
ate the birds from the scientists."[34]

"The poet's pursuit of Nature is the only true one," Burroughs
wrote, paraphrasing Whitman. "The study of natural history, to be
profitable and true, must be grafted on a deep and abiding love of
Nature; not the birds or the plants for themselves, but so far as they
express and stand for the spirit of Nature. Is your delight the same,
if you see no bird or flower? If not, you will never interpret aright
these forms."[35]

Bold as his conversation became, Burroughs feared in his heart
that he was not a poet, or at least not yet. And so the claims he made
for his work early in his career were appropriately modest. In the
preface to the first edition of *Wake-Robin* he wrote, "This is mainly
a book about the Birds, or more properly an invitation to the study
of Ornithology and the purpose of the author will be carried out in
proportion as it awakens and stimulates the interest of the reader
in this branch of Natural History.

"Though written less in the spirit of exact science than with the
freedom of love and old acquaintance, yet I have in no instance
taken liberties with facts, or allowed my imagination to influence
me to the extent of giving a false impression or a wrong coloring. I
have reaped my harvest more in the woods than in the study; what
I offer, in fact, is a careful and conscientious record of actual observations and experiences, and it is true as it stands written, every
word of it."

Two decades later, when Burroughs was a famous author and *Wake-Robin* was being prepared for reissue as part of his collected works, he interpreted his approach to nature writing more fully. "I cannot bring myself to think of my books as 'works,' " he wrote, "because little 'work' has gone to the making of them. It has all been play. I have gone a-fishing, or camping, or canoeing, and new literary material has been the result. My corn has grown while I loitered or slept. The writing of the book was only a second and finer enjoyment of my holiday in the fields or woods. Not till the writing did it really seem to strike in and become part of me."

In fairness to his own ambitions as an artist, however, Burroughs could hardly leave it at that. He knew that careful writing was not merely play, and he had no desire to create the impression that his writing lacked higher merit or meaning. "Literature does not grow wild in the woods," he continued. "Every artist does something more than copy Nature; more comes out in his account than goes into the original experience.

"Most persons think the bee gets honey from the flowers, but she does not: honey is a product of the bee; it is the nectar of the flowers with the bee added. What the bee gets from the flower is sweet water: this she puts through a process of her own and imparts to it her own quality; she reduces the water and adds to it a minute drop of formic acid. It is this drop of herself that gives the delicious sting to her sweet. The bee is therefore the type of the true poet, the true artist. Her product always reflects her environment, and it reflects something her environment knows not of. We taste the clover, the thyme, the linden, the sumac, and we also taste something that has its source in none of these flowers.

"The literary naturalist does not take liberties with facts; facts are the flora upon which he lives. The more and the fresher the facts the better. I can do nothing without them, but I must give them my own flavor. I must impart to them a quality which heightens and intensifies them.

"To interpret Nature is not to improve upon her: it is to draw her out; it is to have an emotional intercourse with her, absorb her, and reproduce her tinged with the colors of the spirit.

"If I name every bird I see in my walk, describe its color and ways, etc., give a lot of facts or details about the birds, it is doubtful if my reader is interested. But if I relate the bird in some way to human life, to my own life,—show what it is to me and what it is in the landscape and the season,—then do I give my reader a live bird and not a labeled specimen."

Burroughs spent ten years in Washington, much of it seated as a clerk before an iron vault in the basement of the Treasury Department, where he kept track of all the bank notes that went in and out. There, in intervals snatched from his working hours, he wrote and dreamed of the Catskills and the Hudson River Valley that he loved. He was good at his job and received promotions regularly, becoming well off if not wealthy. But he felt, he said, like a fowl with no gravel in its gizzard. As time passed, he became hungry for the earth and said he would eat it like a horse if he could only get at it.[36]

Abruptly in 1873, thirty-six years old and finally seeing new opportunities, Burroughs resigned his position and was immediately appointed receiver of a failed bank in upstate New York. At the same time, he became a part-time national bank examiner for the same region. At last he considered himself freed from what he called "eating government dirt." And as he took over his new positions, Burroughs bought a nine-acre farm in West Park, overlooking the Hudson River ninety miles north of Manhattan. There he built a rambling stone house that he christened "Riverby." It would be his family's main residence for the rest of his life.

Part of Burroughs' motive in buying the farm was to make it pay enough to get him out of the bank business altogether and give him time to write. Burroughs wanted, as his biographer Edward Renehan writes, "to be able to spend all of his todays nostalgically re-creating a rural yesterday both on his farm and in his books. He wanted to be able to define himself solely via the creation processes through which he found his most vital link to the past: the processes of farming and writing."[37]

Two years after he moved to Riverby, Burroughs' second book of nature writing was published. Again it comprised essays he had published in popular journals, and again his writing was greeted warmly by readers and critics. Henry James found *Winter Sunshine* "a very charming little book . . . The minuteness of [Burroughs'] observation, the keenness of his perception, give him a real originality, and his sketches have a delightful oddity, vivacity, and freshness." James characterized Burroughs as "a sort of reduced, but also more humorous, more available, and more sociable Thoreau." The *Boston Gazette* hailed Burroughs as "one of the most delightful American essayists, and in the description of our out-door scenes, sports, and observations, we know of no one who excels him."[38]

Thereafter Burroughs published a new book about every other year, twenty-seven altogether. Not all were nature studies; he occasionally wrote philosophical essays and literary criticism, in addition to a biography of Audubon and a second study of Whitman. But it was as a disciplined field naturalist with extraordinary knowledge of his locale that he became a literary figure of national prominence.

For much of his career Burroughs objected to the suggestion that he had been influenced to any significant degree by Thoreau. In the 1880s, though acknowledging that Thoreau had rare descriptive powers and high principles, Burroughs characterized him as "grim, uncompromising, almost heartless." In a popular article on Thoreau, reprinted in his book *Indoor Studies,* Burroughs recounted Thoreau's story of meeting a skunk on one of his walks. "One day he met a skunk in the field," Burroughs wrote, "and he describes its peculiar gait exactly when he says: 'It runs, even when undisturbed, with a singular teeter or undulation, like the walking of a Chinese lady.' [Thoreau] ran after the animal to observe it, keeping out of the reach of its formidable weapon, and when it took refuge in the wall he interviewed it at his leisure." Burroughs told the story not only to credit Thoreau's skill as a writer but also to underscore his aversion to humankind, which Burroughs interpreted as mean-spiritedness. "If it had been a man or a woman he had met" instead of a skunk, he concluded, Thoreau "would have run the other way."[39] Only after he had gained a large readership, toward the end of his life, did Burroughs willingly admit to kinship with Thoreau, and then only with reservations. "I have always read him with keen interest," he said, "but I don't owe him any great debt."[40]

Burroughs never put Thoreau out of his mind, however, and wrote about him and Whitman his entire life—just as he continued to write about Emerson. In his last book, published posthumously in 1922, he devoted a long chapter to Lowell's 1864 diatribe against Thoreau. He took issue with Lowell's criticism, asserting that "both by training and by temperament, Lowell is disqualified from entering into Thoreau's character and aims."[41]

It had taken Burroughs a long time to reach this assessment. In the 1880s he had been saying that Thoreau "was more intent on the natural history of his own thought than on that of the bird. To the last, his ornithology was not quite sure, not quite trustworthy."[42] Even in his final assessment, at the end of his life, Burroughs was disturbed by Thoreau's examination of the self and society—just as many of Burroughs' genteel readers were. Meaning to give Thoreau his due without praising him too highly, Burroughs asserted that "Thoreau was not a great philosopher, he was not a great naturalist, he was not a great poet, but as nature-writer and an original character he is unique in our literature. His philosophy begins and ends with himself, or is entirely subjective, and is frequently fantastic, and nearly always illogical . . . There are crudities in his writings that make the conscientious literary craftsman shudder; there are mistakes of observation that make the serious naturalist wonder; and there is often an expression of contempt for his fellow countrymen, and the rest of mankind, and their aims in life, that make the judicious grieve."[43]

In many ways, however, Burroughs was one of those judicious countrymen Thoreau had been eager to upset with his paradoxes and complications. Almost from the beginning, as a writer, Burroughs intended to upset no one, except perhaps churchgoers, whom he despised, in reaction to the fundamentalism his father had imposed on him as a child. It is to Burroughs' credit, then, that late in his career he acknowledged many of his literary shortcomings that resulted from his eagerness to please. He added in his last assessment that Thoreau was "suggestive of those antibodies which modern science makes so much of. He tends to fortify us against the dry rot of business, the seductions of social pleasures, the pride of wealth and position. He is antitoxic; he is a literary germicide of peculiar power. He is too religious to go to church, too patriotic to pay his taxes, too fervent a humanist to interest himself in the social welfare of his neighborhood."[44] In contrast, Burroughs wrote, "I do not take readers to nature to give them a lesson, but to have a good time."[45] He took no extreme positions to impugn the social respectability of his readers. As Joseph Wood Krutch observed, "The ordinary citizen could read Burroughs with full assurance that he would not be scolded as Thoreau would scold him."[46] In short, Burroughs wrote for people like himself who enjoyed, on their literary nature walks, a felicity of description more than a meteorology of the mind.

Shy and diffident in public, Burroughs preferred his rural home to traveling. Like Thoreau he loved his solitude, and he had an abiding love for the natural world, especially birds. But unlike Thoreau, Burroughs hungered for approval both from the public at large and from his literary peers. He was artistically ambitious, but at the same time he saw no harm in making as much money as possible from his writing, partly to satisfy Ursula and partly to collect for himself the perquisites that came with fame—literary awards, dinners with wealthy patrons, and photo sessions with friendly politicians.

With all these mixed qualities, Burroughs produced a prose that was graceful and literary while expressing an attitude toward nature very much in harmony with what the country and its political leaders wanted to hear. He met all the American literary luminaries of his day, and even hosted Oscar Wilde at his small cabin next to Riverby in the Catskills. In his middle age he allowed his publisher and friends to make him the head of his own nature cult. The elderly John Burroughs, bearded and silver-haired, was known as "John o' Birds," and flocks of schoolchildren joined the John Burroughs Society to celebrate the man and his books. When he journeyed cross-country by train with Teddy Roosevelt in 1903, it was Burroughs as much as the president whom the crowds came out to cheer.

In 1912 the elderly Burroughs wrote several essays commenting on the destructive influence of the latest piece of American technology, the automobile. Burroughs called it a "demon" machine capable of taking people into "even the most secluded nook or corner of the forest and befoul[ing] it with noise and smoke."[47]

Shortly after these essays appeared, Henry Ford wrote to Burroughs thanking him for the many pleasures his books had given him. Ford read very few books in his life, but Burroughs' were among them. "He wants to do something for me," the flattered naturalist reported to a friend. "He wants to present me with an automobile all complete, and send a man to teach Julian [Burroughs' son] how to run it. His sole motive is his admiration for me and my work—there shall be no publicity in connection with it."[48]

The car arrived in January and in fact produced an enormous amount of publicity. A whole series of photographs shows Burroughs and Ford sitting together happily in the Model T. A close and long-lived friendship developed between Burroughs and

Ford, and Burroughs never again wrote critically about the neighing of the iron horse.

The episode is typical of Burroughs' relationships with the powerful and wealthy men of his time. Besides Ford, Burroughs formed friendships with Harvey Firestone, E. H. Harriman, Thomas Edison, Andrew Carnegie, and Theodore Roosevelt. He allowed himself to be photographed blessing hydroelectric power plants with industrialists, then to be captured on publicity newsreels birdwatching with them in the forests they were planning to exploit for natural resources. He called Ford "a lovable man" despite the fact that Ford, like Edison and Firestone, was rabidly anti-Semitic, his factories fouled Detroit's air and destroyed its waterways, and his goons were later dispatched to brutally crush America's budding labor movement. In the autumn of 1913 Burroughs traveled with Ford in a fleet of cars around New England, the first of several trips he would undertake with the carmaker. In this instance the route included a pilgrimage to Concord. Ford's camera crews filmed the two men walking through Emerson's old house. They tramped around Walden Pond and visited Sleepy Hollow Cemetery, where the great transcendentalists were buried. Ford and Burroughs stood together smiling over Thoreau's headstone as newsreel cameras churned.

Regardless of Burroughs' reluctance to criticize the politicians and industrialists who used him for their own ends, his writing engendered a love of nature in millions of Americans that made them conscious of the rapid destruction of natural habitats. He respected facts and was, as one of his friends remarked, "encyclopedic in his knowledge of birds, flowers, trees, rocks"; surely he was "the most serious, passionate, and genuinely intrigued of all amateur natural historians."[49] His writing was well crafted, vivid, and often eloquent, wise in many ways, and seldom sentimental.

If Burroughs is not read much today, it is because in our time there is a great urgency to preserve wilderness, and Burroughs was not much taken by the wild. When the *Atlantic Monthly* published a tribute to him in 1910, to commemorate Burroughs' fifty years of writing for the magazine, fellow nature writer Dallas Lore Sharp considered the differences between Burroughs and Thoreau on just this point.

"If Mr. Burroughs were to start from my door for a tramp over these small Hingham hills he would cross the trout-brook by my neighbor's stone bridge, and nibbling a spear of peppermint on the way, would follow the lane and the cowpaths across the pasture. Thoreau would pick out the deepest hole in the brook and try to swim across; he would leap the stone walls of the lane, cut a beeline through the pasture, and drop, for his first look at the landscape, to the bottom of the pit in the seam-face granite quarry. Here he would pull out his notebook and a gnarly wild apple from his pocket, and intensely, critically, chemically, devouring said apple, make note in the book that the apples of Eden were flat, the apples of Sodom bitter, but this wild, tough, wretched, impossible apple of the Hingham hills united all ambrosial essences in its striking odor of squash-bugs.

"Mr. Burroughs takes us along with him. Thoreau comes upon us in the woods—jumps out at us from behind some bush, with a '*Scat!*' Burroughs brings us home in time for tea; Thoreau leaves us tangled up in the briars.

"It won't hurt us to be jumped at now and then and told to '*scat!*' It won't hurt us to be digged by the briars. It is good for us, otherwise we might forget that *we* are beneath our clothes. It is good for us and highly diverting, but highly irritating too.

"For my part, when I take up an outdoor book I am glad if there is quiet in it, and fragrance, and something of the saneness and sweetness of the sky . . . Thoreau is a succession of showers—'tempests'; his pages are sheet-lightning, electrifying, purifying, illuminating, but not altogether conducive to peace. There is a clear sky to most of Mr. Burroughs's pages, a rural landscape, wide, gently rolling, with cattle standing here and there beneath the trees."[50]

Sharp and many of the readers of the *Atlantic* had no taste for squash bugs, and neither did Burroughs.[51] His gift was to make nature seem available to common people, but he also—for better or worse—made it seem unnecessary that they actually experience the outdoors for themselves, so placid and immediate did nature seem in his prose. Burroughs offered himself as his readers' friendly representative to the natural world: someone who would walk the trails for them, observe closely, then gracefully report back nature's most gentle aspects, where none of the trails were too steep. "Showing somewhere along every open field in Burroughs's book is a piece of fence," Sharp said in both accurately and affectionately summing up Burroughs' work, "and among his trees there is always a patch of gray sloping roof."[52]

Chapter Five

THE WOODCOCK'S LEG

At the turn of the century the sixty-three-year-old John Burroughs was the most venerated nature writer in America. He had a long, grandfatherly beard, and his white hair rose about his balding head like a halo. Angelic in photographs, he was perceived by his readers as gentle and tolerant, perpetually sunny and endearing, "a child in the heart." As his companion in later life, Clara Barrus, wrote, he was "much rhymed about, much painted, modeled, and photographed, and—much loved."[1]

Burroughs was by no means the only American nature writer in 1900, nor the only successful one. In fact such an astonishing number of nature books were being published that a 1903 article in *Outlook* proclaimed, "no sign of the times is more significant of the change in American habits than the number of volumes on flowers, trees, shrubs, birds, which are constantly coming from the press."[2] Dallas Lore Sharp, a prolific nature essayist himself, observed in the *Atlantic* that "nature-writing and the automobile business have developed vastly during the past few years."[3]

In his glib way, Sharp was commenting on the perils for America's wilderness latent in both of these booming, mass-production industries. The dangers from automobiles were becoming all too apparent; the dangers from a certain kind of popular nature book—at least in Burroughs' mind—would soon need to be exposed by Burroughs himself, with the help of the press and his powerful friends.

Between 1870 and 1900 America was rapidly evolving from an agrarian economy into an industrial one. The population doubled to 76 million largely as a result of an influx of immigrants, many driven by necessity from their homelands and hopeful of finding a new life on a boundless continent. By 1900, however, the majority of these immigrants were at work not in the unpopulated outlands of America but in its grim factories and mills, in overcrowded cities choked with foul air, poor sanitation, poverty, and violence.

As conditions in urban centers worsened, Americans in eastern cities looked through the factory smoke outside their windows and longed for a cleaner, healthier life. They remembered—or imagined—a world of harmony and goodness that now seemed nearly gone. In their memories that goodness lay somewhere in the suburban fields or among the wooded lots of the distant farms.

Even though they entertained this "Arcadian myth," a dream set in an idealized rural past—whether in the era of the American Indian or of Gilbert White—few Americans wanted to reject all the conveniences of city life.[4] Material comforts were not to be given up that easily. Instead, the back-to-nature movement that reached national proportions by 1900 tended to mythologize a bygone rural life as it might have existed had there been no effort to real farming. As early as the 1850s this pastoral dream was expressed, according to historian Peter J. Schmitt, as having "brooks murmuring with a contented babble, cattle lazily in groups that need no care, and flowers opening that need no culture."[5]

The centuries-long slaughter of native Americans in the New World complicated the Arcadian myth. Now that these peoples had been nearly eradicated and the survivors removed to reservations, they were thought of as having lived an idyllic existence in an American Eden. Sentimental portraits represented them as emblematic of what America should have been. Their tradition—a life in holistic balance with the environment—was perpetuated in various forms in small communities and in marginal religious and cultural societies.[6] The endurance of the tradition, including the fact that a few native American groups continued to exist in isolated parts of the continent, only underscored the disharmony that the majority of the new industrial settlers felt so keenly.

The destruction of America's native peoples was blamed in part on the scientific paradigms and worldview that had conquered the Western frontier. Science was also blamed for having despoiled the American landscape and for having precipitated America's sense of spiritual loss and fragmentation. A new attitude toward nature was needed, distinct from the mechanistic vision of the universe created by a heartless, reductive science. As John Burroughs phrased it, empirical science had turned human beings out into the cold and made them shelterless against the "eternities and infinities of geological time and sidereal space." What Americans needed was science with a heart, a "spiritual Natural History."[7]

In his concept of "communion with nature" Henry Thoreau offered an antidote to the despair beginning to afflict the new century. Around 1900 Thoreau's work underwent a rediscovery and revival. His journals and letters were published in full for the first time, and he became the subject of sympathetic biographies and essays. Readers began to see that Thoreau had imagined "communion" not in an orthodox religious way, of course, but as the ingestion of a wild, astringent eucharist that had been handed down from the native Americans and that could transform science along with the human spirit.[8] In a sense, Thoreau's lifelong project in natural history had been to imagine the kind of scientist who, in learning "facts," would become not less like a native American but more. In his earliest essay Thoreau had written, "The true man of science will know nature better by his finer organization; he will smell, taste, see, hear, feel, better than other men. His will be a deeper and finer experience. We do not learn by inference and deduction, and the application of mathematics to philosophy, but by direct intercourse and sympathy . . . The most scientific will still be the healthiest and friendliest man, and possess a more perfect Indian wisdom."[9]

Along with their renewed passion for nature and their association of the outdoor life with health, Americans developed an intense interest in "cures" of all kinds, for both mind and body.[10] "Potentizations" of vitality, water cures, Swedenborgian Influx, homeopathy, chiropractic, and vegetarianism blossomed in the American imagination—many of them expressions of the public's fear that life had become terribly disjointed, mechanized, and dispirited. As historian Gail Thain Parker writes, "The All-Supply and the national park system, influx and the strenuous life—these were the dreams of people who felt crowded and pinched."[11]

Americans began to journey out of the cities and into the suburbs and countryside in ever greater numbers for the healthful benefits of blue skies and clean water. In 1872 local "Fresh Air Charities" sprang up as a way to give slum children the benefits of unpolluted atmosphere and nature education. In 1874 the Young Women's Christian Association became the first national organization to encourage outdoor recreation as a "retreat for industrial working girls."[12] The first Young Men's Christian Association camp was established ten years later. By 1895 the Fresh Air Charities were transporting half a million children to summer outings in the country.[13] At the turn of the new century, other long-lived nature groups were formed, including the Boy Scouts, Camp Fire Girls, and Girl Scouts, each advocating the healthy influence of nature on young children. Schools of woodcraft guided by "Buckskin Regulations" sprouted up, and summer camps appeared. Programs ranged from retreats in which youngsters were forced to rough it on Spartan fare to programs in which toddlers were tended by campfire mothers who tucked them in and supervised their proper hygiene. There were Woodcraft Indians, Sons of Daniel Boone, Buckskin Knights, Boy Pioneers, Outdoor Chums, and

Ranger Boys. And a wealth of instructional pamphlets appeared to give them guidance. Soon there were magazines, handbooks, and novels especially for children who went to camp, including the "Bobbsey Twins," created in 1904, "The Outdoor Girls," and "Bunny Brown."[14]

While children of those who could afford a rural escape went to country schools, their parents went to country clubs. These adult symbols of wealth began as suburban hunting clubs, where businessmen could go to shoot or ride in semidomesticated forests. By 1900 country clubs had evolved into places where harried wealthy urbanites played golf on manicured fairways.[15]

But despite their efforts to create patches of green to which they could retreat, Americans could not help fearing that their affection for nature had arrived too late to save many habitats and forms of wildlife. The more interested they became in having the outdoors as an escape from the city, the more destruction of nature they saw resulting from uncontrolled industrialism. Not only had the great tribes of native peoples been killed or removed to distant reservations; the wilderness itself was officially gone, wiped out by westward expansion. Forests that had seemed inexhaustible had been clear-cut and sold or turned into pasture.[16] Vast herds of large mammals in the West had been annihilated. The last great buffalo slaughter had taken place in 1882, the Arizona elk became extinct in 1906, and bighorn sheep in the Badlands were gone by 1908. Brightly plumed birds that once filled the skies by the millions had been hunted to extinction to supply feathers for ladies' hats, eggs for egg collections, and stuffed trophies for natural history cabinets in middle-class homes. The last passenger pigeons were blasted from the sky in 1914.[17]

Shortly after the turn of the century the automobile had become one of the most destructive instruments of wildlife habitats. In 1900 only 4,000 cars were produced; by 1909 more than 3 million had been registered for the road. The automobile enabled hordes of travelers to reach, in a single day, wilderness that had been all but inaccessible except to well-equipped expeditions. Behind the wheels of their autos, motorists by the thousands cut haphazard roads into the forests and wilderness areas, polluting the waters, damaging the underbrush, creating fire hazards, and otherwise destroying the countryside they were frantically trying to embrace.[18]

Out of a recognition of the automobile's destructiveness, the newly established national parks at first banned cars. At Yosemite, visitors arriving by car had to chain their vehicles to logs and turn in their keys at park headquarters. But as the public began to demand easier access as a condition for support of the parks system, the prohibition against automobiles was overturned and the first cars entered Yosemite in 1913. Autos were allowed into Yellowstone two years later, and by 1919 there were 100,000 cars on the newly built roads within the national parks.[19]

Auto camping, known as "sagebrushing," became a national fad. A disgusted observer at the time characterized the sagebrusher as a motorist who "cuts loose from all effeteness," bringing "clothes and furniture and house and food—even the family pup—and lets his adventurous, pioneering spirit riot here in the mountain air."[20] Between 1908 and 1914 Mount Rainier, Crater Lake, Glacier, Yosemite, Sequoia, and Mesa Verde were opened to automobiles and motorcycles, and by 1926 over 400,000 cars rumbled into the national parks. Most visitors to the parks by this time arrived by car rather than by rail or some other means, and the total visitor count for the eleven national parks rose from 69,000 in 1908 to more than a million in 1921; by 1928, it had tripled to 3 million.[21]

When Americans were not driving to the country in their cars, they were reading about nature in books and magazines. Many "nature lovers," as they proudly called themselves, actually preferred to stay home. Going back to nature, they were assured by booksellers, did not mean necessarily going into the wild; they could get a healthful dose of nature just by reading about it. "We go back to nature," wrote Bliss Carman in 1908, "every time we take a deep breath and stop worrying."[22]

Nature books were bought in astonishing quantities and published in astounding varieties, including animal tales for children, wilderness novels, short stories, travelogues, and nature guides. Written for the urban reader, these accounts of wildlife experiences were often idealized rather than factual. They aimed to stimulate the imagination rather than the reason, to entertain with a good tale rather than give instruction in botany or biology.

In this atmosphere, the turn of the century saw the popular development of a new kind of book, partly fact and partly fiction, playing upon the hunger that the public felt for a continuity and even an intimacy with the nonhuman world. A host of short stories and novels appeared in which animals were given major, sympathetic roles in the action. Anna Sewell's *Black Beauty*, published in an American edition in 1890 by the American Humane Education Society, was among the most important. Kipling's *Jungle Book* appeared in 1894. Equally important for establishing the realistic animal story as a new literary form in America was Ernest Thompson Seton's *Wild Animals I Have Known*, published in 1898.[23] More successful than Seton's book were *The Call of the Wild* in 1903 and *White Fang* three years later, novels that established Jack London's reputation and made him a fortune.

Even more profitable than London's work were four sentimental nature novels with animal heroes that between 1900 and 1930 sold more than 1.5 million copies each. All were written by an amateur bird-watcher and nature photographer from Indiana named Gene Stratton Porter. The first, a sentimental romance called *The Song of the Cardinal*, appeared in 1903, just two years after Porter wrote her first magazine article. In the style of this new sentimental nature book, Porter's romance had a pair of cardinals as the protagonists. Her second novel, *Freckles*, sold over 3 million copies, making Porter one of the most popular writers in America.[24] Over

the years Porter wrote ten more novels and eight natural history
books. Before 1915 her books had sold over 9 million copies, and
her earnings exceeded $2 million. So wealthy and successful did
Porter's animal books make her that she moved to Hollywood,
bought a film company, and produced movie versions of her best-
selling works. She died in Hollywood in 1924 when her limousine
was run over by a trolley.

At the turn of the century, nature study had also become an important part of school curriculums. Books of outdoor essays, nature novels, and animal stories were used as reading primers. More
sophisticated nature books made their way onto college reading
lists. Part of their popularity came from the fact that in these works
nature's "laws" were presented from a new, gentler perspective,
quite different from the tooth-and-claw, "survival of the fittest"
version of Darwinism promoted by mainstream scientists and ex-
trapolated into economic theory by conservative social scientists
such as William Graham Sumner. Social Darwinists justified cal-
lousness and ruthlessness by big business as "natural," biologically determined, even beneficial to society, and hence as morally
sanctioned.[25]

In contrast, the popular nature writers portrayed a world of animal compassion and kindness, suggesting that individual animal
behavior was flexible rather than predetermined or mindlessly in-
stinctual, and that even in the animal kingdom morality existed
under "natural conditions." Rather than "lowering" mankind to
the "savage" level of brutes, these writers understood Darwinism
as "elevating" all living things into a holistic community, with
shared qualities of altruism, ethics, and spirituality. Biologist Liberty Hyde Bailey of Cornell University asserted in 1915 that "the
theme of evolution has overturned our attitude" toward nature,
and he called for the establishment of a new, unselfish relationship
with the Earth and all creatures. No longer was the living creation
"exclusively man-centered," Bailey said; it was "biocentric."[26]

Writers of popular nature books glorified animals that displayed virtues previously thought of as exclusively human—the dog's "faithfulness" and the lion's "nobility." But while these portraits created greater sympathy for nature and contributed to the popularity of societies formed to prevent cruelty to animals, the blurred distinctions between animals and humans did not benefit all creatures. Nature books sometimes described animals as though they were little furry or feathered humans rather than species of wildlife. And just as there could be cuddly friends among these creatures, there could be villains in the animal kingdom as well—raptorial birds, for example, and predators such as wolves, coyotes, and cougars. Theodore Roosevelt expressed the popular, anthropomorphic view of predators when he called them "criminal vermin" that ought to be shot on sight. By acting on such prejudices, hunters reduced the wolf population in the United States from 200,000 to only 2,000 by 1908.[27]

The role of instinct in human conduct, the ability of animals to feel and suffer, and the relationship of humankind to wildlife were prominent issues in nature books. But given the complexity of these issues—and especially their appeal to the heart more than the head, as well as their profound implications for societal conditions—disagreements among nature writers were almost inevitable. Disagreements evolved into conflict. And when the big blowup came, it was sparked by the country's leading spokesman for nature, the elderly John Burroughs. The debate inspired by Burroughs' wrath at what he considered slipshod and sentimental nature books reverberated across the country for nearly six years, drawing in many of America's most eminent scientists and writers, and eventually the president of the United States. The highly publicized controversy radically undermined and threatened the general public's faith in nature writing's truthfulness. To a degree, the doubts and confusions persist into the present.

The controversy began in 1902 when a popular nature writer

named William J. Long published a book titled *School of the Woods: Some Life Studies of Animal Instinct and Animal Training*. Long was no more inaccurate or sentimental in his observations than dozens of outdoor writers who wrote about wildlife. Before publishing *School of the Woods*, he had written numerous magazine articles and six books, including *Ways of Wood Folk* in 1899, *Wilderness Ways* in 1900, and *Secrets of the Woods* in 1901. As a naturalist and writer he was highly regarded by the public. But whereas some popular writers on nature subjects, such as Jack London and Gene Stratton Porter, made it clear that they were writing fiction, Long stressed the veracity of his firsthand observations and prided himself on their accuracy of detail. Among his observations Long reported seeing occurrences in nature that strained the imagination, and his interpretations of what he had allegedly seen were even more incredible. To Burroughs, Long stood for all the nature hacks whose work tarnished the reputation of serious nature writers such as himself. In Burroughs' opinion the popularity of "skillful frauds" like Long misled trusting readers about nature's true meaning, a meaning it was crucial to understand.

Disgusted with Long's new book and others like it, and determined to discredit all of them once and for all, Burroughs launched a scathing and sweeping attack in the *Atlantic* in an article titled "Real and Sham Natural History."[28] Although nature books had become very popular in the United States, Burroughs' article began, only "a very small number" of them made "valuable contributions to our natural history literature." Most, he asserted, were written solely for profit and contained no genuine knowledge of the natural world. As an example he singled out William J. Long's *School of the Woods*.

Good nature writing often demanded a literary sensibility, Burroughs acknowledged, room for a subjective style, and the mixing of interpretation with fact. But Long and writers like him went overboard in making their descriptions "literary." To Burroughs, Long epitomized "the danger of making too much of what we see and describe,—of putting in too much sentiment, too much literature,—in short, of valuing these things more for the literary effects we can get out of them than for themselves."

Mixing natural history and a literary style had not been a danger in Gilbert White, Burroughs claimed, because White "always forgets White, and remembers only nature . . . He tells the thing for what it is . . . There is never more than a twinkle of humor in his pages, and never one word of style for its own sake." Long's work, on the other hand, galled Burroughs not only because of its stylistic liberties but because of its content. Long was telling egregious lies merely to sell more books and claiming to have witnessed things Burroughs knew to be impossible. Among these lies, according to Burroughs, were accounts of having observed animals instructing their young much the way humans did. Then, interpreting his observations, Long questioned the role of instinct in animal learning. "After many years of watching animals in their native haunts," Long had written, "I am convinced that instinct plays a much smaller part than we have supposed; that an animal's success or failure in the ceaseless struggle for life depends, not upon instinct, but upon the kind of training which the animal receives from its mother."

Burroughs was outraged. No! he exclaimed, "the crows have no fortresses, or schools, or colleges, or examining boards, or diplomas, or medals of honor, or hospitals, or churches, or telephones, or postal deliveries, or anything of the sort." Birds are not taught by their mothers to build nests any more than foxes are taught in fox schools how to elude traps, Burroughs insisted. Creatures know these things by instinct alone.

And yet Long had written of witnessing what he called a "kingfisher's kindergarten," where he saw adult birds capture minnows and place them in shallow pools. There, Long said, the mother birds taught their young how to dive for their food. He had seen great blue herons break up frogs and scatter the parts on the water as a kind of bait to attract fish and to teach their young the skills of fishing. "If he had said that he saw the parent birds fishing with hook and line, or dragging a net of their own knitting, his statement would have been just as credible," Burroughs replied in scorn.

"There is a school of the woods," Burroughs reiterated, "just as much as there is a church of the woods, or a parliament of the woods, or a society of united charities of the woods, and no more; there is nothing in the dealings of animals with their young that in the remotest way suggests human instruction and discipline. The young of all the wild creatures do instinctively what their parents do and did. They do not have to be taught; they are taught by nature from the start."

Long had apparently observed even more than animal schools and birds fishing with bait. He wrote of porcupines that tucked themselves into balls and rolled downhill to escape predators, of an eagle that died in flight and then glided gently and gracefully to the earth on outstretched wings, and of a particularly cunning fox that captured roosting chickens by running in circles underneath them. The chickens, Long reported, got so dizzy from trying to keep an eye on the fox that they tumbled off their roosts and into the fox's jaws.

"Mr. Long's book," Burroughs concluded, "reads like that of a man who has really never been to the woods, but who sits in his study and cooks up these yarns from things he has read in *Forest and Stream*, or in other sporting journals. Of real observations there is hardly a vestige in his book."

The fact that Long's work made readers interested in nature and sympathetic to wild creatures could not excuse the books' inaccuracies and their "mock natural history," Burroughs concluded. "No pleasure to the reader, no moral inculcated, can justify the dissemination of false notions of nature, or of anything else." And, Burroughs warned menacingly, "the writer who seeks to palm off his own silly inventions as real observations is bound sooner or later to come to grief."

Harsh as Burroughs' published attack was, his original draft of the article had been even more severe. Before sending it to the *Atlantic* he had asked Clara Barrus if it showed too much "bad blood." Barrus advised him to tone it down. He showed it to others, including Dallas Lore Sharp, who suggested that the attack was so harsh it might backfire. Even so, the toned-down version that went to Bliss Perry, editor of the *Atlantic*, was still so "ill-natured" and "peevish," according to Perry, that he sent it back to Burroughs for further revision.[29]

At the time of Burroughs' attack on him in the national media, William J. Long was a thirty-seven-year-old Congregationalist minister living in Massachusetts. Long had studied at Harvard, then in Berlin and Heidelberg, where he had received a Ph.D. in theology. In addition to being an eloquent clergyman, Long was an amateur naturalist and avid camper who spent his summers hiking in the wilds of eastern Canada. As an extension of his passion for the outdoors, Long had thrown himself into a second career by writing on nature subjects. Publishing for both children and adult readers, he had become extremely popular and successful.[30]

Far from being discouraged by the attack on him by America's senior, most beloved, and most respected nature writer, Long sent off a stern rebuttal to Burroughs that appeared within weeks in the *Boston Evening Transcript*. At the same time he prepared a more extensive rebuttal, published two months later in the *North American Review*.[31] In both articles Long attempted to be judicious, but he gave not an inch of ground to Burroughs.

Long's *North American Review* article, "The Modern School of Nature-Study and Its Critics," began by distinguishing between the study of nature and the study of science. Science, Long argued, concerns itself with laws and generalizations. In contrast, nature study recognizes that creatures and life forms are struggling for individuality, and that their unique circumstances make it difficult to define each individual strictly by the rigid laws and generalizations of biology. Nature study is so complex and varied that the best approach to understanding is to appreciate and interpret rather than to classify and define, Long asserted. "The difference between Nature and Science is the difference between a man who loves animals, and so understands them, and the man who studies Zoology; it is the difference between the woman who cherishes her old-fashioned flower-garden and the professor who lectures on Botany in a college class-room."

Long asserted that modern naturalists like himself were more attuned to living creatures than were old-fashioned natural historians like Burroughs. Whereas the older generation saw animals as creatures of instinct and habit only, the new nature writers understood that "animals of the same class are still individuals; that they are different every one, and have different habits; that they are not more alike than men and women of the same class, and that they change their habits rapidly—more so, perhaps, than do either governments or churches—when the need arises."

If you talk to wilderness guides, Long wrote, you will find that each has a story that would seem unbelievable. These guides know more than most naturalists and can recite such stories not because they are liars, but because they have discovered the secret of animal individuality. "If you cannot find two leaves alike on the same elm-tree," he wrote, "you certainly cannot write a list of habits that will cover even two animals perfectly, with their wild free life and their individuality struggling to express itself amidst a hundred dangers and unknown problems."

Long next argued that modern nature writers had learned that "only a book which has style can live." To create such a work, he wrote, nature writers "must have not only sight but vision; not simply eyes and ears and a note-book, but insight, imagination, and, above all, an intense human sympathy, by which alone the inner life of an animal becomes luminous, and without which the living creatures are little better than stuffed specimens, and their actions the meaningless dance of shadows across the mouth of Plato's cave."

Finally, Long faulted Burroughs for believing that all animals behave exactly like the individual animals Burroughs had seen in his own neighborhood. "From the mice and woodchucks of his pasture, where he is at home, [Burroughs] affirms what is true and false of the bear and caribou of the great forest where he has never been," Long chided. And to put a point on his argument, Long cited observational inaccuracies in Burroughs' own work, along with previous instances in which Burroughs had attacked the accuracy of his fellow writers, only to be proved wrong later.

Long's defense had merit and seemed reasonable to a number of readers. But he made one major mistake in his reply. To prove his point that individual animals can behave in rather unexpected ways, he cited the example of two orioles he had witnessed building a nest.

The birds wanted to build in the fork of a tree, but the fork was too wide. The orioles "deliberated plainly upon the matter," Long wrote. Then the birds "brought up a twig from the ground, laid it across the forks, and tied it there with strings as a third support to the nest." Not only did the orioles tie the strings, according to Long; "they took the ends in their beaks and hung their weight upon them so as to draw the knots tight." The birds then were able to build their nest within the smaller triangle in the fork of the tree.

Long had seen these orioles over twenty-five years ago, he said. Then, just last spring, he had witnessed another pair of orioles who were also skilled engineers. This pair, having been driven away from their favorite elm by carpenters, wanted to build in a buttonwood tree. "They wanted a swinging nest," Long wrote, "but the buttonwood's branches were too stiff and straight; so they fastened three sticks together on the ground in the form of a perfectly measured triangle. At each angle they fastened one end of a cord, and carried the other end over and made it fast to the middle of the opposite side. Then they gathered up the loops and fastened them by the middle, all together, to a stout bit of marline." Next, Long wrote, "they carried up this staging and swung it two feet below the middle of a thick limb, so that some leaves above sheltered them from sun and rain; and upon this swinging stage they built their nest. The marline was tied once around the limb, and, to make it perfectly sure, the end was brought down and fastened to the supporting cord with a reversed double-hitch, the kind that a man uses in cinching his saddle." Not yet finished, these highly skilled birds next "tied a single knot at the extreme end lest the marline should ravel in the wind."

Burroughs' rejoinder to Long's article was so harsh that it proved difficult to publish. The *Atlantic* did not want to perpetuate the controversy, so Burroughs persuaded *Century Magazine* to publish it.[32] "The orioles built a nest so extraordinary that it can be accounted for only on the theory that there *is* a school of the woods, and that these two birds had been pupils there and had taken a course in strings," Burroughs wrote. "After such an example as this, how long will it be before the water-birds will be building little rush cradles for their young or rush boats driven about the ponds and lakes by means of leafy sails, or before Jenny Wren will be living in a log cabin of her own construction?"

The fight between the two men might have ended there. The other authors Burroughs had attacked in his original article had all retreated and were unwilling to go against the country's senior nature writer. And meanwhile, President Theodore Roosevelt had written a warm letter of support to Burroughs after the appearance of his original article, beginning a close and very public friendship between them. In his private correspondence Roosevelt made it clear that he did not agree with all Burroughs' points, particularly his insistence that animals learned nothing from their parents' behavior. He advised Burroughs to be less dogmatic in insisting that animals are rigidly "under the domain of absolute nature, or what we call instinct, innate tendency, habit of growth, as are the plants and trees." But the president agreed heartily with the need to excoriate sham naturalists and congratulated Burroughs for the service he was doing natural history and the truth.

Burroughs and Roosevelt, however, had underestimated William J. Long and his few allies. Threatened financially by the public debate, Long's publishers came to their author's defense by distributing a pamphlet—to be passed out in the schools where Long's books were widely used—defending his position. Other writers and editors, offended by what they saw as Burroughs' heavy-handedness and arrogance, also took a position in Long's defense. And while acrimonious editorials and articles by nature writers flew back and forth about oriole architects and boat building wrens, journalists and newspaper cartoonists found the entire affair rich material for satire. Nature writers were fast becoming a national joke in the pages of the country's newspapers and magazines. One wag claimed his next book would be a guide called "How to Tell the Animals from the Wild Flowers." The artist Frederick Church published a drawing of a benevolent Mother Nature surrounded by foxes; in her lap was an open book illustrating traps and snares. The drawing was titled "A Lesson in Wisdom."

Through it all, Long continued to publish articles and books containing instances of animal ingenuity heretofore overlooked by other observers. The most interesting and inflammatory examples were contained in an article published in *Outlook* four months after Long's self-defense in the *North American Review*. Titled "Animal Surgery," Long's new essay asserted that he had seen animals capable not only of learning architecture but also of treating their injuries and illnesses with first aid and "a rude kind of medicine and surgery."[33] Long described witnessing bears and muskrats bandaging their injuries with a coating of pine pitch, spruce resin, and clay to keep the wounds sterile. "When a coon's foot is shattered by a bullet, he will cut it off promptly and wash the stump in running water, partly to reduce the inflammation and partly, no doubt, to make it perfectly clean," Long wrote. Long also knew of beavers that had covered their wounds with thin vegetable matter to promote healing. But his most provocative story concerned the ingenuity and medical acumen of a wild bird.

One day, as Long sat quietly in the reeds beside a brook, he spied an injured woodcock busily tending its leg, which was apparently broken. As Long watched, the bird took wet clay in its bill and smeared it deliberately around its fractured limb. After a while the woodcock "fluttered away on one foot for a short distance and seemed to be pulling tiny roots and fibers of grass, which he worked into the clay that he had already smeared on his leg." The woodcock scooped up more clay and plastered it over the enlarging cast, "working away with strange, silent intentness for fully fifteen minutes, while I watched and wondered, scarce believing my eyes." When the cast had been applied and reinforced with feathers and fibers to make it strong, the bird stood on one leg for a full hour to let the cast set, occasionally smoothing it with its bill. Satisfied with its work, the bird then fluttered away into the thick woods and disappeared.

To support his assertions, Long noted that he had met other woodsmen who had witnessed similar examples of birds applying first aid to themselves. But although Long stressed that not all woodcocks were necessarily capable of the behavior in question, saying that these few individuals were perhaps "woodcock geniuses," his attempts to qualify his claims did not save him from the wrath that followed. This time the storm came from a host of eminent biologists and natural historians, all writing in a February 1904 issue of *Science*.[34]

Among them was the Harvard entomologist William Morton Wheeler, who wrote, under the heading "Woodcock Surgery," that "Mr. Long virtually claims that a woodcock not only has an understanding of the theory of casts as adapted to fractured limbs, but is able to apply this knowledge in practice. The bird is repre-

sented as knowing the qualities of clay and mud, their lack of cohesion unless mixed with fibrous substances, their tendency to
harden on exposure to the air, and to disintegrate in water. Inas-
much as woodcocks have for generations been living and feeding
in muddy places, we could, perhaps, although not without some
abuse of the imagination, suppose the bird to possess this knowledge. But the mental horizon of Mr. Long's woodcock is not
bounded by the qualities of mud. He is familiar with the theories of
bone formation and regeneration—in a word, with osteogenesis,
which, by the way, is never clearly grasped by some of our university juniors."

Professor Wheeler further decried the fact that such stories,
propagated by Long and writers like him, were used in public
schools where, although they "titillate the fancy of the boys and
girls," they only add "to the gayety of comparative psychologists.
Those who are attacking the fads of our educational system will
find plenty of work awaiting them as soon as they turn their attention to the excrescences of 'nature study.'"

Other scientists joined in this fresh attack on Long and "the new
nature writer," by which they meant an amateur who was literary
and popular. Even mistakes made by Burroughs were pointed out
and criticized, though only in passing.[35] Only one reader of *Science*
defended the beleaguered William Long. Professor Ellen Hayes of
the Whitin Observatory in Wellesley wrote in a letter to the editor
that "it is [Long's] critic, Mr. Wheeler, who 'virtually' affirms that
a woodcock could not apply mud to a broken leg without a knowledge of surgery; and it is much as if he should say that a man who
blows on his fingers to warm them or on his tea to cool it has a
knowledge of the laws of thermodynamics and is ready to discuss
entropy or an indicator diagram. It is the merest commonplace
fact that in order to avoid danger, to lessen pain, to save life, to gain
pleasure, human beings are constantly performing acts the underlying principles of which they understand scarcely any better than
a woodcock understands the principles of surgery."[36]

Meanwhile Long continued to fight back on his own behalf. In a May 1904 issue of *Science* he attempted to counter the authorities aligned against him by quoting from a number of affidavits from backwoods witnesses. One was from an Ohio man who had found a woodcock whose fractured limb had "a bandage around it, composed of a hard clay-like substance, interwoven with grass or a woody fiber of some kind. The bone seemed to have been set properly and had knit perfectly." A medical doctor, according to Long, had pronounced the cast better "than nine tenths of the surgeons could do." Another witness had seen not one but four woodcocks with casts, each of them made of clay interwoven with bits of feather and grass to give them support and make them more adhesive. But only Long claimed to have seen a bird actually construct a mud cast.

Eventually Long produced an actual specimen of a bird's leg for his critics to examine. The *New York Times* described it as "the severed leg of a fowl, around which was bound a jacket of feathers glued together with some adhesive stuff." Long claimed that it was "the leg of a grouse which has bound up its wounded limb with a bandage of feathers plucked from its own body and cemented with some sticky substance the nature of which we have not been able to discover." William T. Hornaday, director of the New York Zoological Park, pronounced the lump on the bird's leg to be blood and mud, but the claim that it was somehow the work of bird surgery Hornaday considered "too absurd for serious consideration."[37]

After four years with no relief from this controversy, President Roosevelt himself could no longer resist weighing in against Long and those whom the press had begun calling "nature fakers." In the June 1907 issue of *Everybody's Magazine*, Roosevelt blasted not only Long but also Jack London and several other writers, authors of what he called "unnatural" history.[38] In an article titled "Roosevelt on the Nature Fakirs," the president called Long's books a "genuine crime," especially against the children of the country.

"I don't believe for a minute," Roosevelt wrote, "that some of these men who are writing nature stories and putting the word 'truth' prominently in their prefaces know the heart of the wild things. Neither do I believe that certain men . . . have succeeded in learning the real secrets of the life of the wilderness. They don't know, or if they do know, they indulge in the wildest exaggeration under the mistaken notion that they are strengthening their stories.

"As for the matter of giving these books to the children for the purpose of teaching them the facts of natural history—why, it's an outrage," Roosevelt continued. "There is no more reason why the children of the country should be taught a false natural history than why they should be taught a false physical geography."

The redoubtable William Long, however, was no more cowed by the president than he had been by John Burroughs. In a major article that appeared simultaneously in New York, Boston, Chicago, and several other cities, Long called Roosevelt's attack on him venomous and cowardly.[39] He used Roosevelt's own writings against the safari-loving president, calling him "a man who takes delight in whooping through the woods killing everything in sight."

"Who is he to write, 'I don't believe for a minute that some of these nature writers know the heart of a wild thing'?" Long asked. "As to that I find after carefully reading two of his big books that every time Mr. Roosevelt gets near the heart of a wild thing he invariably puts a bullet through it. From his own records I have reckoned a full thousand hearts which he has thus known intimately. In one chapter alone I find that he violently gained knowledge of eleven noble elk hearts in a few days and he tells us that this was 'a type of many such hunts.'"

Long charged further that Roosevelt could not have got near enough to animals of the forest to know them because, as Long said, "you stop 200 yards away to shoot a deer." In contrast, "I watch my friends from a point perhaps twenty or thirty yards away

. . . I have been so close to wild animals that I could lie and watch their eyelids lift and fall."

The popular press delighted in the fray. The colorful, big-game-hunting president had become locked in battle with bug-catchers, bird-watchers, and a nature writer unwilling to say uncle. The story boosted the sales of newspapers and magazines, in many of which Long was depicted as the David to Roosevelt's Goliath. And it helped that this David was a serious, articulate writer, an ordained minister, and an outdoorsman who sincerely believed in all that he had reported. Cartoonists and pundits portrayed the president as a bully, wasting time on what appeared to be his personal argument with a private citizen while the country suffered from problems far more serious than the purported behavior of lame birds.

Seeing his friend Roosevelt under attack, John Burroughs reentered the battle, again criticizing Long's woodcock stories as ridiculous fantasy. But once again Long promptly struck back, suggesting that the elderly Burroughs was a sycophant, "only too ready to please the president by attacking a brother naturalist." Long concluded this attack on Burroughs by suggesting that the old man was simply jealous and opposed to "every naturalist whose articles were more interesting and successful than his own."[40]

Roosevelt, now feeling that the controversy had to be ended once and for all—for his own good and everyone else's—delivered what he hoped would be the final blow against Long in September 1907. The president quietly arranged the publication of a symposium called "Real Naturalists on Nature Faking," to include testimony from the most important scientists and naturalists in America, all of whom were ready to denounce Long.[41]

William T. Hornaday led the attack. "Whenever Mr. Long enters the woods, the most marvelous things begin to happen. There is a four-footed wonder-worker behind every bush and a miracle every hour. His animals are of superhuman intelligence, and the 'stunts' they do for him surpass all that have been seen by all the real naturalists of the world added together." Hornaday wanted not only to crush Long but also to ensure that his books would be taken from the shelves and destroyed. "In my opinion any board of education which places W. J. Long's books in the schools under its control, or leaves them there after they have found their way in, is recreant to its duty and deserves severe censure. An unqualified approval of Long's books is, in my opinion, a sure index of profound ignorance regarding wild animals, their mental capacities and their ways."

J. A. Allen, curator of mammalogy and ornithology at the American Museum of Natural History, also criticized Long, as did Edward W. Nelson, a government scientist attached to explorations from Alaska to Central America. Nelson wrote that Long deserved "the hearty contempt of all naturalists and others who know and love the truth." C. Hart Merriam, chief of the U.S. Biological Survey, also attacked Long's integrity, as did Frederick A. Lucas, chief curator of the Museums of Brooklyn Institute.

The symposium concluded with an essay by Roosevelt himself titled "Nature Fakers." In it the president called Long and others of his type "object[s] of derision to every scientist worthy of the name, to every real lover of the wilderness, to every faunal naturalist, to every true hunter or nature lover." The writings of Long and his fellow nature fakers were "preposterous" and "worthless," said Roosevelt. Like Hornaday, the president was determined to see to it that Long would cease to be read altogether. Just as Hornaday had warned libraries and schools against buying and holding Long's books, Roosevelt threatened Long's publishers. There will always be liars, Roosevelt announced, but those who publish them are particularly abhorrent and reckless and, like Long, should be stopped.

After the symposium appeared in print, the skirmishes continued briefly, but Long himself was uncharacteristically silent for some time. Rumors spread that he was gravely ill, physically and spiritually broken by the battle. When he finally reemerged, he criticized Roosevelt and Burroughs once again in interviews. But the old fire was gone, and at last the press tired of the story. Long's nature publishing all but ceased. Discredited by the highest authorities in the land, his books were removed from schools and his once-popular work expunged from America's bookshelves.[42]

The effects of the highly publicized nature-faker controversy were long-lasting. The first of several consequences was greater skepticism on the part of the public concerning the accuracy of nature stories, followed by greater scorn on the part of professional scientists toward amateur naturalists. It made no difference that, as a third consequence, writers and publishers became more cautious of what they published and of the claims they made for its accuracy. Long stood for a social evil and an affront against legitimate science that were better forgotten.

To give him his due, however, it must be said that William J. Long courageously supported ideas that were ahead of his time. He abhorred the killing of wolves and other predators, for example, and he opposed hunting for any reason. Both of these positions gave Long the appearance of being on the radical fringe, especially to big-game hunters who, like Roosevelt, were important men, and to their admirers, like Burroughs. Long also raised other ethical questions concerning animals and the relationship of animal and human biology—questions distasteful to many in the sciences and in the conservative press because they smacked too much of anthropomorphism and indirectly challenged social Darwinism's hold on economic policy.

Roosevelt, for his part, actually agreed with certain positions of Long's. He was inclined, for example, to acknowledge the existence of cognitive and social behaviors in animals that were unexplainable by instinct alone, as it was then understood. Had he taken his position to its logical conclusion, however, he would have had to reexamine the ethics of hunting, of using animals for research, and other troubling issues that he preferred to avoid.

Burroughs, even during the first year into the fight, began to realize that he was painting himself too quickly into a corner over the question of animal cognition and learning, and the role of instinct in animal behavior. After some consideration, he saw that to deny that animals reasoned at all was probably a mistake, and in 1905 he published a volume of essays on the subject of animal intelligence in order to clarify his position. In the introduction to *Ways of Nature* Burroughs wrote, "I confess I have not been fully able to persuade myself that the lower animals ever show anything more than a faint gleam of what we call thought and reflection . . . Nearly all the animal behavior that the credulous public looks upon as the outcome of reason is simply the result of the adaptiveness and plasticity of instinct."[43] But by the end of the book Burroughs was still struggling with what he meant: "Instinct is not rigid as cast iron; it does not invariably act like a machine, always the same. The animal is something alive, and is subject to the law of variation. Instinct may act more strongly in one kind than in another, just as reason may act more strongly in one man than in another, or as one animal may have greater speed or courage than others of the same species. It would be hard to find two live creatures, very far up the scale, exactly alike."[44]

In the end, both sides in the controversy may have realized that the natural world is more complex than they had been willing to conceive. We can only wonder what Burroughs and Roosevelt would have made of modern theories of sociobiology, for example, which demonstrate that just as principles of evolution have resulted in fixed action patterns in animal behavior, they have also resulted in the capacity—even among individuals of nonhuman species—to transmit and receive information by signs, language, and imitation. In short, teaching and learning, communication and culture are by no means distinctive to humans but can be found in many living organisms. And we might wonder what they would have made of current studies in cognitive ethology, which explore even more closely the role of thinking, reflection, and creativity in animal behavior.

When he attacked Long's oriole architects, Burroughs was aware of the bower birds of New Guinea and of the weaver birds of Africa, both of which stitch and weave strips of grass and similar material into structures far more elaborate than the nest reportedly made by William Long's birds. Burroughs continued to maintain that "the most ingenious nests in the world, as those of the weaver-birds and orioles, show no more independent self-directed and self-originated thought than does the rude nest of the pigeon or the cuckoo."[45] Yet ornithologists today report that, to build its nest, the male village weaver requires both practice and a period of learning. Until young birds have had the opportunity to observe experienced males build nests, they build partial and irregular structures that are unacceptable to potential mates.[46] And in other recent observations of the fishing techniques of herons, Hiroyoshi Higuchi reports frequently seeing herons use live bait, such as earthworms and flies, to attract fish, while other individual herons have become adept at fishing with lures of their own making, fashioning them from twigs, feathers, bark, and Styrofoam— and they apparently "teach" these techniques to their young.[47] Finally, we might wonder what Burroughs would have made of recent scientific reports of Capuchin monkeys seen treating their own wounds and the wounds of their offspring with plant and liquid materials, even manufacturing the tools with which to apply the treatments.[48]

As a result of the nature-faker controversy, nature writing acquired a reputation for being inaccurate as well as sentimental, a genre for children rather than for serious adults and real scientists. As World War I began and the American public turned to issues other than the genteel countryside, the controversy faded; Roosevelt died in 1919, and John Burroughs in 1921, marking the end of a literary era and of a controversy that had not been entirely settled.

Meanwhile, nature writing was occurring in a larger context; in the far West, a different style of nature writing and activism had been developing, concerned with a landscape unlike those of William J. Long and John Burroughs in temperament and in grandeur, and grappling with environmental issues larger than those suggested by the woodcock's leg.

Chapter Six

MOUNTAIN SELF

Although numerous people disagreed with him, William Tecumseh Sherman predicted in 1860 that if a civil war broke out, the country would be drenched in blood. By 1862 his prediction had come true, and as the war dragged on, the Army of the Potomac in particular suffered ghastly defeats. Two years into the war, volunteer enlistment plummeted; soldiers who had enlisted eagerly at the onset of the conflict went back to their farms when the time came to reenlist, wanting no more of army life and hideous carnage. Young men like John Burroughs, at home in the Catskills, thought hard about becoming soldiers. Despite his sympathy with the Union cause, Burroughs eventually wrote to a friend that he would not enlist. The generals of the North were so incompetent, he complained, that there was "not one . . . I would serve under without compulsion."[1] To raise enough recruits to continue the war, Congress in July 1862 passed the Militia Act as a first step toward universal conscription. All males aged eighteen to forty-five were compelled to enroll for the draft, and within months the first call went out to the states for 300,000 fresh soldiers.

Not only U.S. citizens were obligated under the new conscription laws to serve in the Union army. Immigrants who had at any time declared an intention of becoming citizens—and having voted or owned land was proof of such intention—were also required to register for the draft. In some regions, such as the Midwest, where as much as half the population was foreign born, there was tremendous opposition to the federal government's war. It was not that the immigrants necessarily favored the Confederacy; most of them simply had no intention of dying for a country that they had only recently adopted and that was now sending its young men to slaughter.[2]

Fourteen years earlier, in 1848, Daniel and Anne Muir had moved from Dunbar, Scotland, and settled on the edge of the Midwestern frontier with their seven children. Driven by Daniel's iron will and by grit and sweat, they cleared a portion of the Wisconsin woods and meadows near Portage. In 1857 their frugality and unrelenting hard work made it possible for Daniel to buy a second farm, and the entire family had made it, too, profitable through backbreaking labor and discipline. Now, with the children grown, Daniel Muir deeded the original farm to his married daughter, Sarah, leased the second, and moved his household into Portage.

The Muir family wanted no part of the Civil War. Facing the possibility of being drafted, the youngest son, Dan, followed the lead of other immigrant boys who were too poor to hire a substitute or to pay a commutation fee to get out of the war: he fled to Canada. The Muirs' oldest son, John, also feared having to fight in the war but stayed behind for the time being. Despite his poverty and the strong objections of his father, John desperately hoped to get an education that would enable him to break free from the soul-killing labor inherent in farming.

The harsh conditions of farm life had made John tough and disciplined, capable of outdoor work that would have broken someone less robust and determined. But one of the worst things he endured was his father's whippings, not labor on the land. A member of the Disciples of God—a sect of Scot Campbellites, woefully grim[3]—Daniel Muir viewed the world as a fallen, transitory place, where delight in nature was a sign of sinfulness. By meting out severe thrashings, enforcing long days of backbreaking labor, and denying his family simple household comforts, Daniel Muir attempted to etch this solemn lesson into his children. "We were called into the morning at four o'clock and seldom got to bed before nine," John Muir remembered, "making a broiling, seething day of seventeen hours long loaded with heavy work, while I was only a small stunted boy."[4]

Despite this severe upbringing, John was apparently immune to his father's brimstone-and-ashes temperament. Quick-witted, as clever at arguing from the Bible as his father, John looked at the world with astonishing good cheer, romping with his brothers in the Wisconsin woods and wildflowers, delighting in the nearly pristine wilderness around the family farm and in its animals, birds, and open skies. Of his boyhood, spent working on the farm instead of going to school, he wrote, "how utterly happy it made us! Nature streaming into us, wooingly teaching, preaching her glorious living lessons, so unlike the dismal grammar ashes and cinders so long thrashed into us."[5]

Twenty-four years old in 1862, Muir finally caught a glimpse of a social world beyond his father's hardscrabble farm, at the small state university in Madison. In contrast to the rigid household of his youth, at college he found encouraging teachers, intellectual openness, and opinions not filtered through a hellfire interpretation of the Bible. Unschooled except in the Bible from ages eleven to twenty-two, he was undoubtedly an eccentric student. But this work-hardened Scottish farm boy impressed his teachers with an endless curiosity and appetite for learning. As a young man he was a resourceful inventor and machinist, fabricating ingenious clocks, door locks, water wheels, barometers, and automatic horse-feeders out of wood. In his small room at the college, intent on wasting no time, he built an alarm-clock bed that woke him in the early morning by pitching him onto the floor. Next to the bed he constructed a study desk rigged with clockwork and cog wheels. The desk's conveyor assembly would thrust a series of open textbooks in front of him at preset intervals. Seated there with the mechanism turning, reading as fast as he could, Muir appeared to his fellow students "as if chained, working like a beaver against the clock and desk."[6]

When one of Muir's professors introduced him to chemistry, he turned his dormitory room into a chemistry laboratory. The following spring, when a fellow student introduced him to botany, his room became a herbarium. The study of plants electrified him and became an obsession; he started a botanical journal and went into the countryside on long exploratory treks. One of these Muir arranged down the Wisconsin River valley and into Iowa, in the summer of 1863. Partly he planned to enjoy the seasonal beauty of the land, but partly, in the face of possible conscription, Muir was trying to decide what turn his life should take next.

From Madison Muir and two friends went by train to a point above the Dells, where they felled trees and built a raft. Launching their craft onto the slow-moving river, the young men drifted by the steep sandstone cliffs above Madison and floated downstream with the current, exhilarated by the landscape, exulting in the joy and freedom of their summer adventure.

Although they gloried in the wonder and beauty on the river and in the meadows and woods along the banks, war occupied the minds of all three friends. While they leisurely rafted on the water, a protracted battle in and around the village of Gettysburg, Pennsylvania, was killing and maiming 51,000 young soldiers, the majority of them farm boys like themselves. Gazing into the rapids, Muir saw metaphors of combat. In his letters home he described the river rapids, swollen by the melted snows of the previous winter, as "fierce legions": "All in one they rush to battle clad in foam, rise high upon their ever-resisting enemy, and with constant victory year by year gain themselves a wider and straighter way."[7]

Botanizing in ravines containing "the most perfect, the most heavenly plant conservatories I ever saw," Muir wrote to his sister Sarah that he was awed by so much natural beauty: "We traveled two miles in eight hours, and such scenery, such sweating, scrambling, climbing, and happy hunting and happy finding of dear plant beings we never before enjoyed. No human language will ever describe them," he concluded. Even many years later, when he had become a celebrated writer, a charter member of the National Institute of Arts and Letters, with honorary degrees and distinguished books to his credit, he would sound this refrain concerning the wonders he had seen.

Carefree as it all seemed, Muir knew the trip would have to end and decisions be made. He thought he might go back to the university in the fall to study medicine. Then again, he might return to Scotland, where wartime conscription was no threat, or go exploring in South America or Africa, like his heroes Alexander von Humboldt and Mungo Park. He might even work for his sister and brother-in-law on the old family farm—this time for the pleasure of the outdoors, away from the tyranny of his father.

Muir returned to Madison to news of violent antidraft riots in New York and Boston. Over the summer riots had broken out in his home state and throughout the Midwest. Confidence in President Lincoln had fallen to an all-time low as citizens protested corruption in recruitment practices, profiteering by legislators and generals, and the ability of the wealthy to buy their way out of the draft. And through it all, the end of the bloody war seemed nowhere in sight.

Hesitant, Muir lingered through the autumn and winter, farming and chopping wood instead of going to school. Then on February 1, Lincoln issued a call for 500,000 more soldiers. Muir could wait no longer for his name to be drawn. In March, like so many other young men of Wisconsin, he decided simply to disappear across the border into Canada. With streaming eyes, as he phrased it later, he was leaving one university for another: "the Wisconsin University for the University of the Wilderness."[8]

Having crossed into Canada near Sault Sainte Marie, Muir explored along the shores of Lake Huron, along North Channel and

Georgian Bay, and south again toward Lake Ontario. The tamarack and evergreen swamps of Canada, though rich with botanical wonders, were hard going for an impoverished young man on foot with few provisions. "Land and water, life and death, beauty and deformity, seemed here to have disputed empire and all shared equally at last," he wrote later. "I will not soon forget the chaos of fallen trees in all stages of decay and the tangled branches of the white cedars through which I had to force my way; nor the feeling with which I observed the sun wheeling to the West while yet above, beneath, and around all was silence and the seemingly endless harvest of swamp."[9]

Muir hiked alone through dense forest bogs, and when his money gave out he worked at chopping, clearing, and harvesting, for whatever wages the suspicious Canadian farmers would pay this gaunt, odd-looking wanderer with a shaggy reddish beard and bright blue eyes. Often he slept far away from the towns and farmhouses, bedded down by a solitary campfire that he kept ablaze to discourage the approach of wolves.

During these bleak months in the swamp Muir had an experience he would remember for the rest of his life. For hours he had been wading through icy water in a particularly impenetrable evergreen bog. With darkness falling, he feared the night would overtake him before he reached dry land and shelter. Without light in the swamp, he would have to make his bed in the trees, and there would be no chance of gathering dry wood for a fire or a warm meal. In the gloom, he recalled the allegorical sloughs in *Pilgrim's Progress* and Adam's despair in *Paradise Lost*. He had said when he had left Wisconsin that he felt like Milton's Adam exiled into the wilderness; now he felt his loneliness as never before.

Just when he was most discouraged and miserable from slogging through the darkening mist, Muir saw on the mossy bank of the mire a single white flower, standing alone on its small stem. One of the rarest of wild orchids of the north, the blossom of *Calypso borealis* rose like a tiny beacon just above a tuft of yellow moss. "The flower was white and made the impression of the utmost simple purity like a snowflower," Muir recalled later. "I sat down beside it, and fairly cried for joy." How long he sat beside the luminous small flower he could not remember. But "hunger and weariness vanished," he wrote, "and only after the sun was low in the west I plashed on through the swamp, strong and exhilarated as if never more to feel any mortal care."[10]

Forty-five years later, Muir still referred to the experience as "more memorable and impressive than any of my meetings with human beings excepting, perhaps, Emerson and one or two others." Calypso's beauty comforted him, nourished him, and carried him forward. In the future, intimate and deeply felt experiences of natural beauty—no matter how small—would sustain Muir through many other isolated treks in the wilderness. But perhaps he remembered this one so well because it was the first time he had felt such an intense—if not a mystical—light marking a way into the natural world. Muir would become the most exuberant lover of nature and wilderness that American writing has witnessed—a lover of small, unassuming swamp flowers and of monumental glaciers, of spring showers and of violent winter storms, of the light through purple meadow grasses and of thundering earthquakes. His vaulting optimism, first in his letters and later in essays and books, showed itself to be consistently boundless, jubilant, and irrepressible.

His encounter with *Calypso borealis* resulted in Muir's first published nature writing. Jeanne Carr, the wife of his natural history professor at the University of Wisconsin and a lifelong influence, together with his former teacher James Davie Butler stitched together parts of Muir's letters and sent them to a Boston newspaper. "I never before saw a plant so full of life; so perfectly spiritual, it seemed pure enough for the throne of its Creator," the article reported Muir rhapsodizing in his letters. "Could angels in their better land show us a more beautiful plant? . . . I cannot understand the nature of the curse, 'Thorns and thistles shall bring forth thee.'

Is our world indeed worse for this 'thisly curse?' Are not all plants beautiful? or in some way useful? Would not the world suffer by the banishment of a single weed? The curse must be within ourselves."[11]

Over the course of his life as a writer, explorer, natural historian, farmer, bronco rider, sheepshearer, mountaineer, and political activist, John Muir would reiterate some of these sentiments often. He would extol the rewards of direct encounters with nature, and through disciplined scrutiny he would establish himself as a serious field scientist, primarily in glaciology. He would argue for the ecological interdependence of all living things, from the smallest weed to the largest trees and mammals. And he would continue to stress the spiritual and religious qualities of nature, demonstrating through the example of his own rich life the profound "usefulness" of beauty and wonder.

Returning to the United States from Canada after the war was over, Muir went to work in a factory in Indianapolis, where his genius for invention was put to profitable use. Hired as a menial woodworker in a factory that produced brooms and rakes slowly by hand, Muir quickly invented a machine that produced 23,000 broom handles a day. He invented another machine for making rake teeth, "and another for boring them, and driving them, and still another for making the bows, still another used in making the handles, still another for bending them—so that rakes may now be made nearly as fast again," he wrote a friend.[12] Remembering his factory work later in life, he asserted, "I might have been a millionaire, but I chose to become a tramp."[13]

His choice of tramp over millionaire came about partly as the result of an accident. One day, bent over one of his machines, pulling hard on the laces of the belt mechanism, Muir felt the apparatus kick. Suddenly, the nail-like end of a file he was holding was driven into his right eye. As the liquid inside the lacerated eye dripped out into his cupped hands, Muir's other eye quickly went blind in sympathy. "My right eye is gone," he murmured aloud, "closed forever on all God's beauty." Lying in bed the following weeks with both eyes bandaged, uncertain if he would ever recover his sight, Muir realized he had taken the wrong path, that factory work had caused him foolishly to turn away from God's beauty, perhaps permanently and before he had experienced even a small part of its glory.[14]

Although the right eye would always be scarred and slightly off, within a matter of months, remarkably, both eyes healed. Given a second chance, Muir decided to abandon mechanical inventions and the world of business, "to devote the rest of my life to the study of the inventions of God." Leaving behind an offer to make him a partner in the successful firm for which he had invented many profitable machines, Muir once again set out on an extended trek, this time, as he said, to answer "some restless fires" that were driving him from noisy commercial centers toward "my *real* wishes."[15]

In September 1867, the twenty-nine-year-old Muir departed from Louisville, determined to walk a thousand miles to the southernmost tip of America. From Florida he planned to sail to South America, to drift down the Amazon to its mouth, and, finally, to lose himself in the rain-forest wilderness. He intended to follow "the wildest, leafiest, and least trodden way I could find."[16] Having given in to his deepest wishes and his restless nature, to all its extravagance and unreasonableness, "I wish I knew where I was going," he confessed to Jeanne Carr. "Doomed to be 'carried of the spirit into the wilderness,' I suppose. I wish I could be more moderate in my desires," he added, "but I cannot, and so there is no rest."[17] Never had he planned a trip so solitary, wild, and far from the home he knew. Even the dismal swamps of Canada had at least skirted the countryside he had grown up exploring. Now, as he prepared a small leather-bound notebook to carry with him, he inscribed his new address on the flyleaf: "John Muir, Earth-planet, Universe."

Not until late in life did Muir come back to the journal he faithfully kept on this trip south. When he did, he dictated minor revisions to a stenographer, then put it aside again. Immersed in a host of other projects, he did not see it published before he died. The journal eventually appeared as *A Thousand-Mile Walk to the Gulf*, and though written in the past tense, it retains its rhapsodic youthfulness. It also records Muir's intellectual coming of age and his developing sense of the moral meaning in natural phenomena.

Confronted by hardships and dangers on the long journey, curious encounters with wildlife and humans (the gentle and the predatory in both cases), Muir again expressed doubt that language could adequately render experiential knowledge or the intelligence gained from physical ordeals in the wilderness. After tramping through the mountains and forests of Kentucky, Tennessee, and Georgia, Muir arrived in Florida, where, he wrote, "it is impossible to write the dimmest picture of plant grandeur so redundant, unfathomable." Even the lowly grasses struck him as glorious. "All of them are beautiful beyond the reach of language," he marveled. Yet in the same paragraph of his journal he found the vivid words he needed to paint those very grasses. "Here are panicles that are one mass of refined purple; others that have flowers as yellow as ripe oranges, and stems polished and shining like steel wire. Some of the species are grouped in groves and thickets like trees, while others might be seen waving without any companions in sight. Some of them have wide-branching panicles like Kentucky oaks, others with a few tassels of spikelets dropping from a tall, leafless stem."[18]

Moving seamlessly from description of grasses to questions of moral perception, Muir wrote, "How strangely we are blinded to beauty and color, form and motion, by comparative size! For example, we measure grasses by our own stature and by the height and bulkiness of trees. But what is the size of the greatest man, or the tallest tree that ever overtopped a grass! Compared with other things in God's creation the difference is nothing. We all are only microscopic animalcula."[19]

Muir's equation of the large and small in nature, of the human
and nonhuman, melded into a vision of the living world's interdependence—a conviction that later became fundamental to the
wilderness preservation movement he began, and has been cited
as one of the founding principles of modern environmental ethics.[20]

Walking through Florida's Cedar Keys and encountering predatory reptiles, poisonous snakes, plants with leaves like sharpened bayonets, tropical disease, and starvation, he reflected on the
absurd tendency of humans to view themselves as the center of
creation, imposing their will on nature, and destroying whatever
in God's dominion they considered noxious or unusable. "The
world, we are told, was made especially for man—a presumption
not supported by all the facts," Muir wrote. "A numerous class of
men are painfully astonished whenever they find anything, living
or dead, in all God's universe, which they cannot eat or render in
some way what they call useful to themselves . . . it never seems to
occur to these far-seeing teachers that Nature's object in making
animals and plants might possibly be first of all the happiness of
each one of them, not the creation of all for the happiness of one.
Why should man value himself as more than a small part of the one
great unit of creation? And what creature of all that the Lord has
taken the pains to make is not essential to the completeness of that
unity—the cosmos? The universe would be incomplete without
man; but it would also be incomplete without the smallest trans-
microscopic creature that dwells beyond our conceitful eyes and
knowledge."[21]

In the words of his recent biographer Michael P. Cohen, Muir in
his late twenties "was beginning to think of human life, his own included, from an eternal perspective. He was beginning to see his
limits as a man. He was learning the humility necessary to any true
vision of Nature."[22] Muir's embrace of nature extended even to
varmints and predators, like the alligators that he saw Floridians
slaughtering at every opportunity, out of fear of the beasts. In a

passage that reveals Muir's developing compassion for life as well as his amusement at human folly, he offered the alligators this benediction: "Honorable representatives of the great saurians of an older creation, may you long enjoy your lilies and rushes, and be blessed now and then with a mouthful of terror-stricken man by way of a dainty!"[23]

Like animals, plants too might have sentience, Muir reasoned, and purposes separate from humankind's: "How little we know as yet of the life of plants—their hopes and fears, pains and enjoyments!" The Florida palms had such a grandeur about them that they must contain some kind of knowledge, moral or spiritual in nature. People tell us, he wrote, "that plants are perishable, soulless creatures, that only man is immortal, etc.; but this, I think, is something that we know very nearly nothing about. Anyhow, this palm was indescribably impressive and told me grander things than I ever got from human priest." Having gone so far as to allow that plant life might have spirit, Muir saw no reason to deny a similar respect to the nonliving parts of nature: the very rocks. "Plants are credited with but dim and uncertain sensation, and minerals with positively none at all," he wrote. "But why may not even a mineral arrangement of matter be endowed with sensation of a kind that we in our blind exclusive perfection can have no manner of communication with?"[24]

Out of money, poorly nourished, and exhausted, having often slept in the open, near swamps, in the mosquito-infested night air, and even in graveyards, in Cedar Keys Muir collapsed from malaria and lay unconscious and untended for several days. He would certainly have died from his illness had it not been for the kindness of a mill owner and his family who took him in. For three months he hallucinated, shook with fever and night sweats, and was so weak he could only crawl. But as soon as he had recovered enough to go on, he booked passage to Cuba, still intending to reach South America. His health did not improve, however, and after a month of feebly wandering the beaches and sleeping aboard ship, Muir was forced to give up his plans. He caught a little schooner out of Havana loaded with oranges and sailed to New York. From there he knew he could find a vessel going wherever he wished. Within days of landing, he headed south again. Traveling steerage on the ship *Nebraska*, across the Isthmus of Panama by rail, then north by boat again, at the age of thirty Muir reached San Francisco.

When he arrived in San Francisco in early spring of 1868, Muir asked directions to "the nearest way out of town to the wild part of the State,"[25] and at once set out on foot toward the mountains. Muir would remain forever entranced by what he found in the Sierra Nevada range. In Yosemite Valley, where he quickly settled, he discovered towering coniferous forests and snows still six feet deep in early summer. He wrote later that these mountains should not be called Sierra Nevada, which means Snowy Range, but the Range of Light. "I have crossed the Range of Light, surely the brightest and best of all the Lord has built," he proclaimed. The range was "so gloriously colored, and so radiant, it seemed not clothed with light, but wholly composed of it, like the wall of some celestial city."[26]

For the next six years Muir lived as a shepherd, sawyer, and handyman in the valley and foothills of Yosemite. Becoming a passionate mountaineer and guide, he began to make important geological discoveries at the higher altitudes and in the nearly inaccessible passes he climbed. Among the most important of these discoveries was living glaciers, which were thought not to exist in the Sierra, and he began to understand the influence of glaciation on Yosemite's formation.

Through his continuing connections with Jeanne Carr, who had moved with her husband to Oakland, Muir met eminent scientists who came with their students to explore Yosemite Valley. All were startled by the knowledge and enthusiasm of this tall, blue-eyed sawyer, with his tangled beard and hair, who lived year-round in a rough shed in the mountains.

In 1871, again through Jeanne Carr, Muir met his most important mountain visitor, Ralph Waldo Emerson. Sixty-eight years
old and plagued by a failing memory, Emerson arrived in Yosemite
surrounded by devoted friends who had accompanied him from
the East. Muir found these friends to be "affectionate but sadly civilized," and they prevented Emerson from camping with Muir under the trees in Mariposa Grove. Muir and Emerson nevertheless
spent several afternoons together, and their meeting made a tremendous impression on Muir. "I was excited as I had never been
excited before, and my heart throbbed as if an angel direct from
heaven had alighted on the Sierran rocks," Muir recalled later, "so
great was my awe and reverence."[27] Emerson was also impressed
by Muir. After Emerson returned home the two men continued to
correspond, and the elderly sage urged Muir to move to Concord
to be near him and his New England friends. In his journals at the
end of his life, Emerson added Muir's name to a short list—also
containing the names of Thoreau, Carlyle, and Agassiz—labeled
"My Men."[28]

Despite the flattering invitation from one of America's most
eminent writers, Muir had no intention of leaving his mountain
home; he had too many high mountain passes still to explore and
many a glacier to cross, he said. Besides, as he wrote Jeanne Carr,
"I have been too long wild, too befogged to burn well in [New England's] patent, high-heated, educational furnaces."[29] As much as
anything, Muir loved what he called "the Godful solitude" among
the high cliffs and domes of Yosemite, "as elaborately and thought-
fully carved and finished as a crystal or shell."[30]

Muir passionately desired to avoid the world outside Yosemite,
but during his visit Emerson had urged him to communicate
his scientific findings and unique intelligence to society at large.
Jeanne Carr implored him in the same way. And so did John D.
Runkle, president of the Massachusetts Institute of Technology,
who visited the valley a few months after Emerson. When Muir explained his geological theories of Yosemite's formation by glacia-

tion to Runkle, he insisted Muir write down his scientific observations so they could be shared with the Boston Academy of Science.

Tempted as he was to write, Muir found it difficult and time-consuming. He did not want to be distracted from what he called his "main work," his field observation. In contradiction to the accepted theories of such noted scientists as California state geologist Josiah Whitney, Muir had found that Yosemite had been formed not by cataclysm, but that "each dome and brow and wall, and every grace and spire and brother is the necessary result of the delicately balanced blows of well directed and combined glaciers against the parent rocks which contained them."[31]

Muir had little money to support his solitary explorations. Often he went for days and weeks with no more provisions than a crust of bread and a handful of tea. Muir hardly considered such deprivations a hardship, and poverty by itself might never have brought him out of the mountains. But soon Muir found his glacial theories—which he explained at length to every mountain visitor—being appropriated and published by others, none of whom had applied his method to understanding mountains. "Patient observation and constant brooking above the rocks, lying upon them for years as the ice did, is the way to arrive at the truths which are given so lavishly upon them," he wrote.[32]

Within months of meeting Emerson, Muir completed his first major essay, "Yosemite Glaciers," and saw it quickly accepted by the influential New York *Daily Tribune*.[33] It was not the purely objective scientific paper Professor Runkle had wanted him to write. Instead, as was typical of all his later work, the essay described in an engaging, first-person voice a journey along high Sierra Nevada ridges, along the shores of radiant blue lakes, through stands of bright trees, and across breathtaking meadows. While the article contained exact scientific data—much of it a significant contribution to glaciology in the region—it also surrounded the reader with exhilarating detail, visions of towering mountains, dazzling snow, tranquil meadows, the sounds of rumbling rapids, roaring waterfalls, and singing rain showers.

In the essay Muir employed "book of nature" and palimpsest images, which he frequently used in his journal entries and letters, to describe the glacial landscape. "Two years ago," he began, "when picking flowers in the mountains back of Yosemite Valley, I found a book. It was blotted and storm-beaten; all of its outer pages were mealy and crumbly, the paper seemed to dissolve like the snow beneath which it had been buried; but many of the inner pages were well preserved, and though all were more or less stained and torn, whole chapters were easily readable. In this condition is the great open book of Yosemite glaciers today; its granite pages have been torn and blurred by the same storms that wasted the castaway book. The grand central chapters of the Hoffman, and Tenaya, and Nevada glaciers are stained and corroded by the frosts and rains, yet, nevertheless, they contain scarce one unreadable page."

Muir applied his anthropomorphism to the rocks and ice not only because he wanted to help the reader understand glacial action, but also because he felt profoundly that all of nature was alive in some complex way as yet not understood. "There is sublimity in the life of a glacier," he wrote. "Water rivers work openly, and so the rains and the gentle dews, and the great sea also grasping all the world: and even the universal ocean of breath, though invisible, yet speaks aloud in a thousand voices, and proclaims its modes of working and its power: but glaciers work apart from men, exerting their tremendous energies in silence and darkness, outspread, spirit-like, brooding above predestined rocks unknown to light, unborn, working on unwearied through unmeasured times, unhalting as the stars, until at length, their creations complete, their mountains brought forth, homes made for the meadows and the lakes, and field for waiting forests, earnest, calm as when they came as crystals from the sky, they depart."

He moved through the landscape with a pace even a tender-footed reader could maintain and, when necessary, stopped to rest and sleep. "Last evening I was camped in a small round glacier meadow, at the head of the easternmost tributary of the cascade," Muir wrote. "The meadow was velvet with grass, and circled with the most beautiful of all the coniferae, the Williamson spruce. I built a great fire, and the daisies of the sod rayed as if conscious of a sun. As I lay on my back, feeling the presence of the trees—gleaming upon the dark, and gushing with life—coming closer and closer around me, and saw the small round sky coming down with its stars to dome my trees, I said, 'Never was mountain mansion more beautiful, more spiritual; never was moral wanderer more blessedly homed.' When the sun rose, my charmed walls were taken down, the trees returned to the common fund of the forest, and my little sky fused back into the measureless blue. I was left upon common ground to follow my glacial labor."

In pursuit of glaciation, Muir took his reader with him through the narrow mountain passes, pointing out crystal lakes and smooth purple grasses, the shy deer and wild bear. And at the essay's end, he again lay down to rest beside a blazing fire, surrounded by pine, silver fir, and spruce, as if acknowledging the importance of meditation, repose, and dreams to any expedition. Resting and gazing at the night sky was also an acknowledgment of his own frailty—no matter how tireless his pace along the trail sometimes seemed—and a time to allow the human and the spiritual to enter the world of the essay. In a carefully rendered moment of ecstasy, he said, "I have set fire to two pine logs, and the neighboring trees are coming to my charmed circle of light." The sensory presence of the wilderness came down to embrace him and, by proxy, his reader. Then, having taken in the night as fully as he had taken in the day, he lay back, concluding the essay with a farewell: "Good-night to my two logs and two lakes, and to my two domes high and black on the sky, with a cluster of stars between."

"Yosemite Glaciers" was purchased for $200, a substantial sum in Muir's time. Moreover, it was read and remarked upon by leading naturalists in New York and Boston. Its favorable reception, both as graceful essay and as significant exposition of glaciology, launched Muir's career as a writer. He began writing for the New York *Weekly Tribune* as well as the *Daily Tribune*, two of the largest newspapers in the country, and soon began a long association with the prestigious and well-paying *Overland Monthly*.

Muir acknowledged two writers in particular as influences upon his style. The first was John Ruskin. Like Thoreau, however, Muir felt that Ruskin lacked a real spiritual or moral understanding of nature; "You never can feel that there is the slightest union betwixt Nature and him."[34] He felt a closer affinity with Thoreau, committing long passages of his writing to memory. Frequently in his prose Muir would give a nod to one of his favorite passages. In his second article for the *Overland Monthly*, "Twenty Hill Hollow," Muir echoed the beginning phrase of Thoreau's essay "Walking," writing, "I wish to say a word for the great central plain of California in general and for Twenty Hill Hollow, in Merced County, in particular."[35]

For the next four years Muir attempted to maintain his life in the mountains while keeping up with his writing commitments. He climbed Mount Ritter and Mount Whitney and explored the high region around Yosemite, and from these trips developed an important series of descriptive and scientific articles for the *Overland Monthly* titled "Studies in the Sierra." He also wrote for *Harper's*, and steadily for the San Francisco *Daily Evening Bulletin*.

In all of this work and in his work generally it would be hard to overstate Muir's appeal as an affectionate narrator and mountain guide. Part of that appeal, his readers and admirers have often noted, comes from Muir's tendency, no matter what philosophical point he was making or what life-threatening mountain adventure he was describing, always to efface himself. "It is not obliteration, but the careful pose of an usher: one who takes his experience as in

no way unique; one who speaks as the representative of his readers," according to scholars Robert Engberg and Donald Wesling.
"That voice is an achievement of maturity, and if we hear it properly we hear a voice continuously protecting its utterance from
being selfish or thrusting or hectoring in his father's style. There is
no wish to dominate the reader and turn the reader into a child. His
is a tact, to let the reader alone, based on a larger and finer tact,
which is that of letting the natural world alone."[36]

Like Thoreau, Muir knew the importance of a fact—that, seen
properly, it might flower into truth. And he likewise knew the importance of imagination. "How infinitely superior to our physical
senses are those of the mind! The spiritual eye sees not only rivers
of water but of air," he wrote in his journal. "It sees the crystals of
the rock in rapid sympathetic motion, giving enthusiastic obedi-
ence to the sun's rays, then sinking back to rest in the night. The
whole world is in motion to the center.

"So also sounds," he continued. "We hear only woodpeckers
and squirrels and the rush of turbulent streams. But imagination
gives us the sweet music of tiniest insect wings, enables us to hear,
all round the world, the vibration of every needle, the waving of
every bole and branch, the sound of stars in circulation like parti-
cles in the blood. The Sierra canyons are full of avalanche debris—
we hear them boom again, for we read past sounds from present
conditions. Again we hear the earthquake rock-falls. Imagination
is usually regarded as a synonym for the unreal. Yet is true imagination healthful and real, no more likely to mislead than the
coarser senses. Indeed, the power of imagination makes us infinite."[37]

Even as his strength as a writer grew, Muir continued to prize
direct experience over descriptive language and over the hard labor that he found writing to be. No matter how exactly he might
succeed in making words work for him, and despite the steady demand for his articles, Muir continued to doubt his abilities as a
writer and the abilities of language in general to convey his expe-

riences. As he was being convinced to undertake his "Studies in the Sierra" for the *Overland Monthly*, he wrote in a Christmas letter to Jeanne Carr: "Book-making frightens me, because it demands so much artificialness and retrograding. Somehow, up here in these fountain skies [of Yosemite] I feel like a flake of glass through which light passes, but which, conscious of the inexhaustibleness of its sun fountain, cares not whether its passing light coins itself into other forms or goes unchanged—neither charcoaled nor diamonded! Moreover, I find that though I have a few thoughts entangled in the fibres of my mind, I possess no words into which I can shape them. You tell me that I must be patient and reach out and grope in lexicon granaries for the words I want. But if some loquacious angel were to touch my lips with literary fire, bestowing every word of Webster, I would scarce thank him for the gift, because most of the words of the English language are made of mud, for muddy purposes, while those invented to contain spiritual matter are doubtful and unfixed in capacity and form, as wind-ridden mist-rags."[38]

Despite his love of solitude and wilderness, Muir found it increasingly difficult to remain in the mountains and do the writing that now seemed to him his obligation to society and his destiny: writing that would "entice people to look at Nature's loveliness" and to understand the soul-healing importance of the wild.[39] "Heaven knows that John Baptist was not more eager to get all his fellow sinners into the Jordan than I to baptize all of mine in the beauty of God's mountains," he wrote.[40]

To complete the "Studies in the Sierra" series, Muir moved to Oakland in 1873. It was a wrenching move, and he needed to return to the mountains repeatedly for brief periods to regain what he called his "mountain self" and his "glacial eye." With each trip back to Yosemite he was appalled by the increased destruction from fires set by sheepherders and from the hydraulic mining that ripped out enormous living sections of the Tuolumne. He would write later of the horror he felt watching sawyers blast down giant sequoia with dynamite for cheap lumber and, even worse, the destruction by the "hoofed locusts," domestic sheep, herded into the mountain meadows where they would overgraze every bit of wild vegetation. At the same time, nothing he saw could dim his untiring delight in the mountains and in his mountaineering solitude.[41]

In November 1874 Muir climbed Mount Shasta alone. After reaching the peak through all but impassable drifts, he met violent winds that blew streaming banners of loose, dry snow from the tops of the surrounding peaks, some of the banners "more than a mile long, shining, streaming, waving with solemn exuberant enthusiasm as if celebrating some surpassingly glorious event." Descending to his solitary base camp, he buried himself in a "storm-nest" to wait out the weather. The storm continued for three days. Rather than feeling a sense of danger, Muir experienced only a "wild exhilaration." Having given explicit instructions that he was to be left alone on the mountain no matter what, he was sorely disappointed when, though he was not lost, "rescuers" eventually found him.[42]

After the descent, exploring on the Yuba, Muir ventured into yet another storm, drawn by its "passionate music." Silver pines 200 feet high vibrated down to their foundations and waved like goldenrods, "chanting and bowing low as if in worship." The force of the gale was so great that he could hear large trees falling around him every two or three minutes, uprooted or broken straight across. In the midst of the roaring tumult, Muir climbed to the top of a 100-foot spruce and braced himself in the highest slender branches as they "flapped and swished in the passionate torrent, bending and swirling backward and forward, round and round, tracing indescribable combinations of vertical and horizontal curves." He clung there "like a bobolink on a reed." When it was all over, having listened to the great orchestra of wind, having drunk the fragrance of the torrents steeped like tea in the forest's rich bed of plant life and mineral, he wrote, "We all travel the milky way together, trees and men; but it never occurred to me until this storm-day, while swinging in the wind, that trees are travelers, in the ordinary sense. They make many journeys, not extensive ones, it is true. But our own little journeys, away and back again, are only little more than tree-wavings—many of them not so much."[43]

Despite these brief sojourns into high mountain weather, Muir's life now gave him less and less time to explore. His path had turned down toward civilization and to a new kind of work. Although he continued strenuously to explore and botanize, taking expeditionary trips to Utah, Nevada, and an extended journey to Alaska, the solitary years in the mountains were essentially over.

One week before his forty-second birthday, to the amazement of many of his friends, the reclusive and foot-loose John Muir married Louie Strenzel, the only child of a wealthy fruit rancher in a valley far below the mountain crests. He took up residence on his father-in-law's 2,600-acre ranch near Martinez, at the mouth of the Sacramento River, and turned his intense powers of concentration to the duties of husband, father, householder, and rancher.

It was nearly ten years before Muir returned to his writing in earnest. Despite his silence, his reputation as a writer had persisted, and in late May 1889 the fifty-one-year-old mountaineer-turned-rancher met Robert Underwood Johnson, an editor of the nation's leading monthly, *Century Magazine*. Johnson came to San Francisco from the East intentionally seeking out Muir, determined to get him back into the writing business. When they met, Johnson discovered that Muir was as formidable with agriculture as he had been with writing, turning his vineyards and orchards into one of the most successful ranches in the valley. Muir was also a devoted father and husband. Nevertheless he longed to return to his "real work," up in the wilderness, looking after Yosemite.[44]

Louie, watching her husband chafe under the responsibilities of ranch work, had urged Muir for several years to resume writing.

It was with her blessing that Johnson and Muir rode from the ranch together and into Yosemite Valley, headed for Soda Springs. The two men packed into the high meadows by mule, and Muir gave Johnson the whole tour. Late at night on a bed of spruce needles, under stars as big as snowballs in the clear mountain air, the two men lamented the disgraceful mismanagement and neglect of Yosemite's resources by the state of California. Between them they devised a foolishly optimistic plan—to lobby the federal government to acquire control of the valley once and for all, and to convert Yosemite into a national park.

At the time, only Yellowstone was a national park in name. Designated as "worthless"—that is, without any resources to plunder—Yellowstone had been set aside not as a wilderness preserve but as a "pleasuring ground for the benefit and enjoyment of the people."[45] Johnson and Muir had preservation in mind for Yosemite's wilderness, too. Johnson agreed to promote the idea in his magazine and to lobby his friends in Congress, and Muir agreed to write two articles for *Century* celebrating the valley's beauty and proposing the outlines for its boundaries as a park.

Muir's first article, "The Treasures of the Yosemite," appeared in *Century* in August 1890. Lavishly illustrated and written with a keen sense of mission, it contains some of Muir's finest prose, arguing for preservation of "wilderness pure and simple." The second article, "Features of the Proposed Yosemite National Park," appeared the following month, and within weeks President Benjamin Harrison signed into law a bill that, generally following the recommendations of Muir's article, set aside 1,500 square miles of forest surrounding Yosemite—the first national preserve specifically designated for protecting wilderness.[46]

The victory was far from total. Yosemite Valley itself was not included in the new park but rather remained in state control.[47] But the success of the national campaign waged by Johnson and Muir, along with the enormous readership Muir's articles in *Century* received, made Muir a national figure. On the strength of that noto-

riety, intoxicated by hope for the success of his preservationist ideals, Muir now joined in some of the most furious political debates
of the period, including further efforts to have all of Yosemite come
under federal control, and later the national fight to save Hetch
Hetchy from being flooded for a municipal reservoir for San Francisco. Two years after the *Century* articles, he rallied two dozen
friends to found, for the purpose of defending the new park and
preserving other features of the Sierra Nevada mountains, a group
calling itself the Sierra Club.

Muir's reputation rose dramatically as he produced a stream of
articles praising America's forests and wilderness. He was willing
to battle any individual or group contributing to the destruction of
the public lands. In 1897 he closed a long essay in the *Atlantic* with
one of his typically impassioned calls for preservation. "Any fool
can destroy trees," he wrote. "They cannot run away; and if they
could, they would still be destroyed,—chased and hunted down
as long as fun or a dollar could be got out of their bark hides,
branching horns, or magnificent bole backbones . . . Through all
the wonderful, eventful centuries since Christ's time—and long
before that—God has cared for these trees, saved them from
drought, disease, avalanches, and a thousand straining, leveling
tempests and floods; but he cannot save them from fools,—only
Uncle Sam can do that."[48]

Always outspoken and fearless when defending the land, Muir
met Theodore Roosevelt shortly after he took office as president
and convinced him to save, through national legislation, greater
tracts of wilderness lands and national treasures, including the
Grand Canyon and the Petrified Forest. Muir met John Burroughs,
the other leading nature writer of the period, and scolded him
for shrinking from political activism, for being too impressed by
famous men to chide them into doing their part to save the forests.
(Burroughs had said of Yellowstone, while visiting there with
Roosevelt, "The most interesting thing in that wonderful land
was, of course, the President himself."[49] Muir, in contrast, had

dared to tell railroad magnate E. H. Harriman, with whom he traveled to Alaska at Harriman's expense, that he was richer than Harriman because he knew how much money he really needed and Harriman did not.[50]) Muir scolded not only Roosevelt but his powerful commissioners, such as Chief Forester Gifford Pinchot, for what Muir regarded as their inadequate regard for conservation; he also scolded Roosevelt's successor, William Howard Taft.

Despite Muir's independence and confrontational ways—exaggerated in the press because of the final, bitter fight he waged, and finally lost, to save Hetch Hetchy—Muir's fundamental generosity and good humor kept him on friendly terms with many of the same men who disagreed with him, including Burroughs, Harriman, and Roosevelt.[51] None of them could deny Muir's passion and dedication or the effectiveness of his writing.

In a letter to Robert Underwood Johnson in 1889, Muir defined himself succinctly, and in doing so gave definition to that species also known as the American nature writer: a "self-styled poetico-trampo-geologist-bot. and ornith-natural, etc!!!" In his "etc!!!" were several additional facets of John Muir, including artist, evangelist for nature, political activist, farmer, explorer, and mystic.

John Muir had the rigorous learning and discipline of a scientist. He discovered and described numerous new species of plants and insects, recognized the presence of geological processes and glaciers in the Sierra Nevada and in Alaska, and was the first to explore with scientific precision certain regions in both Alaska and California. But he wanted science to include more than objectivity; he did not want to separate from scientific observation the passionate physical and spiritual impressions he had gained through direct contact with the world. In *The Mountains of California*, his first book, published when he was fifty-six years old, Muir wrote, "The influences of nature seem to be so little known as yet, that it is generally supposed that complete pleasure of this kind, permeating one's very flesh and bones, unfits the student from scientific pursuits in which cool judgment and observation are required. But the effect is just the opposite. Instead of producing a dissipated condition, the mind is fertilized and stimulated and developed like sun-fed plants."[52]

Later he wrote, "The man of science, the naturalist, too often loses sight of the essential oneness of all living beings in seeking to classify them in kingdoms, orders, families, genera, species, etc. taking note of the kind and arrangements of limbs, teeth, toes, scales, hair, feathers, etc., measured and set forth in meters, centimeters, and millimeters, while the eye of the Poet, the Seer, never closes on the kinship of all God's creatures, and his heart ever beats in sympathy with great and small alike, as 'earth-born companions and fellow mortals' equally dependent on Heaven's eternal love."[53]

Muir is known not only as the father of the national parks, but also as a hero and a visionary. He saw the continuity and interrelatedness of the world in a manner ahead of his time and with an ecstatic optimism that was hardly short of religious and mystical. His vision of the universal interdependence of the natural world—along with his activism in favor of national parks, his books, his exhortation to "get these glorious works of God into yourself"—is an essential part of his legacy.

Muir delighted in testing the limits of sensual and physical experience, and the intensity of eye and limb. Through sheer physical endurance, he discovered the great and small in the wilderness terrain and portrayed them in writing to a public that, until it saw the natural world through Muir's eyes, regarded nature as something to be dominated, used, or admired only for its most tame, genteel, and passive qualities.

Muir's most significant discovery, according to his biographer Frederick Turner, was "a way to love the land and to extend that love to the society at large." Perhaps more than Thoreau and Emerson, Muir in his life "reconciled the conflict between democratic individualism and participatory democracy."[54] In this reconciliation, Muir extended the legacy of Thoreau by becoming not only a lover of the American wild and an influential writer on the philosophy of wildness, but also a force asserting that an appreciation of wilderness was synonymous with an active and even aggressive pursuit of beauty. "One must labor for beauty as for bread, here as elsewhere," he wrote from the mountains of Yosemite.[55]

In his journal, just before he died on Christmas Eve at age seventy-six, Muir reaffirmed the optimism and largeness of spirit that had sustained him throughout his life: "*This grand show is eternal*," he wrote. "It is always sunrise somewhere; the dew is never all dried at once; a shower is forever falling; vapor is ever rising. Eternal sunrise, eternal sunset, eternal dawn and gloaming, on sea and continents and islands, each in its turn, as the round earth rolls."[56]

Chapter Seven

IN THE EYE OF THE WOLF

By the spring of 1903 John Muir was meeting often in San Francisco with his Sierra Club friends to discuss, among other things, the federal government's shifting attitudes toward conservation. Some of these shifts had been brought on by dramatic events two years earlier, when an innocent-looking young man had approached President William McKinley in a crowd at the Pan-American Exposition in Buffalo and shot him point-blank with a pistol. Eight days later McKinley died, and his vice president, Theodore Roosevelt, assumed office.

Roosevelt loved hunting, fishing, mountain climbing, and wilderness camping on a robust scale. While vice president it seemed he was more often on safari than in Washington. He had helped found the Boone and Crockett Club, a sportsman's association dedicated to preserving wild game by promoting a degree of restraint, a so-called etiquette, among sport hunters, although some of his own safaris were anything but restrained.[1] Roosevelt was also an avid amateur naturalist; as an undergraduate at Harvard he had intended to make natural history his profession, and he continued to write on the subject even after entering politics. For these reasons, preservationists like Muir were cautiously optimistic that during a Roosevelt administration the Sierra Club's point of view would at least be heard in Washington.

Two years into Roosevelt's term, however, it was becoming clear that the national parks, so important to Muir, were not going to be saved merely by the fact that the president loved hunting and the outdoors. Although Roosevelt asserted federal control for the first time over vast areas of public lands, his close advisers argued that those lands, regardless of their designation as national parks, national monuments, or forest preserves, should be managed principally as timber, grazing, and mining resources. Among the most powerful and vocal of these advisers was Gifford Pinchot, soon to be chief of the U.S. Forest Service. Scenic and aesthetic qualities in nature did not interest Pinchot, nor did wilderness for its own sake. A utilitarian, scientific-minded man of his times, Pinchot declared that "the first duty of the human race is to control the earth it lives upon."[2] In a speech to the Society of American Foresters in March 1903, Pinchot summed up his position by asserting that "the object of our forest policy is not to preserve the forests because they are beautiful or wild or the habitat of wild animals; it is to ensure a steady supply of timber for human prosperity. Every other consideration comes as secondary."[3] Roosevelt and the majority of pragmatic, efficiency-minded Americans seemed to agree with Pinchot.

This was not the kind of conservation the Sierra Club had in mind. But just as Muir began girding himself for the political fight he anticipated over protection of the forests, the new president himself wrote to Muir asking for a private meeting. "I do not want anyone with me but you," Roosevelt said in his message, "and I want to drop politics absolutely for four days, and just be out in the open with you."[4] Muir immediately canceled plans to tour Asia so that he might educate the president on subjects he felt passionately about. In particular, as unsympathetic as federal policy had been to preservation, state policy was even worse. California jurisdiction over Yosemite had resulted in the grazing of hundreds of thousands of sheep on pristine mountain meadows; Muir described them as "hooved locusts." He wanted Roosevelt to protect the valley from such abuses by receding control of it to the federal government.

For three days and nights Muir and Roosevelt camped alone in Mariposa Grove, discussing the fate of Yosemite and the surrounding forests. The old mountaineer led the president through flowering meadows among 300-foot-high sequoias and ardently articulated the necessity of preserving habitat for the water ouzels and golden eagles, the wild primrose and rock ferns, the Douglas squirrels and mountain honeybees. Roosevelt apparently conceived a genuine liking for Muir and relished this time together. "It was clear weather, and we lay in the open," he reported later, "the enormous cinnamon-colored trunks rising about us like the columns of a vaster and more beautiful cathedral than was ever conceived by any human architect."5 By the end of his time in the valley, Roosevelt had decided to extend federal protection to the areas around Yosemite and, if Congress would agree, to put the valley under federal control. Before long, however, Pinchot and his zealous resource managers regained Roosevelt's ear; utilitarianism would prevail in the hardest-fought battle of all, the damming of Hetch Hetchy Valley.

Muir was now sixty-five years old, weathered but still wiry and agile. His gray beard had grown weedy, but his intense blue eyes crackled when he railed against sheep ranchers, loggers, and politicians opposed to preservation. His eyes would soften only when he began one of his long, mountain monologues on the beauty of Alaska or the Sierra Nevada. He found occasions to do both at the congenial homes of men like writer and attorney Theodore Hittell. Among such friends, Muir planned strategy to combat the exploiters of the national park lands, even as he socialized in his usual convivial manner with other writers.

One evening at Hittell's in the spring of 1904, Muir was introduced to a broad-featured woman in her mid-thirties with thick, waist-length brown hair. She had small eyes and heavy eyelids, a wide mouth, and a brooding face deeply tanned by desert life. Strong-willed, Mary Austin had been toughened by years of having to make her own way with little help from others, and it showed in her features. A writer herself, she knew Muir's wilderness books well and had been thirsty to meet him.

As on other evenings, the loquacious Muir did most of the talking, soliloquizing about nights spent on unstable glaciers or under thundering cataracts, encounters with grizzlies, and hair's-breadth escapes from mountain cliffs. Austin later recalled having been swept away by the old mountaineer's declaration, familiar by now to his friends, that in his most perilous moments in the wild, angels had come to help him find his footing along a steep ledge, a handhold as he dangled by his fingertips above a waterfall, or safe passage across an icy crevasse. His unpretentious faith in fundamental mysteries rang true to Austin. She too had been in the company of angels, and, she told Muir, they aided her when she wrote. Like Muir's angels in the wild, hers came to give her guidance. They were mystical Presences, tall but invisible, and she had felt them near her since she was five years old.[6]

When she met Muir, Austin's regional stories and poems had already appeared in the *Atlantic, Out West,* and *Overland Monthly,* journals that were also publishing Muir's work. She had been invited to the Hittells' because of the success of her first book, a collection of interwoven essays and vignettes describing the southern desert of California between the Sierra Nevada and Death Valley. Bliss Perry, editor at both the *Atlantic* and Houghton Mifflin, had published it in October of the previous year.

The Land of Little Rain, as the book was called, drew immediate critical acclaim, and for Austin it was just the encouragement she needed to make a full break from her marriage and to launch a full-time writing career living on her own. Before she died, some thirty-five years later, Austin would publish more than twenty-five additional books, including novels, short story collections, children's tales, plays, feminist and religious philosophy, literary theory, Indian legends, ethnography, an art book in collaboration with Ansel Adams, and natural history—plus hundreds of pieces for more than sixty periodicals.[7] But *The Land of Little Rain*, a rather small book of observations on the desert's sparse flora and fauna, and on the human inhabitants who scraped out an austere living there, would be her most enduring work.

Austin had come to the edge of California's Mojave Desert when she was just twenty, in the company of her mother and siblings. Just out of college in the Midwest, she had resisted the move, but her objections carried no weight with her mother. From the time Mary's father had died, when Mary was ten, her mother had been standoffish and cold to her, perhaps frightened by her daughter's odd intellectual interests and willfulness. She avoided touching Mary or giving her any physical comfort, and when Mary's sister died the same year as her father, her mother wished aloud that it had been Mary who died instead.

Mary found it difficult to conform to Midwestern female propriety, and therefore ever to satisfy her mother's expectations and demands. Her mother sternly discouraged Mary's "childish" love for nature, for instance. She informed Mary that respectable young men who might come calling, if they ever did, would not be attracted to a young lady with such interests. "Especially you must not talk appreciatively about landscapes and flowers and the habits of little animals and birds to boys; they didn't like it," Austin remembered her mother telling her. "You must not quote; especially poetry and Thoreau. An occasional light reference to Burroughs was permissible, but not Thoreau."[8]

Only one other person in Austin's hometown of Carlinville, Illinois, was known to care about natural history subjects. Mary first heard the man's name because of the pity the ladies in town offered the man's wife, who was, according to Austin, "if not humiliated, at least rendered unpleasantly self-conscious by his queerness." Austin wrote later that people spoke of this man's love for nature "only a little less disparagingly than they would if it had been a weakness for cards, or a too great conviviality, a little the way they spoke of a man who played the piano for a living."[9]

After her father's death, Mary's older brother, Jim, became the head of the family. When Jim eventually decided to homestead in California, Mary and her mother, in large part out of economic dependency, followed him. After traveling tourist class to Los Angeles in a Union Pacific coach, Mary's mother and brother loaded themselves and all their belongings into a cramped wagon. Mary was put on horseback, and the family set out to cross the desert, looking for Jim's homestead stake. Ill equipped to make a go of desert agriculture, and unfamiliar with the arid landscape, as the family drove farther into the desert they grew increasingly homesick for "the glory of the October hills of Illinois." Yet the more parched and uninhabited the land became, the higher Austin's spirits rose. Notwithstanding the tarantulas and coyotes, the rats that ate the meager crops, and the corpses of famine-racked cattle in the homesteaders' waterholes, she found herself falling in love with the rhapsodic beauty and freedom of the land. She became "spellbound," she said, constantly alert "not to miss any animal behavior, any bird-marking, any weather signal, any signature of tree or flower."[10]

Her brother's attempts at agriculture soon failed. Worse for Austin, however, was the cruelty of her family. They found her temperament strange, and their prejudice against her spoiled what would otherwise have been a happy existence in that radiant landscape she had grown to love. To save herself from her family's mistreatment, she soon found an intelligent but ineffectual young man to marry. Though not without lapses, she would stick by this well-meaning, desultory husband for more than ten years. Through a series of failed ventures into the desert south of Bakersfield, into stark little towns without water or hope, and eventually to Independence, in the Owens Valley, Austin and her husband patched together a difficult living in a miserable, loveless marriage.

Rather than giving her comfort, Austin's marriage produced only a profoundly retarded child, named Ruth, and additional obstacles to her aspirations to be a writer. Nevertheless, she began to dedicate every available moment to her stories, poems, and essays, often to the neglect of those around her. Finally, after the publication of *The Land of Little Rain*, Austin extricated herself from Ruth, whom she institutionalized, and from her husband, whom she simply left behind. She first sought out literary companionship in Los Angeles and San Francisco, then moved to Carmel, on the California coast. In this newly founded colony of bohemian artists and writers she met such luminaries as Jack London and Ambrose Bierce and became infatuated with the poet George Sterling. She moved into a log cabin and built a platform in the branches of an old oak, where she would go to write, wrapped theatrically in "long Grecian robes, with her hair hanging to her waist," or dressed in a leather gown as though she were an Indian princess.[11] She wrote and published prodigiously, and the more rapidly her notoriety grew, the more she wrote.

At age thirty-seven, not long after moving to Carmel, Austin toured Europe and England for two years, where she met, among others, Shaw, Yeats, Conrad, H. G. Wells, and Isadora Duncan. Although she herself had little money, she lived stylishly in London with Herbert Hoover and his family. At least one acquaintance thought she was developing "an empress complex," impressed with her own fame and genius.[12]

Increasingly radical in her political and feminist views, Austin next moved to New York, where she lived more than a dozen years. She saw her play *The Arrow Maker* produced, and her social connections expanded to politicians, journalists, and anarchists. In Greenwich Village she became a prominent feminist theorist and a highly regarded literary force—a socialist, a poet, a suffragist, and a mystic—always emphasizing her Western point of reference by wearing colorful Indian apparel and chastising the New York literary elite for their neglect of Western writers and subjects.

In particular, she was outraged by and bitter about their sexist treatment of her work.

Eventually, in her late fifties, Austin returned to the desert West for good, settling for the last decade of her life in an adobe house on the Camino del Monte Sol, overlooking Santa Fe. She enjoyed the company of writers and artists such as Willa Cather and Georgia O'Keeffe, but she also loved the presence of the native American people, whose traditions she cherished. "It is a mountain country, immensely dramatically beautiful," she said, "with its appeal of mystery and naked space, and it supplies the element of aboriginal society which I have learned to recognize as my proper medium."[13]

By the time Austin wrote *The Land of Little Rain*, Muir had already explored the Sierra range and shown how the keen eye of the naturalist might be compatible, in that lush wilderness, with a transcendental spirit. Before Austin described the desert, however, few had embraced that desolate land to the south of Muir's Range of Light in a literary and loving way. Like Muir, Austin wanted to unite the ineffable spirituality she saw in natural processes with the hard-won facts she obtained firsthand at the dusty waterholes and on the gray manzanita hills and windy mesas. In a chapter in *The Land of Little Rain* devoted to unpredictable desert storms, she evoked Muir's visionary glow and drew on his descriptive richness, turning an anecdote into a moral.

"Weather does not happen," she wrote. "It is the visible manifestation of the Spirit moving itself in the void. It gathers itself together under the heavens; rains, snows, yearns mightily in wind, smiles; and the Weather Bureau, situated advantageously for that very business, taps the record on his instruments and going out on the streets denies his God, not having gathered the sense of what he has seen. Hardly anybody takes account of the fact that John Muir, who knows more of mountain storms than any other, is a devout man."

Of the few other writers who had cared to take the California desert for their subject matter, the most notable was Austin's contemporary John C. Van Dyke, whose book *The Desert* appeared the same year as *The Land of Little Rain*.[14] An art historian from New Jersey, Van Dyke purportedly wandered alone in the arid Southwest for three years, often sick and near death. In fact, the hardships he described were probably fictitious; he rode in Pullman cars and stayed in luxury hotels whenever possible. Nevertheless, Van Dyke's love for desert aesthetics was real and his descriptions are compelling. At a time when Americans saw their deserts as "wasteland," Van Dyke wrote, "Nature's work is all of it good, all of it purposeful, all of it wonderful, all of it beautiful."

For all his love of the desert, however, Van Dyke's book lacked the consistent eloquence and unity of Austin's. Austin's literary ambitions were higher than Van Dyke's, and they were also higher than those of an earlier California desert writer, Bret Harte. In *The Land of Little Rain*, Austin radiated affection for the people of the region—poor Mexican immigrants, an old Paiute basketmaker, prospectors, mule drivers, and sheepherders. Unlike Harte, Austin saw the native people and desert inhabitants not as eccentrics and examples of local color, but as fellow creatures adapting with dignity to the desert world she had grown to love.

"None other than this long brown land lays such a hold on the affections," Austin wrote in her opening chapter. "The rainbow hills, the tender bluish mists, the luminous radiance of the spring, have the lotus charm." To observe the desert, she hunkered down close to the level of pocket gophers and kangaroo rats: "Getting down to the eye level of rat and squirrel kind, one perceives what might easily be wide and winding roads to us if they occurred in thick plantations of trees three times the height of a man. It needs but a slender thread of barrenness to make a mouse trail in the forest of the sod. To the little people the water trails are as country roads, with scents as signboards." She added, "It seems that man-height is the least fortunate of all heights from which to study trails."

In this book as in her life, Austin preferred the outback and the odd to the garden plot or the tamed. In the third chapter of *The Land of Little Rain*, devoted to scavengers, she praised wolves, coyotes, and even the buzzards that arrived black and thick as plague when carrion was plentiful. "On clear days they betook themselves to the upper air, where they hung motionless for hours," she wrote. "That year there were vultures among them, distinguished by the white patches under the wings. All their offensiveness notwithstanding, they have a stately flight. They must also have what passes for good qualities among themselves, for they are social, not to say clannish."[15]

For Austin, it was not buzzards and coyotes that were clumsy and out of place in nature but ordinary men who came as trespassers to the wild. "No other except the bear makes so much noise," she wrote. "Being so well warned before hand, it is a very stupid animal, or a very bold one, that cannot keep safely hid. The cunningest hunter is hunted in turn, and what he leaves of his kill is meat for some other. That is the economy of nature, but with it all there is not sufficient account taken of the works of man. There is no scavenger that eats tin cans, and no wild thing leaves a like disfigurement on the forest floor."

Austin never again succeeded in writing about nature with such appealing simplicity and clarity. Driven by a restless hunger for literary recognition and multiple outlets for her genius, she went on to other literary interests and to work for social reform. Throughout her life, however, she always retained, as part of her writing and political activism, a reverence for native American people and a spiritual kinship with the land as she imagined it manifested in their religion.

It was this reverence, and a continuing desire to defend Indian arts and culture against further degradation, that brought Austin back finally to the desert Southwest. There, at age sixty-five, still writing and lecturing, still resentful over being denied the full recognition she felt her work deserved, lonely but seeking as ever for deep connection and community with the natural world, Austin died in her sleep of heart disease. A woman of powerful personality who impressed with her genius and eccentricity all those she met, she concluded her autobiography by writing, "At the core of our Amerindian life we are consummated in the dash and color of collectivity. It is not that we work upon the Cosmos, but it works in us."[16]

Mary Austin was one of three important nature writers in succession to come from the Midwest. John Muir, in the generation just before her, had been raised in Wisconsin's cornfields and pine forests. And just as Austin was preparing to leave for the California desert with her family, the most important nature writer of the next generation, Aldo Leopold, was born in Iowa, on the western banks of the Mississippi. Like Austin, he would leave the Midwest for the southern desert while in his early twenties. And once he arrived, Arizona's diverse creatures and arid expansiveness would enthrall him.

Leopold was different from all the nature writers before him in one significant regard: he came to the West as a trained scientist, and he came, as he believed, to do good for the land, to protect its creatures, and to see that it was managed properly. As a young man he had been educated in the new economic management theories of Gifford Pinchot; only by participating in abuses to the environment as a result of following these theories, by serving the land badly at times without realizing it, did he later develop a broader, less utilitarian understanding of the natural world. From that understanding came his enduring contribution to nature writing and to ecology—a single great book, modestly titled *A Sand County Almanac*.

Born in 1887 and raised in a large Victorian house that stood above the town of Burlington looking out over the Mississippi, Leopold acquired a love of nature from his father. On family camping trips ranging from the Illinois bottomlands to the northern edge of Lake Huron, Aldo, who was the oldest of four children, hunted ducks along riverbanks with his shotgun and his dog or sat beside green lakes fishing with his friends. When he was thirteen Teddy Roosevelt was in the White House, and outdoor stories by Jack London and Ernest Thompson Seton were the rage with schoolboys. He was precocious and adventurous, and his love for this life made him resolve to pursue an education in forestry.

At eighteen Leopold enrolled as an undergraduate at Yale and went on to enter Yale's newly established and prestigious Forest School, the first graduate program in the country to train young men in the science of utilitarian forestry, as advocated by Gifford Pinchot. Four years later, with a master of forestry degree, Leopold took up his first assignment with the U.S. Forest Service, stationed in the Apache National Forest in southeastern Arizona Territory.

None of Leopold's camping trips with his father, his hunting expeditions with friends in the East, or his Ivy League education had prepared him for the sprawling mesas, the yellow ponderosa pine forests, and the windblown dust he found on the southern rim of the Colorado Plateau that first July as a professional forester. He rode into the backcountry of Apache National Forest on a newly bought horse wearing all-new cowboy gear—leather chaps, jeans, bandanna, and a broad-rimmed hat. Full of idealism and confidence, the twenty-two-year-old Leopold had hardly ever been on a horse.[17]

Within a month the Forest Service put Leopold in charge of a six-man team assigned to map timber in the tangled, uncharted canyons along the wilderness border between Arizona and New Mexico. The wild country of piñon and juniper, scrub lowlands, and high, amber-colored marshes was home to whitetail deer, gray wolves, grizzly bear, and wild cattle, but few settlers. Leopold and his team, only two of whom had any experience in the region, canvassed the canyons and forested hills on horseback, establishing baselines for surveys, estimating the quantity of standing timber, inspecting private lumber mills, and counting the game animals.

At night the call of the wolves rebounded through the mountains. Around their campfires young Leopold and his raw foresters listened intently to the living darkness that resonated with wilderness sounds.

"A deep chesty bawl echoes from rimrock to rimrock, rolls down the mountain, and fades into the far blackness of the night," Leopold wrote, remembering that wolf country nearly four decades later in *A Sand County Almanac*. "It is an outburst of wild defiant sorrow, and of contempt for all the adversities of the world . . . It tingles in the spine of all who hear wolves by night, or who scan their tracks by day. Even without sight or sound of wolf, it is implicit in a hundred small events: the midnight whinny of a pack horse, the rattle of rolling rocks, the bound of a fleeing deer, the way shadows lie under the spruces. Only the ineducable tyro can fail to sense the presence or absence of wolves, or the fact that mountains have a secret opinion about them."[18]

Within a matter of weeks Leopold got one of his first lessons in the secret opinion of mountains. As fall came on, he camped for lunch one afternoon with a member of his crew in the wooded canyons above a turbulent river.[19] "We saw what we thought was a doe fording the torrent," he wrote later, "her breast awash in white water. When she climbed the bank toward us and shook out her tail, we realized our error: it was a wolf. A half dozen others, evidently grown pups, sprang from the willows and all joined in a welcoming mêlée of wagging tails and playful maulings. What was literally a pile of wolves writhed and tumbled in the center of an open flat at the foot of our rimrock."

Forest Service policy was based on the "scientific" view that the fewer predators there were on the land, the better it was for the "beneficial," that is, income-producing, wildlife and grazing herds. In line with that policy, foresters had been instructed to exterminate all wolves on sight. "In a second," Leopold wrote, "we were pumping lead into the pack, but with more excitement than accuracy." Leopold and his companion fired until their rifles were empty, their shots ricocheting and reechoing in the canyon, then clambered down the slope to survey their work. When he reached the dead and dying wolves, Leopold prodded the crippled she-wolf with his rifle butt. With the last of her strength, the old wolf snarled and lashed out. In her eyes, Leopold saw something totally unfamiliar, an ancient green fire still smoldering and still defiant until the moment she died.

That light did not convert Leopold to a philosophy of preservation, but it planted in his mind the seed of a doubt. "I realized then, and have known ever since," he wrote many years later, "that there was something new to me in those eyes—something known only to her and to the mountain. I was young then, and full of trigger-itch; I thought that because fewer wolves meant more deer, that no wolves would mean hunters' paradise. But after seeing the green fire die, I sensed that neither the wolf nor the mountain agreed with such a view."

The howl of a wolf meant many things, Leopold realized later, depending on the listener's perspective. "To the deer it is a reminder of the way of all flesh, to the pine a forecast of midnight scuffles and of blood upon the snow, to the coyote a promise of gleanings to come, to the cowman a threat of red ink at the bank, to the hunter a challenge of fang against bullet. Yet behind these obvious and immediate hopes and fears there lies a deeper meaning, known only to the mountain itself. Only the mountain has lived long enough to listen objectively to the howl of a wolf."

The mountain's knowledge—distinct from mankind's—came slowly to Leopold. He, his foresters, and the U.S. Forest Service would know soon enough what a wolfless mountain was like: a defoliated, overgrazed wasteland scattered with the bleached skulls of starved deer. Without predators to cull the herds, the deer multiplied beyond the capacity of the range to support them. The scarred and wounded mountain that resulted would teach Leopold a lesson in game management—and then a deeper lesson about the limitations of applied science and the result when humans disregard all viewpoints except the economic one.

Many years later Leopold would conclude of the experience, "I now suspect that just as a deer herd lives in mortal fear of its wolves, so does a mountain live in mortal fear of its deer. And perhaps with better cause." In the howl of the wolf, in the green eye of the predator, knowledge beyond human reason was at work. To comprehend it, Leopold would have to learn "to think like a mountain." That first encounter in wolf country was only the beginning.

As a young man, any doubts Leopold had about the wisdom of Gifford Pinchot's sustained-yield theory of environmental management he kept to himself. Besides, during his first year in Arizona personal matters were more pressing than any desire to buck the system. Leopold was handsome and spirited, with sandy hair, a broad forehead, and blue-green eyes, and soon after his arrival in Arizona he met the twenty-year-old daughter of a prominent New Mexico family. Estella Bergere was one of twelve siblings whose lineage, on their mother's side, extended back to eleventh-century Spanish nobility. Leopold proposed to her four months after they met, and they married a year later.

Among the wedding presents the couple received was the eleven-volume Riverside edition of Thoreau's works.[20] Six months after the wedding, a spring blizzard caught Leopold in the high San Juan mountains. Lost in the Apache Reservation on unfamiliar ground, unprepared for the bitter weather, Leopold fell gravely ill from exposure to the cold. By the time he reached a doctor in Santa Fe, an inflammation in his legs had worsened into acute nephritis, or Bright's disease, and he almost died. During nearly eighteen months of recuperation, he turned many times to his books—those by Muir, Burroughs, Francis Parkman, and Edward Thomas Seton—and particularly to the volumes by Thoreau.

This extended period of reading and rest forced Leopold to get out from among "thickets of detail and box canyons of routine," as he wrote in a letter, and to look around from a higher vantage point.[21] Among the books that gave him that vantage point was William Temple Hornaday's newly published *Our Vanishing Wild Life*. Hornaday's persuasive and uncompromising argument for preserving endangered wild populations struck home with Leopold. When he finally returned to work, he began to devote himself wholeheartedly to issues of wildlife conservation, or, as it was called then, "game management."

At this point Leopold was still an avid hunter and continued to think of wildlife as "game." But the more he saw of the landscape firsthand, the more he saw that the scourge of overgrazing and the management of animal populations solely for their economic and sporting uses had destroyed the high desert's fragile equilibrium. The ruined land forced him to reevaluate standard management practices and to ponder the interrelated issues affecting the total Southwest environment—issues yet to be studied by scientific theories of utility and efficiency. To be sure, land deterioration was influenced by plant and animal ecology, disciplines barely understood. But Leopold began to realize that land degradation was also influenced by cultural and social variables such as attitudes toward wilderness, education, and political policy. Beyond these, even more imponderable influences, such as aesthetics and morality—human attitudes about what is beautiful or ugly in nature—determined what was valuable or expendable.

After twelve years in the Southwest Leopold rose to high positions in the Forest Service in reward for his energy and brilliance in enforcing game laws and for his writings on management issues. In a remarkable essay in 1923 titled "Some Fundamentals of Conservation in the Southwest," he expressed his deepening awareness of environmental relatedness and his early doubts about the management philosophy he had made his career.[22] The essay began conventionally by discussing economic resources in the Southwest—minerals, water, forests, and range land—and their depletion by weather, erosion, and human use. Toward the end, however, Leopold made an abrupt leap from economics to

Ezekiel, quoting the Old Testament prophet's questions: "Seemeth it a small thing unto you to have fed upon good pasture, but ye just tread down with your feet the residue of your pasture? And to have drunk of the clear waters, but ye must foul the residue with your feet?" Through the rest of the essay Leopold focused on moral and ethical issues that transcended economic determinism and were clearly outside his professional training. "It is possible," he continued, "that Ezekiel respected the soil, not only as a craftsman respects his material, but as a moral being respects a living thing." And as Leopold wrote these words, he found himself needing to redefine what is living and what is dead.

Leopold had read such early plant ecologists as Frederick Clements and Henry Cowles, but in researching his paper he found scant scientific data to support the idea of a living, holistic environment.[23] He therefore turned to philosophy for help in his argument, and particularly to the Russian writer P. D. Ouspensky. In his recently translated *Tertium Organum*, Ouspensky suggested that many things that appeared to be dead matter were in a more profound sense alive and conscious: "In organic nature where we see life it is easier to assume the existence of a psyche. But life belongs not alone to separate, individual organisms," Ouspensky asserted; "anything indivisible is a living being. There can be nothing dead or mechanical in Nature . . . life and feeling . . . must exist in everything."[24]

In his essay Leopold struggled to reconcile land-management theories with this philosophy. He noted that the complex environment of the Southwest comprised parts so integrated that none could continue to function without the others. Soil, mountains, rivers, atmosphere, plants, and animals all needed one another to exist, and elimination of the smallest part had unpredictable consequences throughout the interrelated system. "If we could see this whole, as a whole, through a great period of time," he asserted, "we might perceive not only organs with coordinated functions, but possibly also that process of consumption and replacement which in biology we call the metabolism, or growth. In such a case we would have all the visible attributes of a living thing, which we do not now realize to be such because it is too big, and its life processes too slow. And there would also follow that invisible attribute—a soul, or consciousness."

The Earth and all its parts—its soil, mountains, rivers, forests, climate, plants, and animals—should not be regarded as a dead resource, Leopold argued, but "as a living being, vastly less alive than ourselves in degree, but vastly greater than ourselves in time and space—a being that was old when the morning stars sang together, and, when the last of us has been gathered unto his fathers, will still be young." And if the Earth and its parts are "alive" in this holistic sense, Leopold wondered, then what should be our relationship to nature?

In answer, he cited John Muir's assertion that rattlesnakes and other "vermin" have a right to exist even if they have no benefit to man, simply because all living things have an equal right to life. It was an idea that contrasted profoundly with the policy currently pursued by the Forest Service, of exterminating diverse species of plants and animals solely because they were an economic inconvenience to one species, humans.

"If there be, indeed, a special nobility inherent in the human race—a special cosmic value, distinctive from and superior to all other life," Leopold asked in a series of questions at the end of his essay, "by what token shall it be manifest?

"By a society decently respectful of its own and all other life, capable of inhabiting the earth without defiling it? Or by a society like that of John Burroughs' potato bug, which exterminated the potato, and thereby exterminated itself?" He concluded, "As one or the other shall we be judged in 'the derisive silence of eternity.' "

By linking ethics and ecology, and science with mystical philosophy, Leopold was voicing heresies in more than one sense. By training and by career choice, he was what environmental historian Donald Worster has called an "imperial" ecologist, devoted to conserving but also controlling and dominating nature.[25] In his sympathies, however, Leopold was gradually coming to be, at least so far as this essay was concerned, with the tribe of Thoreau and Muir—subjective, intuitive, bio-centered. It is no wonder that he tucked this paper into his files and left it there, unpublished; it remained in typescript until after his death.[26]

As an accomplished field scientist, Leopold knew very well how to write a professional paper, and, having hidden this one away, he began to search for empirical arguments rather than intuitive or philosophical ones to support his changing ideas about wilderness and wildlife. At the same time, he began using a new metaphor in his writing: "land health." It was a term that would become, as he slowly clarified it in his own mind, the cornerstone of his mature work, what he later called a "land ethic." The concept of a living Earth and a moral responsibility to nature, however, would have to evolve slowly, and it would remain unarticulated in his published writing for another ten years.[27]

In the meantime, putting aside these tentative thoughts about a biocentric world, Leopold accepted a new assignment with the Forest Service. A year after he wrote "Some Fundamentals of Conservation in the Southwest" he was transferred to Madison, Wisconsin, to the Forest Service's Products Laboratory. There, uprooted with his family from the Southwest he had grown to love, Leopold began the second half of his career.

The move to Madison brought many changes to Leopold's life and thought. He grew increasingly uncomfortable with the economics of forestry, especially as stressed in the products laboratory where he worked, and four years later he resigned from the Forest Service. To support his growing family, he took on consulting assignments for private interests. He worked for the Sporting Arms and Ammunition Manufacturers' Institute, preparing game surveys across several Midwestern states, and took assignments for state agencies in Iowa and Wisconsin. During the Depression he returned to the Southwest briefly to supervise erosion control for the Civilian Conservation Corps. And in 1933, at age forty-six, he published *Game Management*, a book that became the standard text in the field for several decades. In the same year Leopold was appointed head of game management in the Department of Agricultural Economics at the University of Wisconsin, a job he held for the rest of his life.

Some ten years after moving to Madison, and a year after starting work at the university, Leopold and his brother Carl took one of their frequent fishing trips to nearby Waushara County. They decided to explore the Endeavor Marsh on the upper Fox River near Portage, not far from where John Muir's father, nearly a century earlier, had built a log shanty and farmed 160 acres of rolling hills dotted with oaks. Remembering his boyhood, Muir had exclaimed, "Oh, that glorious Wisconsin wilderness!" Rich in deer, partridges, and jacksnipes, the land's beauty had overwhelmed young Muir. "Nature streaming into us, wooingly teaching her wonderful glowing lessons," Muir wrote. Among the birds Muir saw were bluejays, bluebirds, woodpeckers, hen-hawks, kingbirds, nighthawks, and "the long-legged, long-billed" sandhill cranes.[28]

Aldo and Carl found a greatly changed environment. Most of the Wisconsin marshes had been drained and farmed to exhaustion. Out of neglect and ignorance on the part of the settlers, the drained marshes had been allowed to catch fire, and "great pockmarks were burned into field and meadow," Leopold wrote in describing them; "the scars reaching down to the sands of the old lake, peat-covered these hundred centuries." The once-great forests had been plundered for timber, wheat farming had depleted the sandy soil, and overgrazing had brought erosion and "blowouts," leaving shifting, infertile sand dunes.

As an expert in environmental resources at the University of Wisconsin, Leopold was principally concerned with how to sustain the forests for timber and wild game for hunting. He had little professional reason to be interested in nongame animals and birds. But he had heard reports that a remnant band of sandhill cranes was breeding in the Endeavor Marsh, one of the few marshes that had not been drained or reduced to ashes and weeds.[29] He also knew there were perhaps only twenty breeding pairs of the great birds in the entire state.

Driving to the end of a rutted dirt road, the Leopold brothers met a farmer who had lived near the marsh for sixty years. The farmer was glad to direct them to a spot where they might find a pair of cranes. Hiking quietly through a stand of oaks, scanning the marsh with field glasses, Leopold and Carl were suddenly startled by a loud clamoring. Breaking from the rushes directly before them, the great, trumpeting birds abruptly rose on broad gray wings, beating the air with a slow, noble detachment that stunned Leopold's senses. In the flurry of wings and soaring bodies, a sudden recognition came to him of some essence in those birds—an essence he had never emotionally or intellectually encountered before. With the birds rising suddenly before his eyes, he saw in that moment back to the Wisconsin of a hundred years earlier, then back to the deep evolutionary past that had created those ancient, endangered creatures.

Leopold's biographer, Carl Meine, suggests that seeing the sandhill cranes that day "flipped a mental switch in Leopold's mind. Over the next few years, he sought out cranes in the marshes and in books, and he devoted much thought to their role in nature's scheme. But Leopold's pursuit of the crane went even beyond this. As he learned more about the tall, gray denizen of the wild marshes, Leopold explicitly drew the connection, heretofore only implicit in his appreciation, between a natural object's beauty and its evolutionary history. The value of a creature lay not in its appearance alone, but in its story as a species."[30]

The she-wolf that Leopold had killed in Arizona as a youth and the sandhill cranes he now saw with his full attention would become emblematic and figure prominently in Leopold's great work, *A Sand County Almanac*. He would say of that ancient bird, "Our appreciation of the crane grows with the slow unraveling of earthly history. His tribe, we now know, stems out of the remote Eocene. The other members of the fauna in which he originated are long since entombed within the hills. When we hear his call we hear no mere bird. He is the symbol of our untamable past, of that incredible sweep of millennia which underlies and conditions the daily affairs of birds and men."

Six months later, shortly after Leopold turned forty-eight, he planted roots in that land himself by purchasing some eighty acres of sandy, depleted farmland and marsh as a retreat from the town of Madison for himself and his family. By most estimates the land he bought was worthless, mostly sandhills and pines. The only structure still standing on the old farm was a dilapidated chicken coop, which Leopold, Estella, and their five children soon converted into a weekend cabin that they dubbed "the shack." Looking out from its windows over barren soil and old groves of white pine and scrub aspen, Leopold began to write the essays he would later shape into his most memorable book.

At the University of Wisconsin Leopold trained his students in the applied science of game management more or less as he had learned it at Yale and as a working professional. But the older and more experienced he became, the greater need he felt to augment science with intuitive, philosophical, and aesthetic knowledge. In an address to the Wildlife Society titled "The State of the Profession," six years after his encounter with the sandhill cranes, he publicly lamented the barrier between science and literature.[31]

"The definitions of science written by, let us say, the National Academy, deal almost exclusively with the creation and exercise of power," he told his audience. "But what about the creation and exercise of wonder, of respect for workmanship in nature?"

"Few wildlife managers have any interest or desire to contribute to art and literature," Leopold continued, "yet the ecological dra-

mas which we must discover if we are to manage wildlife are infe-
rior only to the human drama as subject matter for the fine arts. Is
it not a little pathetic that poets and musicians must paw over
shopworn mythologies and folklores as media for art, and ignore
the dramas of ecology and evolution?

"There are straws which indicate this senseless barrier between
science and art may one day blow away, and that wildlife ecology,
if not wildlife management, may help do the blowing . . . In our
profession, and on its fringes, are a growing number of painters
and photographers who are also researchers. These intergrades in
human taxonomy are perhaps more important than those which
so perplex the mammalogists and ornithologists Their skulls are
not yet available to the museums, but even a layman can see that
their brains are distinctive."

Writers who could combine science with art would have the
power to change people's ideas about what is ultimately valuable
in the land, Leopold argued, and "to change ideas about what land
is for is to change ideas about what anything is for."

All his life Leopold had worked with people—settling disputes
on the range, giving speeches to civic and professional groups, establishing organizations, serving on committees and boards. He
contributed to nearly a hundred conservation and professional organizations, including the Wilderness Society, which he helped to
found in 1935. But now he was more certain than ever that an even
larger number of people needed to be reached in a language that a
layman could understand, to change *people* and not just *policies*.

Leopold was fifty-four years old when an editor at Knopf suggested that he write a "warmly, evocatively, and vividly written"
introduction to ecology for the layman. It was just the opportunity
that Leopold had been looking for to reach a wide readership. Over
the next seven years he gathered together what he called his "phil-
osophic essays," written in his forties, and began to compose new
essays for this project.[32] Eventually, in its final scheme, he divided

the essays into three parts, all supporting his fundamental goal—
to change minds about the land in order to change minds about life
itself.

Leopold wrote the first part of the book as an "almanac,"
with monthly sketches describing his family's life at "the shack"
from January to December.[33] Beginning with January's thaw, the
sketches contained his close observation of the recovering farmland, his identification with the muskrats and chickadees on his
property, and his attempts to read the "autobiography" of the land
in its lumber piles and in the growth rings of old oaks. He included
an account of his transformation from a hunter and game manager
to a man searching for the point of view of the hunted. He had
grown to know his plant and animal neighbors by name, as per-
sonalities. He anticipated their seasonal comings and goings, he
knew their histories on the land, and he foresaw their futures.
When any creature disappeared, it was not merely the erasure of a
name in a textbook, but a loss to his farm's community. "We grieve
only for what we know," he wrote.

In "April" Leopold watched the woodcocks drumming and fluttering in the sky dance over their peenting ground. "The woodcock is a living refutation of the theory that the utility of a game
bird is to serve as a target, or to pose gracefully on a slice of toast,"
he wrote. "No one would rather hunt woodcock in October than I,
but since learning of the sky dance I find myself calling one or two
birds enough. I must be sure that, come April, there be no dearth
of dancers in the sunset sky."

In the second part of his book, "Sketches Here and There," Leopold related the story of his personal and professional transformation. He began and ended this part with an elegy for the abused
Wisconsin marshlands. Here he recalled the awakening in himself
triggered when the sandhill cranes broke from the tamaracks before his eyes one late July and hoisted their ungainly forms into the
air, "flailing the morning sun with mighty wings." Empathizing
with a creature in nature begins with experience and perception,

he wrote; not with the "cold-potato mathematics" of abstract science, but with the vision of a creature's beauty. "Our ability to perceive quality in nature begins, as in art, with the pretty," Leopold asserted. "It expands through successive states of the beautiful to values as yet uncaptured by language. The quality of cranes lies, I think, in this higher gamut, as yet beyond the reach of words." Like Thoreau, Leopold realized that aesthetic understanding is deeply commingled in the human heart with a quality that can only be called wildness—a recognition, a wonderment, and a deep certitude in an experience so fundamental that the ancients called it sacred. "The ultimate values in these marshes is wildness," Leopold wrote, "and the crane is wildness incarnate."

Leopold was never a sentimentalist. He disliked "nature lovers" who stuck to the paths, got their nature from books, and wrote "bad verse on birch bark." An outdoorsman and sportsman all his life, Leopold in "Sketches Here and There" confessed the love he had had since childhood for hunting—a love he never gave up. He recalled his first kill as a young boy while duck hunting, feeling "unspeakable delight when my first duck hit the snowy ice with a thud and lay there, belly up, red legs kicking."

In describing the role he had played as a young forest ranger in mistakenly exterminating predators in the Southwest, Leopold recalled how a local rancher had found, half buried on his land, a dagger engraved with the name of one of Coronado's captains. "We spoke harshly of the Spaniards," he recalled, "who, in their zeal for gold and converts, had needlessly extinguished the native Indians. It did not occur to us that we, too, were the captains of an invasion too sure of its own righteousness."

Leopold returned again to the relation between aesthetics and ecology. "The physics of beauty," he wrote, "is one department of natural science still in the Dark Ages. Not even the manipulators of bent space have tried to solve its equations. Everybody knows, for example, that the autumn landscape in the north woods is the land, plus a red maple, plus a ruffled grouse. In terms of conventional physics, the grouse represents only a millionth of either the mass or the energy of an acre. Yet subtract the grouse and the whole thing is dead. An enormous amount of some kind of motive power has been lost.

"It is easy to say that the loss is all in our mind's eye, but is there any sober ecologist who will agree? He knows full well that there has been an ecological death, the significance of which is inexpressible in terms of contemporary science."

As did Thoreau and Muir, Leopold also recognized that aesthetics, like ecology, requires the cognitive ability to see things whole, to see the details without losing sight and sense of a greater unity. As Donald Worster phrases it, "aesthetic apprehension is the ability to look beyond the level of isolated details and perceive their underlying cohesion. The details remain important, but the habit of looking at them too closely for too long can atrophy the aesthetic faculty. One loses the awareness of how things are joined together, how they form patterns with one another, how fitness is achieved. Nature then ceases to please the eye, and in the saddest cases the eye does not even know it should be pleased. When the aesthetic awareness is well developed, on the other hand, one sees easily and surely the deeper harmony within, and the pleasure it affords is intense. Words like 'beauty' and 'integrity' come readily to mind. Indeed, such qualities become the most significant realities that exist and their perception and enjoyment is the highest form of living."[34]

To effect a change in the way people perceive, Leopold had come to believe, would require time. "Ecological science has wrought a change in the mental eye," he wrote. Educating people to perceive and respect nature's beauty, however, would be a job not of "building roads into lovely country, but of building receptivity into the still unlovely human mind."

In the third part of *A Sand County Almanac*, titled "The Upshot," Leopold added a final element to the interweaving of almanac, autobiography, aesthetics, and ecology. So far he had written in the familiar, personal voice of earlier nature writers such as White, Thoreau, Burroughs, and Muir—although he had perhaps more sins to confess than many of his predecessors. In "The Upshot" he asserted that the degradation of nature is not merely economically wasteful and aesthetically tragic, but morally and even religiously indefensible. He was ready now to lay out his notion of a "land ethic."

Leopold's argument was what philosopher J. Baird Callicott calls "the first self-conscious, sustained, and systematic attempt in modern Western literature to develop an ethical theory which would include the whole of terrestrial nature and terrestrial nature *as a whole* within the purview of morals."[35] Nature writers before Leopold had developed a moral environmentalism, embracing nature in a holistic way. Muir, for example, was the first American to use the word "rights" in connection with nature, by asserting that even the rocks and soil have rights.[36] But in the final section of *A Sand County Almanac* Leopold proposed, as few had done before him, the need for a redefinition of American institutions and American morality with regard to nature.

Human history, Leopold wrote, has been the slow evolution of ethical conduct. When Odysseus returned from Troy and hanged all his slave girls on the mere suspicion of their disloyalty, he did so not because he lacked moral propriety, but because it was his right to treat his slaves as property. It was Odysseus' right, as "owner," to treat his wife in the same manner. Since that time, Leopold asserted, civilization has developed a finer sense of right and wrong with respect to individual human life. But as yet civilization has not recognized a moral obligation to nature that supersedes the rights of individual "ownership" of the land.

"What we call wilderness is a civilization other than our own," Thoreau had written. In elaborating on Thoreau and others, Leopold said, "In short, a land ethic changes the role of *Homo sapiens* from conqueror of the land-community to plain member and citizen of it. It implies respect for his fellow-members, and also respect for the community as such." With respect come obligations, and the extension of social conscience "from people to land."

"It is inconceivable to me," Leopold concluded, "that an ethical relation to land can exist without love, respect, and admiration for land, and a high regard for its value. By value, I of course mean something far broader than mere economic value; I mean value in the philosophical sense . . . There is no other way for land to survive the impact of mechanized man, nor for us to reap from it the esthetic harvest it is capable, under science, of contributing to culture."

Leopold took seven years to craft and shape his essays for *A Sand County Almanac*, rendering in them a lifetime of thought and experience. During that time Knopf and other publishers repeatedly rejected his drafts of the manuscript; the writing was not warm enough, they said, too pessimistic, too "philosophical."

Out of frustration, after many revisions, in December 1947 Leopold sent the latest draft of his manuscript to Oxford University Press. Four months later the company's editor notified him by telephone of Oxford's acceptance.[37] Leopold, who was sixty-two years old, had nearly given up ever seeing the book in print.

A week later, still ecstatic over his book's pending publication, up at dawn as usual on his sandhill farm, Leopold went to the marsh and counted the wild geese as they flew over. He witnessed a remarkable number of them on the wing, more than eight hundred. He made notes in his journal, then walked back to the shack and joined his wife and daughter for a light breakfast. They laughed together as he delightedly reported the number of geese to them. At midmorning the April wind rose, and Leopold spotted smoke near his neighbor's house. Because it was only trash burning, he put it out of his mind.

But the trash fire spread to dried leaves in the neighbor's farmyard. Seeing the threat to his neighbor's barn and milk pens, and to his own marsh, Leopold called Estella and his daughter, and the

three of them rushed to help fight the blaze. Other neighbors
joined them as the flames reached a stand of alders and the dry border of the marsh. In the excitement the little group spread out,
each taking a position with buckets and brooms in various parts of
the burning yard. Wetting down the edges of the flames with a
hand-held pump, out of sight of the others, Leopold was seized by
a heart attack. In pain, he lay down on his back, folded his hands
across his chest, and within a matter of minutes died. The flames,
now weakened and no longer a threat, swept silently over his still
body and burned themselves out.

Chapter Eight

SMALL WINGED FORMS

ABOVE THE SEA

Writer and environmentalist Wallace Stegner, summarizing Aldo Leopold's impact on American culture, notes, "it was not for its novelty that people responded to Leopold's call for a land ethic. It was for his assurance, an assurance forecast much earlier in the work of George Perkins Marsh and John Wesley Powell, that science corroborates our concern, not our optimism: that preserving the natural world we love has totally practical and unsentimental justifications."[1]

As a scientist engaged in field research, Leopold concluded that humans are but one part of an interrelated biotic community, and that greater potential to alter the environment gives humankind not more license but more obligations to behave wisely. At the same time, Leopold realized the limitations of applied science and tried to warn against overconfidence in making environmental changes that could alter critical balances among a multitude of biotic systems.

Leopold searched for empirically based general principles that could guide human behavior. But these general principles, he concluded late in his career, must derive from ethics and aesthetics as well as from science; otherwise they would never become integrated into the entire complex of human behavior. To this end, Leopold developed in *A Sand County Almanac* a general rule for any land-use decisions: "It is right," he stated, "when it tends to preserve the integrity, stability, and beauty of the biotic community. It is wrong when it tends otherwise."

Leopold became part of the long tradition of nature writing when, after a lifetime of personal experience, he saw beyond so-called empirical considerations. He clarified for himself his changing perceptions as a scientist by turning to the poets and prophets. His writing summoned up the work of John Burroughs, who was still widely read and respected by many Americans in the 1930s and 1940s. Burroughs had written in his last book, *Accepting the Universe*, that "creation is no more exclusively for [humans] than for the least of living things," and that "life, then, in all its forms is for its own sake. It is an end in itself."[2] Leopold also recalled in his writing John Muir's conviction that every species, whether wolf or rattlesnake, merited respect. "Men," Leopold asserted in *A Sand County Almanac*, "are only fellow voyagers with other creatures in the odyssey of evolution."

Despite the eloquence of his arguments, just after World War II, when Leopold's best work was published, Americans were luke-warm to his call for an ethical link with the natural world. Popular interest in "nature lovers" generally had cooled, especially in those calling for restraint, simplicity, and humility even toward predators. Hadn't the world war been fought against "predators"? Having sacrificed and grieved, having endured hardships and material shortages during the conflict, Americans wanted a return to the progress that had been interrupted by the Depression and the war. They wanted a "better life" made easier by science.

As historian Roderick Nash points out, "what [Leopold] proposed would have necessitated a complete restructuring of basic American priorities and behavior . . . The conquest and exploitation of the environment that had powered America's westward march for three centuries was to be replaced as an ideal by cooperation and coexistence. The land ethic, in short, placed unprecedented restraints on a process that had won the West and lifted the nation to at least temporary greatness as a world power. Leopold's philosophy abruptly curtailed the accustomed freedom with which Americans had hitherto dealt with nature."[3]

To many Americans, the natural world had come to seem quaint and backward compared with the marvelous conveniences that American industry and technology provided in the 1950s. Moreover, American industry needed peacetime markets for its manufacturing capabilities and more consumers to buy more products. This was not the time to simplify, simplify. To the majority of consumers, industry's stockpiles of goods and innovations—many of which had helped to win the war—seemed clearly "beneficial."

But although new industrial products had saved lives during the war, among them were potent synthetic chemicals that were untested for peacetime applications. When DDT was invented in 1939 and used successfully in World War II to kill disease-spreading insects, for instance, the public was told that DDT required no further testing, that it was a "miracle" insecticide—devastating to bugs and completely harmless to humans.

This proved not to be the case. The nature writer who would awaken Americans to the environmental consequences of these lethal chemicals, sold and distributed by some of the most powerful interest groups in the country, turned out to be a shy but determined marine scientist named Rachel Carson.

Indeed, we associate Carson now with her most controversial book, *Silent Spring*, written about the hazards of DDT. And what many people know about her today may still be tainted by the malicious, concerted attacks on Carson in the early 1960s by governmental and industrial proponents of untested chemical insecticides. For advocating a more cautious approach to biocides—many of which contaminated the environment globally and perhaps irreversibly—she was labeled a "hysterical woman," an old maid, and "not a real scientist." One government official quipped, "I thought she was a spinster; what's she so worried about genetics for?" Another government leader dismissed her as part of the "vociferous, misinformed group of nature-balancing, organic-gardening, bird-loving, unreasonable citizenry." The head of Montrose Chemical Corporation of California called her not a scientist but "a fanatic defender of the cult of the balance of nature." Other powerful industrial opponents suggested that she was a Communist, influenced by "sinister parties." University researchers, funded by the chemical industry, called her work "hogwash," "a hoax," and "more poisonous than the pesticides she condemns."[4]

Carson so alarmed her enemies in industry, in government, in universities, and in the American Medical Association that they attacked her relentlessly in an organized assault that swept through the public media. At the peak of this assault, the main spokesman for the pesticide industry, Dr. Robert White-Stevens of the Research and Development Department of American Cyanamid Company, issued a new attack on her every forty minutes of every day. Even after her death, ignoring the irrefutable data in her carefully reasoned and meticulously researched book, *Time* magazine continued in its obituary to defame her. "Despite her scientific training," the anonymous writer asserted, "she rejected facts that weakened her case, while using almost any material, regardless of authenticity, that seemed to support her thesis. Her critics, who included many eminent scientists, objected that the book's exaggerations and emotional tone played on the vague fears of city dwellers, the bulk of the U.S. population, who have limited contact with uncontrolled nature and do not know how unpleasantly hostile it generally is [without the use of DDT and pesticides]."[5]

By effectively arguing against indiscriminate dumping of powerful chemical agents onto America's towns, farmlands, and waterways, *Silent Spring* was as important to stirring up the American conscience as Tom Paine's *Common Sense*, Upton Sinclair's *The*

Jungle, and Harriet Beecher Stowe's *Uncle Tom's Cabin*.[6] The book argued from a scientific perspective what Muir and Leopold had already asserted: just as it is immoral to treat human life as a commodity—as was done in the American slave trade—so does all nonhuman life deserve ethical consideration.[7]

The book's real threat to its opponents was not merely that it revealed the long-lived toxicity of chlorinated hydrocarbons, such as DDT, dieldrin, aldrin, and endrin, and of organic phosphates, such as parathion and malathion. The book challenged the unregulated freedom being given to industry and government agencies—dominated by special interests—to determine what was done to the natural environment. *Silent Spring* challenged the right of industry and government, in the words of historian Donald Worster, to regard nature as "mainly for the purpose of supplying an endless line of [industrial] goods and absorbing the byproducts of waste and pollution." And it challenged the notion that "whatever has not been produced by some industry and placed on the market for sale" has no value.[8]

By awakening many Americans to the idea that this aggressive, environmentally destabilizing, and economically centered attitude must be restrained, *Silent Spring* encouraged the birth of the modern environmental movement. Nevertheless, despite its enormous importance, *Silent Spring* is only a part—and not an entirely representative part—of Carson's achievement as a nature writer.

Rachel Carson was born in Springdale, Pennsylvania, in 1907 in the Allegheny Valley, eighteen miles from Pittsburgh. In that year small towns like Springdale, with a population of less than 2,000, were being choked by pollution from unregulated coal mining, iron and steel production, and other forms of manufacturing. This pollution would eventually ruin the pristine hills and streams of the Allegheny Valley. Out West, meanwhile, the sixty-nine-year-old John Muir began locking horns in his long battle to save another valley, Hetch Hetchy, from being flooded for a municipal reservoir. And in the Northeast the young Aldo Leopold, as yet unschooled by the wolves of the desert Southwest, labored through his last years of forestry studies at Yale.

Carsons' family had little income but owned sixty-five acres of apple orchards and forest. Her parents encouraged Rachel, the youngest by far of three children, to roam in the woods and along the streams, to learn the names of the birds and flowers, and to get acquainted with the family's few horses, cows, and chickens.

Carson's love of nature was fostered especially by her mother, a woman so solicitous of animal life that she would not allow the Carson children to kill insects that got into the house; they had to be caught and released outside.[9] This gentle and bookish mother, who was thirty-seven when Carson was born, also fostered her daughter's love of writing. Frequently absent from school because of poor health, Carson developed an intellectual and emotional intimacy with her mother that would keep the two of them in the same household until her mother's death at nearly ninety years of age.

Like many children, Carson read the popular nature books of the period, including Gene Stratton Porter's *Freckles*. But by age ten she had decided to write her own books. In fourth grade she won the Silver Badge and ten dollars for a story she sent to *St. Nicholas*, a national magazine for children; over the next twelve months, she won several more prizes with her stories and essays.

In high school Carson excelled in English, and after graduation she received a scholarship to attend the nearby Pennsylvania College for Women. There she joined the literary club and wrote for the college paper. She also wrote poetry and submitted her work frequently to such journals as *Poetry*, the *Atlantic Monthly*, and the *Saturday Evening Post*. None of her verse, however, ever got into print.

In her second year at college, during a required biology course taught by an inspired teacher, Carson's childhood love of nature suddenly revived and intensified. Everyone had assumed that she would graduate in English and become a writer; now she wondered whether she might prefer becoming a scientist instead. "I thought I had to be one or the other; it never occurred to me, or apparently to anyone else, that I could combine two careers," she wrote later.[10] Over the objections of her college counselors and even the college president, all of whom thought science an inappropriate field for a woman, Carson by her junior year had committed herself to majoring in zoology.

To send her to college, Carson's father had had to mortgage his land. Even with the help of a scholarship and a frugal lifestyle, Carson's undergraduate education put her and her family into serious debt. With her heart now devoted to science, however, she persisted, graduating *magna cum laude*. Again she borrowed money and spent her first summer after college studying at Woods Hole Marine Biological Laboratory in Massachusetts. With the continued help of her family and with another scholarship, in the fall Carson entered Johns Hopkins University's graduate school in science.

Before going to college Rachel Carson had never seen the ocean, except in her imagination, in picture books, and in poetry. Until she was a young adult, her only physical sensation of the ocean was the sound she heard in seashells. But the books, seashells, and poetry, as she said later, had made her fascinated by everything relating to the sea.[11] Finally in its presence at age twenty-one, she experienced the real, physical wonder of the ocean that had exerted a powerful grip on her intellect. She did not know it yet, but she was to become the ocean's "biographer."

Before completing her master's thesis on marine zoology, Carson was already teaching part-time at the University of Maryland and at the Johns Hopkins Summer School. She enjoyed teaching, but the work was in fact necessary to help her family and to repay her loans. Her financial obligations mounted to the extent that in 1935, three years after graduation, it was imperative that she find full-time employment. On July 6 of that year, her father died suddenly, leaving her the sole support of her mother. Shortly afterward her older sister divorced and moved into the household with Carson, bringing with her two small daughters, Marjorie and Virginia; they too needed Carson's financial support.

The depressed economy made it difficult to obtain work of any kind, and even in more prosperous times her chances of finding a full-time career in science—a domain traditionally reserved for men—would have been slim. Thus, several months later, Carson considered herself doubly lucky to land not only a full-time job but one in her field. Her employer was among the few organizations willing to hire a woman scientist: the federal government. The security of the job turned into even more of a godsend when, within a year, Carson's sister, Marian, died at age forty, leaving Carson and her mother the task of raising Marjorie and Virginia on Carson's salary.

At the U.S. Bureau of Fisheries in Washington, D.C., Carson's duties involved fieldwork as an aquatic biologist, but her primary responsibilities consisted of writing and editing. She wrote a series of radio scripts on marine life, booklets promoting wildlife conservation, the usual array of government informational pamphlets, technical papers, and other publications the bureau assigned her.

A year into the job, her chief, Elmer Higgins, asked Carson to write an introduction to the radio series she had already completed, which the bureau planned to publish as a booklet. As Carson remembered it, "I set to work, but somehow the material rather took charge of the situation and turned into something that was, perhaps, unusual as a broadcast for the Commissioner of Fisheries. My chief read it and handed it back with a twinkle in his eye. 'I don't think it will do,' he said. 'Better try again.' Then he added, 'But send this one to the *Atlantic*.'"[12]

Though soft-spoken and diminutive in person, Carson was bold when it came to sending off her writing. To her amazement the *Atlantic*—one of the nation's most important literary magazines—promptly accepted her submission. The short essay, titled "Undersea," appeared in September 1937 and generated enthusiastic responses. Among them came a letter from Quincy Howe, editor-in-chief of Simon and Schuster, asking if Carson had ever considered writing a book about the ocean. Shortly afterward the shy writer and the seasoned publisher met for dinner at the Connecticut home of Hendrik Willem van Loon, then famous as the author of *The Story of Mankind*. The next day she met with Howe again in the publisher's offices, and that evening Carson began work on *Under the Sea-Wind*, the first of three books she would publish on the marine environment.

Engaged by her job during the day, Carson had time to work on her first book only at night, often writing in her second-floor bedroom while her mother and two young nieces were asleep. She had determined from the beginning that her book should not be just an introduction to oceanography. She wanted it to be engaging and accessible to nonscientists, to make the ocean "as vivid a reality for those who may read the book as it has become for me during the past decade," she said.

With such a vast subject, the book would need to be dramatic, with characters the reader could understand and be concerned about. "The entire book must be written in narrative form," she told Henrik van Loon. "The fish and the other creatures must be the central characters and their world must be portrayed as it looks and feels to them . . . nor must any human come into it except from the fishes' viewpoint as a predator and destroyer."[13]

In its final form, three years later, *Under the Sea-Wind* presented an almost mythic world, alive in the great, eternal sweep of evolutionary time and place, inhabited by wonderfully diverse creatures and powerful forces, interlocked and eternal. She wrote in her foreword to the first edition that the sea had existed "before ever man stood on the shore of the ocean and looked out upon it with wonder; [these forces] continue year in, year out, through the centuries and the ages, while man's kingdoms rise and fall."

In the opening paragraphs of her *Atlantic* article, "Undersea," she had written, "Who has known the ocean? Neither you nor I, with our earth-bound senses, know the foam and surge of the tide that beats over the crab hiding under the seaweed of his tidepool home; or the lilt of the long, slow swells of midocean, where shoals of wandering fish prey and are preyed upon, and the dolphin breaks the waves to breathe the upper atmosphere . . . To sense this world of waters known to the creatures of the sea we must shed our human perceptions . . . and enter vicariously into a universe of all-pervading water."

Carson guided her readers through this universe by tracing the fates of representative creatures to which she gave names. She wanted her readers to empathize with them and follow them as they instinctively negotiated their environment—shorebirds in the air, large fish in the open ocean, and eels in the rivers that lead into the sea.

Carson created first a black skimmer she called Rynchops (the scientific name for black skimmers is *Rynchops niger*). "Rynchops and his kin had arrived on the outer barrier strip of sand between sound and sea," she wrote in the opening chapter. "They had journeyed northward from the coast of Yucatan where they had wintered. Under the warm June sun they would lay their eggs and hatch their buff-colored chicks on the sandy islands of the sound and on the outer beaches. But at first they were weary after the long flight and they rested by day on the sand bars when the tide was out or roamed over the sound and its bordering marshes by night."

Having evoked Rynchops' windy and wave-swept universe, Carson introduced Silverbar and Blackfoot, a pair of sanderlings; Oopik, a snowy owl; Tuyllugak, a raven; Pandion, a fishhawk; and White Tip, a bald eagle. Expanding on the technique of naming and creating sympathy for wild creatures, a technique she had learned from Henry Williamson's best-selling nature book *Tarka, the Otter*, Carson sparked to life the ocean world's nonhuman forces. She wrote poetically and cinematically, creating a "human" and understandable drama; yet she also remained absolutely faithful to the known scientific facts.

Carson wanted to lift her readers out of a human-centered perspective and place them, albeit vicariously, into another—to open readers' minds to an awareness of the otherness of animals, just as Leopold had become awakened to the lives of wolves and mountains. She knew that this all-but-impossible exercise of the imagination called for familiar human analogies to make it work, and she knew she had to avoid sentimentality and distortion. "We must not depart too far from analogy with human conduct if a fish, shrimp, comb jelly, or bird is to seem real to us—as real a living creature as he actually is," she wrote in the book's foreword. "For these reasons I have deliberately used certain expressions which would be objected to in formal scientific writing. I have spoken of a fish 'fearing' his enemies, for example, not because I suppose a fish experiences fear in the same way that we do, but because I think he *behaves as though he were frightened*. With the fish the response is primarily physical; with us, primarily psychological. Yet if the behavior of the fish is to be understandable to us, we must describe it in the words that most properly belong to human psychological states."

While the use of animal characters and poetic language risked sentimentality at every turn, Carson knew her facts and refused to distort them merely to enthrall her readers. Several years after completing the book, speaking of facts and their use, she wrote, "If facts are the seeds that later produce knowledge and wisdom, then the emotions and the impressions are the fertile soil in which the seeds grow."[14]

Unfortunately, the timing of the publication of *Under the Sea-Wind* could hardly have been worse: it arrived in bookstores in November 1941. One month later, the United States entered the war in the Pacific, Americans turned their attention to the war effort, and in six years the book sold fewer than 1,600 copies.[15] Though disappointed, Carson was at least encouraged that the Scientific

Book Club had adopted *Under the Sea-Wind* as a selection for its members. More important, she received supportive mail from respected scientists. The best of these letters came from William Beebe, the prominent oceanographer and undersea explorer. Beebe selected parts of Carson's book for inclusion in his collection *The Book of Naturalists: An Anthology of the Best Natural History*, published several years later. Beebe's collection, which began with Aristotle and Pliny and included Gilbert White, Thoreau, Darwin, and many prominent scientists, culminated, to her great delight, with Carson.

But even with Beebe's strong endorsement and favorable reviews, Carson's earnings from *Under the Sea-Wind* did not amount to much. The book was soon forgotten, and with reluctance Carson returned to writing and editing for the Bureau of Fisheries, now called the Fish and Wildlife Service.

During the war Carson advanced rapidly in her job. By war's end she was editor-in-chief of the Information Division and had even less time for her own writing. She enjoyed the part of her work that kept her close to marine biology and up-to-date on current research, but she was also restless and anxious to try her hand at another book. She tried in vain to find a job outside the federal government, one in which she might have more time to begin such a book. Frustrated, she resumed writing during the only time she had to herself—late at night when the rest of her household was asleep.

The new book she had in mind would also be about the sea, but she wanted it to be larger and more ambitious than the first, incorporating the many advances in marine science that had occurred as an outgrowth of the war and were now being declassified. "The book I am writing is something I have had in mind for a good while," she informed Beebe. "I have had to wait to undertake it until at least a part of the wartime oceanographic studies could be published, for I wanted it to reflect some of the new concepts of the ocean which that research had developed . . . I am much impressed by man's dependence upon the ocean, directly, and in

thousands of ways unsuspected by most people. These relationships, and my belief that we will become even more dependent
upon the ocean as we destroy the land, are really the theme of the
book and have suggested its tentative title, 'Return to the Sea.' "[16]

Remembering her disappointment with the sales of her first
book, this time Carson decided she needed a professional agent
and soon found Marie Rodell, who would become a lifelong friend.
Through Rodell's efforts, Oxford University Press offered Carson
a contract in May 1949 on the basis of sample chapters. A year
later—nine years after publication of *Under the Sea-Wind*—Carson completed a manuscript titled *The Sea Around Us*.

The publishing history of *The Sea Around Us* contrasts dramatically with that of Carson's first book. The American reading public's concerns had altered since 1941. The war had made Americans more aware of the role of science and technology in their lives
and given them an international perspective. They were ready
to think globally and to see how events worldwide could affect
people locally. In particular, the development of the atomic bomb
had made it plain that technology had reached new levels of potential destructiveness. After Hiroshima and Nagasaki, the previously separate domains of technology and morality could not have
been more clearly linked.[17]

As Carson's book neared publication, she began to release chapters to magazines. One of these chapters, "The Birth of an Island,"
was taken by the *Yale Review* in 1950 and immediately won the
George Westinghouse Science Writing Award from the American
Association for the Advancement of Science—a good portent for
the book as a whole. Even more surprising and gratifying to Carson, the editor of the *New Yorker*, William Shawn, enthusiastically
accepted nearly half of the book to run as a three-part "Profile"
the following summer. Ordinarily, *New Yorker* profiles were life
stories of people; Carson's was to be the life story of the sea.

According to Paul Brooks, who was Carson's editor later at

Houghton Mifflin and also her biographer, the *New Yorker* profile of *The Sea Around Us* generated a greater response than any other piece the magazine had ever printed.[18] When the book appeared one month later, *The Sea Around Us* soared to the top of the *New York Times* best-seller list. By Christmas the *Times* voted it "the outstanding book of the year," and it remained on the best-seller list for more than eighty weeks, selling well over 250,000 copies during that time alone.

The book's phenomenal reception overwhelmed the author and publisher.[19] The following spring Carson received first the National Book Award, then the John Burroughs Medal for the year's most outstanding new book in the field of natural history. She received honorary doctorates, was made a fellow of the Royal Society of Literature in England, and was elected a member of the National Institute of Arts and Letters. RKO Studios bought the movie rights to *The Sea Around Us*; despite Carson's unhappiness with the script, the subsequent film won an Oscar for the best full-length documentary of 1953.

Meanwhile Carson bought back her rights to *Under the Sea-Wind* from Simon and Schuster. Oxford University Press quickly reissued it, and that long-forgotten and overlooked volume immediately joined *The Sea Around Us* on the *New York Times* best-seller list. Reviewers praised the book as "comparable in every way to *The Sea Around Us* . . . a book from a mind able to fuse poetry and science into that rare commodity known as literature." The *New York Times* stated, "Its pages reveal the identical gifts that today have captivated readers: a scrupulous scholarship, a firsthand, warm, individual knowledge of the ocean, and a poetic sensibility."[20] Few reviewers remarked that when *Under the Sea-Wind* had been published in 1941, almost none of them had noticed it.

Carson rapidly became not only a literary celebrity but also one of the country's most prominent and sought-after interpreters of science and the natural world to a general audience. Her modesty at finding herself in that position, along with her faith in the kind of writing she had always been doing, showed in her acceptance speech for the National Book Award.[21]

"Many people have commented with surprise on the fact that a work of science should have a large popular sale," she told her audience. "But this notion, that 'science' is something that belongs in a separate compartment of its own, apart from everyday life, is one that I should like to challenge. We live in a scientific age; yet we assume that knowledge of science is the prerogative of only a small number of human beings, isolated and priest-like in their laboratories. This is not true. The materials of science are the material of life itself. Science is part of the reality of living; it is the what, the how, and the why of everything in our experience. It is impossible to understand man without understanding his environment and the forces that have molded him physically and mentally.

"The aim of science is to discover and illuminate truth. And that, I take it, is the aim of literature, whether biography or history or fiction; it seems to me, then, that there can be no separate literature of science . . . If there is poetry in my book about the sea, it is not because I deliberately put it there, but because no one could write truthfully about the sea and leave out the poetry."

Carson went on in her speech to emphasize the dangers of the human-centered perspective on nature, which she saw as all too prevalent. Too many people viewed the world as if through the wrong end of a telescope, she said. "We have looked first at man and his vanities and greed, and at his problems of a day or a year; and then only, and from this biased point of view, we have looked outward at the earth and at the universe of which our earth is so minute a part. Yet these are the great realities, and against them we see our human problems in a new perspective. Perhaps if we reversed the telescope and looked at man down these long vistas, we should find less time and inclination to plan for our own destruction."

In an address to Theta Sigma Phi the following year, Carson

noted another consequence of distorted perspectives. With her quiet, dry humor she observed how difficult some people found it to believe that the author of *The Sea Around Us* was both a woman and a scientist. Despite her unambiguously female given name, one male reader had written to her in simple obstinacy, "I assume from the author's knowledge that he must be a man." Another, while addressing her as "*Miss* Rachel Carson," she reported, "nevertheless began his letter 'Dear Sir': He explained his saluta- tion by saying that he had always been convinced that the males possess the supreme intellectual powers of the world, and he could not bring himself to reverse his conviction."[22] These preju- dices, though they did not prevent Carson from receiving world- wide acclaim and recognition, dogged her for the rest of her life.

Like *Under the Sea-Wind*, Carson's new book combined a sense of mythic drama and wonder with accurate factual information. In the first part of *Under the Sea-Wind*, called "Mother Sea," Carson took the reader back to the genesis of time and to the formation of the oceans. "Beginnings are apt to be shadowy," she wrote, "and so it is with the beginnings of that great mother of life, the sea."

But unlike *Under the Sea-Wind*, *The Sea Around Us* used no per- sonified animal characters. Carson had learned to create drama in scientific prose without resorting to devices apt to be sentimental. The book would create its drama not through the lives of individ- ual creatures, but through the excitement of exploration being carried out by field scientists. Occasionally using the first-person voice, Carson became the reader's faithful interpreter between mystery and fact, fable and discovery. She helped the reader dis- tinguish among historical beliefs, theories supported by evidence, and speculations about present-day areas of research. From the general and theoretical she moved gracefully to the specific ex- ample; and from folklore accounts she moved to the latest scien- tific data gathered by newly invented technology.

Time and again Carson demonstrated the close connection between the human world and nonhuman life in the sea. Early in the first chapter she wrote, "Fish, amphibian, and reptile, warm-blooded bird and mammal—each of us carries in our veins a salty stream in which the elements sodium, potassium, and calcium are combined in almost the same proportions as in sea water. This is our inheritance from the day, untold millions of years ago, when a remote ancestor, having progressed from the one-celled to the many-celled stage, first developed a circulatory system in which the fluid was merely the water of the sea . . . And as life itself began in the sea, so each of us begins his individual life in a miniature ocean within his mother's womb, and in the stages of his embryonic development repeats the steps by which his race evolved, from gill-breathing inhabitants of a water world to creatures able to live on land."

In the second part of *The Sea Around Us*, "The Restless Seas," Carson focussed on the physical forces that act upon the oceans: winds, waves, and tides. As in her first book, she elevated her prose at times to the level of myth while imparting the known facts of currents, tides, and wave formation, emphasizing the ecological balance between the largest cycles of nature and the processes within living cells. Her closing example of this balance was the emblematic convoluta, a small worm that lives in sandy beaches and is host to a green algae inside its body. Each time the tide recedes, the worm emerges from the sand so its algal cells can carry on photosynthesis; when the tide returns, the worm sinks back into the sand to avoid being washed out to sea.

Placed in an aquarium with no tides, the convoluta continues to rise into the sun twice a day. "Without a brain, or what we would call a memory, or even any very clear perception," Carson observed, "Convoluta continues to live out its life in this alien place, remembering, in every fiber of its small green body, the tidal rhythm of the distant sea."

In the final part of *The Sea Around Us*, "Man and the Sea about Him," Carson presented more specifically the relationship between the sea and human concerns. Taking the reader across place and time, she described climatic changes, tides, and their effects on human history, the natural resources in the sea, the economic motivations for their harvesting, and the mystery of their origins. The ocean surface has been explored and mapped, she pointed out, and yet the majority of what is below the sea's surface, and in the sea's chemistry, is still unknown. "In its mysterious past," she wrote, "[the sea] encompasses all the dim origins of life and receives in the end, after, it may be, many transmutations, the dead husks of that same life. For all at last return to the sea—to Oceanus, the ocean river, like the ever-flowing stream of time, the beginning and the end."

The Sea Around Us gave Carson financial freedom for the first time in her life. She resigned her government job to devote herself to writing. Two years after the book's publication, she used her earnings to buy an acre and a half of land in West Southport, Maine, overlooking Sheepscot Bay, and there built a summer cottage. In the rocky beauty of that landscape she began work almost at once on a new book, this time about the ocean shore, a marine subject she had not paid much attention to in her previous writing.

The new project invigorated Carson. She could support her household, she had her privacy, and she could spend her days quietly exploring the part of the universe that had always fascinated her. "Writing a book about the shore," she said, "as I am doing now, has given me an excuse to spend a great deal of time in places I love very much . . . I can't think of any more exciting place to be than down in the low-tide world, when the ebb tide falls very early in the morning, and the world is full of salt smell, and the sound of water, and the softness of fog."[23]

Carson and her small family took great delight in the cottage. Her niece Marjorie was now grown and had a son of her own, named Roger. With the two of them and her aging mother, Carson trekked through the tide pools and along the rocky margins of

Sheepscot and Boothbay Harbor. To her friend and agent Marie Rodell Carson wrote about the joy she felt during that first summer in Maine. Her letters reveal her intense love of the seashore, her sense of humor, her devotion to her extended family, and, again and again, her reverence for the life she found in the sea.

"Yesterday morning Marjie and I went out about seven for the most extraordinary low we've had, and brought back a 10-inch starfish to photograph Roger holding it," she wrote. "By the time the fog lifted enough for photography, the tide was too high to return the starfish to his happy home. When we got back from putting M. and R. on the train, the tide was low, but also it was about dark. I took the flashlight and went slithering down to the low tide line and it was quite spooky. The big crabs that usually stay down in crevices and under ledges in the daytime were out scampering around, and a drained anemone cave, by flashlight, with all the anemones hanging down, was quite Charles Addamish."[24]

Four years after *The Sea Around Us*, Carson published *The Edge of the Sea*.[25] Conceived at first as only a field guide, to be called "Guide to Seashore Life on the Atlantic Coast," it had quickly grown into something richer and more complex. "To understand the shore, it is not enough to catalog its life," she wrote in the preface. "Understanding comes only when, standing on a beach, we can sense the long rhythms of earth and sea that sculptured its land forms and produced the rock and sand of which it is composed; when we can sense with the eye and ear of the mind the surge of life beating always at its shore—blindly, inexorably pressing for a foothold."

More explicitly than ever, Carson wanted to stress the ecology of the sea and the sea's connection with all other life forms. "To understand the life of the shore," she continued in her preface, "it is not enough to pick up an empty shell and say, 'This is a murex,' or 'That is an angel wing.' True understanding demands intuitive comprehension of the whole life of the creature that once inhabited this empty shell: how it survived amid surf and storms, what were its enemies, how it found and reproduced its kind, what were its relations to the particular sea world in which it lived." All of this knowledge was necessary to understand even the smallest living things. "I have tried," she went on, "to interpret the shore in terms of that essential unity that binds life to the earth."

Once again Carson's writing task involved telling a story that would enthrall her readers, and once again she summoned her artistic sense of drama and her scientific sense of interrelatedness. In a speech describing the book's plan she said, "I am telling something of the story of how that marvelous, tough, vital, and adaptable something we know as LIFE has come to occupy one part of the sea world and how it has adjusted itself and survived despite the immense, blind forces acting upon it from every side."[26]

Like *The Sea Around Us*, this book too was a best-seller. Carson was now forty-eight years old and reaching the peak of her abilities. Publishers, the public, and even television and movie producers sought her out. But Carson remained shy and retiring, reluctant even to appear at the ceremonies and dinners given in her honor. She preferred her cottage in Maine, walking along the shore, and corresponding with friends. She would occasionally grant interviews, but they were often brief. In one interview, shortly before publication of *The Edge of the Sea*, she revealed her self-effacing humor. Rather than being the great Ocean Mother some of her readers imagined her to be, she admitted to the reporter, "I don't swim very well . . . I am only mildly enthusiastic about seafoods, and do not keep tropical fish as pets."[27]

The next two years were the happiest of Carson's life. In her personal letters, more than in her books, where she kept a careful distance and a pose of objectivity, Carson did not censor her uninhibited love of the ocean's wildness.

In a remarkable letter to friends Carson wrote, "We are now having the spring tides of the new moon, you know, and they have traced their advance well over my beach the past several nights.

Roger's raft has to be secured by a line to the old stump, so Marjie and I have an added excuse to go down at high tide. There had been lots of swell and surf and noise all day, so it was most exciting down there toward midnight—all my rocks crowned with foam and long white crests running from my beach to Nahards. To get the full wildness, we turned off our flashlights—and then the real excitement began. Of course you can guess—the surf was full of diamonds and emeralds, and was throwing them on the wet sand by the dozen. It was the night we were there all over, but with everything intensified: a wilder accompaniment of noise and movement, and a great deal more phosphorescence. The individual sparks were so large—we'd see them glowing in the sand, or sometimes caught in the in-and-out play of water, just riding back and forth. And several times I was able to scoop one up in my hand in shells and gravel, and think surely it was big enough to see—but no such luck.

"Now here is where my story becomes different. Once, glancing up, I said to Marjie jokingly, 'Look—one of them has taken to the air!' A firefly was going by, his lamp blinking. We thought nothing special of it, but in a few minutes one of us said, 'There's that firefly again.' The next time he really got a reaction from us, for he was flying so low over the water that his light cast a long surface reflection, like a little headlight. Then the truth dawned on me. He 'thought' the flashes in the water were other fireflies, signaling to him in the age-old manner of fireflies! Sure enough, he was soon in trouble and we saw his light flashing urgently as he was rolled around in the wet sand—no question this time which was insect and which the unidentified little sea will-o'-wisps!

"You can guess the rest: I waded in and rescued him (the will-o'-wisps had already had me in icy water to my knees so a new wetting didn't matter) and put him in Roger's bucket to dry his wings. When we came up we brought him as far as the porch—out of reach of temptation, we hoped."[28]

Carson began planning new projects for her writing. At the

same time she dreamed of somehow preserving in a public trust at least a part of the Maine coastline she had fallen in love with. But in February 1957 personal tragedy again struck her family, and tragedy would dog her for the remaining years of her life. In that month Marjorie, whom she had raised from early childhood, died suddenly from pneumonia. For years Marjorie had been frail and had suffered from arthritis to the point of near disability. Because of these infirmities, Carson and her elderly mother, who was also severely arthritic, had helped raise Marjorie's son, Roger. Now, with Marjorie dead, Carson adopted five-year-old Roger. She was two months from turning fifty, and her frail mother was now eighty-eight.

To write her last and most influential book, *Silent Spring*, required sacrifices beyond what Carson could have ever foreseen. Many of her friends doubted the wisdom of embarking on a project about, of all things, pesticides, a dark, unappealing subject that seemed utterly removed from the joy and light of her previous work. In addition, she soon realized that the book would take her several years to complete and most of those years, of necessity, would be spent in libraries and laboratories rather than at the seashore. Moreover, when it was finished the book was certain to draw severe criticism from powerful interest groups.

The subject of unregulated pesticide use had long been on Carson's mind, however. Indeed, she had proposed writing on the dangers of DDT and other chemical agents as early as 1945. In 1958 she declared, "There would be no peace for me if I kept silent."[29]

In that year Olga Huskins, a resident of Duxbury, Massachusetts, wrote to Carson asking for help in contacting officials in Washington to whom she could complain about the indiscriminate aerial spraying of DDT mixed with fuel oil over her residential neighborhood. A mosquito control plane hired by the state had begun crisscrossing Huskins' town near the marshes, leaving in its wake the corpses of songbirds, honeybees, and harmless insects. The mosquitoes, which were the target of the spraying, only grew more voracious and hardy despite all this collateral death. Huskins had tried scrubbing the poison from the birdbaths, but, as she wrote in her letter of protest, "YOU CAN NEVER KILL DDT."

Literally billions of pounds of dangerous synthetic pesticides had been dumped over the countryside across America since the end of the war. Chilling stories about the poisoning of streams and rivers—resulting in the deaths of millions of fish and wild creatures—had been suppressed by the news media, as Carson well knew.[30] But at last the public was taking notice, and perhaps this was her chance to speak out.

At first Carson thought she could write a short book that would, again, be condensed for the *New Yorker*. But she quickly recognized that this highly technical subject would require enormous research and exacting citation of fact to withstand the well-financed opposition the book would incite. There would be other obstacles too. In December 1958, shortly after she began to write in earnest, her mother died. As she grieved for her mother that winter, Carson herself fell ill, as did little Roger. Nevertheless, she plunged ahead with her research.

When spring came, even more obstacles were thrown in her way: Carson underwent a biopsy on her breast. The tumor reportedly was benign, but at year's end her doctors reluctantly revealed the truth of their findings. For months they had refused to tell Carson that the tumor in her breast was cancerous and had begun to metastasize, "even though I asked directly," she told her friends. Just before Christmas, she flew to Cleveland for consultation and to begin radiation therapy. "I hope to work hard and productively," she told Paul Brooks, her editor. "Perhaps even more than ever, I am eager to get the book done."[31] But Carson knew that she was dying of cancer.

In 1960, discouraged by the radiation treatment, she underwent a radical mastectomy. Early the next year she became bedridden with a staphylococcus infection in her knees and ankles. In addition to her cancer treatments, she suffered continually from arthritis. She had also developed an ulcer, then iritis, which made it difficult and sometimes impossible to see. "It would be easy to believe in some malevolent influence at work, determined by some means to keep the book from being finished," she wrote to her friends. Then jokingly she added that she felt like the Red Queen, who had to run as fast as she could to stay where she was.

Somehow Carson remained cheerful throughout her physical and emotional trials, and she continued working. After another year—the fourth since she had begun—the manuscript could at last be shown to her publisher. In late January 1962 she received a long-awaited letter from William Shawn at the *New Yorker*. Shawn enthusiastically agreed to profile the new book. "It was odd," she wrote to a friend. "I really had not been waiting breathlessly for Mr. Shawn's reaction, yet once I had it I knew how very much it meant to me. You know I have the highest regard for his judgment, and suddenly I knew from his reaction that my message would get across. After Roger was asleep, I took Jeffie [her cat] into the study and played the Beethoven violin concerto—one of my favorites, you know. And suddenly the tension of four years was broken and I let the tears come. I think I let you see last summer what my deeper feelings are about this when I said I could never again listen happily to a thrush song if I had not done all I could. And last night the thoughts of all the birds and other creatures and all the loveliness that is in nature came to me with such a surge of deep happiness, that now I had done what I could—I had been able to complete it—now it had its own life . . ."[32]

In addition to the massive public vilification of Carson when *Silent Spring* appeared, including scurrilous attacks on her character and on her competence as a scientist, she also received a share of honors and awards. After all the hard labor and personal tragedy that accompanied the book's gestation, the public tributes meant a great deal to her. Among the most important awards was the Albert Schweitzer Medal of the Animal Welfare Institute. Carson had dedicated *Silent Spring* to Schweitzer and had long admired his life and writings. In her speech accepting the award—one of the few public ceremonies she was able, because of her health, to attend—she recounted the moment of Schweitzer's sudden awakening to the concept of what he termed "reverence for life." From his small medical outpost in Africa the doctor had been traveling by slow barge laboriously upstream to visit a patient. On the third day, at sunset, he wrote in his autobiography, "we were making our way through a herd of hippopotamuses," when "there flashed upon my mind, unforeseen and unsought, the phrase, 'Reverence for Life.' The iron door had yielded: the path in the thicket had become visible. Now I had found my way to the idea in which world- and life-affirmation and ethics are contained side by side! Now I knew that the world-view of ethical world- and life-affirmation, together with its ideals of civilization, is founded in thought."[33]

Carson went on to recount her own moments of insight into the living connectedness among all parts of the natural environment.[34] "I thought of the sight of a small crab alone on a dark beach at night, a small and fragile being waiting at the edge of the roaring surf, yet so perfectly at home in its world. To me it seemed a symbol of life, and of the way life has adjusted to the forces of its physical environment. Or I think of a morning when I stood in a North Carolina marsh at sunrise, watching flock after flock of Canada geese rise from resting places at the edge of a lake and pass low overhead. In that orange light, their plumage was like brown velvet. . . .

"Dr. Schweitzer has told us that we are not being truly civilized if we concern ourselves only with the relation of man to man," she added in summing up. "What is important is the relation of man to all life. This has never been so tragically overlooked as in our present age, when through our technology we are waging war against the natural world. It is a valid question whether any civilization can do this and retain the right to be called civilized. By acquiescing in needless destruction and suffering, our stature as human beings is diminished."

Slowly, a year after publication of *Silent Spring*, Carson saw the public battle begin to shift in her favor. Congressional hearings on pesticides followed a favorable report from the President's Science Advisory Committee—all sparked by a comment in support of Carson by President Kennedy at a news conference. Because of Kennedy's remarks, the Department of Agriculture and the Food and Drug Administration had to reverse their public positions against *Silent Spring*. Prominent scientists who were not on the payroll of the chemical industry spoke out in Carson's behalf. And throughout the world *Silent Spring* was appearing in translations, spreading to nearly every nation Carson's warning against chemically poisoning the environment.

As the book succeeded, Carson's health continued to deteriorate. "I keep thinking," she wrote to a friend, "if only I could have reached this point ten years ago! Now, when there is an opportunity to do so much, my body falters and I know there is little time left."[35]

In the summer and fall of 1963, a year after publication of *Silent Spring*, Carson returned to her cottage in Maine and recorded in a letter her last days spent contemplating the rocky shoreline. She watched the restless Atlantic surge and break, and the seabirds wheel overhead in the fresh autumn brightness.[36]

"This is a postscript to our morning at Newagen," she wrote to her neighbor Dorothy Freeman at the end of that final visit to Maine. "Something I think I can write better than say. For me it was one of the loveliest of the summer's hours, and all the details will remain in my memory: the blue September sky, the sounds of wind in the spruces and surf on the rocks, the gulls busy with their foraging, alighting with deliberate grace, the distant views of Griffiths Head and Todd Point, today so clearly etched, though once seen in swirling fog. But most of all I shall remember the Monarchs, that unhurried drift of one small winged form after another, each drawn by some invisible force. We talked a little about their life history. Did they return? We thought not; for most, at least, this was the closing journey of their lives.

"But it occurred to me this afternoon, remembering, that it had been a happy spectacle, that we had felt no sadness when we spoke of the fact that there would be no return. And rightly—for when any living thing has come to the end of its cycle we accept that end as natural. For the Monarch butterfly, that cycle is measured in a known span of months. For ourselves, the measure is something else, the span of which we cannot know. But the thought is the same: when that intangible cycle has run its course it is a natural and not unhappy thing that a life comes to its end.

"That is what those brightly fluttering bits of life taught me this morning. I found a deep happiness in it—so, I hope, may you. Thank you for this morning."

Carson's words are deeply reminiscent of Thoreau's final contemplations on the brightly colored leaves that glided and fluttered to the ground around him in a September just one hundred years earlier. "It is pleasant to walk over the beds of these fresh, crisp, and rustling leaves," Thoreau wrote in "Autumnal Tints," his posthumously published meditation on death. "How beautifully they go to their graves! how gently lay themselves down and turn to mold!—painted of a thousand hues, and fit to make the beds of us living."

The following spring Carson died of cancer at age fifty-six. At the end, she understood that all her books had been unified around a single theme. In a speech shortly before her death she said, "In each of my books I have tried to say that all the life of the planet is interrelated, that each species has its own ties to others, and that all are related to the earth. This is the theme of *The Sea Around Us* and the other sea books, and it is also the message of *Silent Spring*." And then she added, "We have already gone very far in our abuse of this planet."[37]

Carson had begun her writing career by speaking about the sea scientifically, but with a tone of wonder. More and more her books challenged her readers' ability to understand and empathize with the nonhuman world—through emotions and through intellect, with common sense, scientific reasoning, and a moral vision. She called herself a "reporter and interpreter of the natural world," but she also embodied a fearless rage at what she termed the "tranquilizing doses" of misinformation and "soothing reassurances" coming from government and industry, all designed to lull the public to sleep. *Silent Spring*, she said, by its meticulous amassing of fact and its powerful use of language, was her wake-up call from that sleep.

Chapter Nine

THE MOON-EYED HORSE

Sometimes, after writing long into the night, Rachel Carson would read a few pages from Thoreau in order to relax her mind before going to sleep. She may have turned often to the passage in *Walden* about hope and awareness: "We must learn to re-awaken and keep ourselves awake not by mechanical aids, but by an infinite expectation of the dawn, which does not forsake us in our soundest sleep."

Carson's final task as a writer was to craft a public alarm to America both about the perils of environmental poisoning and about the responsibilities that each of us has to act. She would have preferred spending her quiet summers in retreat with family and friends, exploring the tide pools along her favorite shoreline in Maine. Instead, she was impelled to become a warrior, to join the tradition of activist nature writers whose zeal projected them into the public eye, and whose language grew more emphatic as they saw the natural environment increasingly threatened. The battle took her away from the quiet contemplation of the small, bright diatoms and wisps of living sea lace that sparked her boundless curiosity and that she loved to observe; and her early death prevented her from pursuing to the end the elusive meanings of those fragile life forms.

Four years after Carson died, a new and equally fervent wake-up call was sounded in another part of the country. Like Carson's, it was driven by love for the natural world, but it also bristled with imperatives. Unlike Carson's writing, this new alarm made its point with outrageous humor and fantasy; and the language in which it was couched guarded its author's privacy by appearing, paradoxically, to be baldly autobiographical.

In temperament Edward Abbey could not have been more dissimilar to Carson. By the time she was in high school, Carson was inclining toward the Northeast, drawn to the Atlantic seashore by her love of the ocean. Abbey, born twenty years later and raised not far from Carson's birthplace in Pennsylvania, turned westward to the deserts of Arizona, New Mexico, Nevada, and Utah. There he discovered as literal fact what Henry Thoreau had meant as allegorical truth—that the West is "but another name for the Wild."

Thoreau himself might have traveled farther into the territories had he lived beyond the age of forty-four. A year before his death, Thoreau journeyed by rail and riverboat into Illinois and Wisconsin, then crossed the Mississippi, stopping in Redwood, Minnesota, near the South Dakota line. Though seriously ill on this trip, he took notes, gathered specimens, and botanized at every opportunity. Turning homeward two months after he began, he passed by train through Madison, Wisconsin, where John Muir was a first-year student and hardly knew the word "botany."[1] On this trip, Thoreau saw things he had never seen before, including the sand dunes below Lake Michigan and the rolling prairies of Iowa; he even traveled westward far enough to meet Sioux Indians. But despite this taste of the frontier's physical reality, the West remained mythic for Thoreau rather than becoming literal, and the following summer he died.

One hundred years later, the West that Edward Abbey discovered was still as symbolic and mysterious as the one Thoreau had described in metaphor; for Abbey, however, it was also a hard-rock landscape whose physicality he learned to know well. Thoreau had said that in the West a person's soul would have room enough to expand and not "rust in a corner." Expressing the same feeling, Abbey called the West a place "for all who wish to rediscover the nearly lost pleasures of adventure . . . not only in the physical sense, but also mental, spiritual, moral, aesthetic and intellectual adventure. A place for the free." Out West, Abbey said, "you may yet find the elemental freedom to breathe deep of unpoisoned air, to experiment with solitude and stillness, to make the discovery of the self in its proud sufficiency which is not isolation but an irreplaceable part of the mystery of the whole."[2]

Not since Thoreau had there been an American nature essayist as playful with language and as irreverent as Abbey. No author since Thoreau expressed in nature writing such hilarity, such laughter in service to indignation, such an aggressive sense of irony, and such irate hostility—which he vented through satire— to America's rape of the natural world. Abbey would never be accused—as he described another nature writer—of being "a first-rate reporter, but too mild, too nice, too cautious—no point of view."[3] If that description fitted the average nature writer, then Abbey wanted no part of the label.

More than once, impatient with the categorizing of his essays, Abbey disclaimed affiliation with nature writing altogether. "Much as I admire the work of Thoreau, Muir, Leopold, Beston, Krutch, Eiseley and others," he said, "I have not tried to write in their tradition. I don't know how. I've done plenty of plain living, out of necessity, but don't know how to maintain a constant level of high thinking. It's beyond me."[4]

Abbey made his own road into the West, and he traveled it with a maverick spirit. He worked at being elusive much of the time, in order to keep his independence, and he loved to surprise his readers, to better effect "the shock of the real" that would startle his audience into alertness. He refused to be corralled by literary categories or to give in to self-importance and purple prose—although he would happily adopt any posture, including outlandish egotism, or prose of any hue, including desert purple, if it suited his subversive, satiric, or celebratory purpose.

Abbey's usual persona was that of an uncomplicated, plainspoken, and spontaneous man. "Though a sucker for philosophy all my life, I am not a thinker but—a toucher," he asserted. "A feeler, groping his way with the white cane of the senses through the hairy jungle of life. I believe in nothing that I cannot touch, kiss, embrace—whether a woman, a child, a rock, a tree, a bear, a shaggy dog. The rest is hearsay. If God is not present in this young prickly pear jabbing its spines into my shin, then God will have to get by without my help. I'm sorry but that's the way I feel. The message in the bottle is not for me."[5]

But despite his insistence that he was a simple man, Abbey, like Thoreau, was complex and more full of contradictions than the surface of his language indicated. This complexity was compounded by the same duality in consciousness with which Thoreau wrestled, what Abbey termed "paradox and bedrock": subjective existence and empirical reality interacting to create the fabric of lived experience.

From his home in the Allegheny Mountains, Edward Abbey took his first trip to the West in 1944, the summer before graduating from high school. "I started out with twenty dollars in my pocket," he recalled. "I was seventeen: wise, brown, ugly, shy, poetical; a bold, stupid, sun-dazzled kid out to see the country before giving his life in the war against Japan. A kind of hero, by God! Terrified but willing."[6]

By the time Abbey reached Chicago, his money had run out, but he continued thumbing west across Iowa and the central plains. He stacked wheat in South Dakota, washed dishes on a ranch in Montana, and took any odd job that came his way in order to pay for his meals. He crossed the Badlands and reached the wide-open skies of Wyoming, where he caught his first glimpse of the Rocky

Mountains "floating like a rampart of clouds across the western horizon. To me who had never seen hills higher than 2,000 feet above valley level, it seemed a fantastic sight." The mountains rose above the land with "an impossible beauty, like a boy's first sight of an undressed girl," he mused; "an image of those mountains struck a fundamental chord in my imagination that has sounded ever since."[7]

Abbey hitched into Yellowstone's high forests, continued across Idaho, then reached Seattle and the Pacific Ocean. Penniless but full of the high spirits of the adventure, he turned southward, working briefly in the pecan orchards and peach canneries of California. Like John Muir he tramped into Yosemite Valley, and like Mary Austin he ventured to Lone Pine in the Owens Valley, then to the sweltering deserts around Barstow and farther south to Needles and Havasu.

By midsummer Abbey had learned the trick of catching freight trains, a mode of transportation often more reliable than hitchhiking, particularly in a region where a person could stand with his thumb out for days under a withering Mojave sun and never see an automobile. Then, as summer ended, he turned eastward again out of the California desert, toward home, watching from the open door of a clattering boxcar the glorious pine forests and redrock canyons of Arizona's Colorado Plateau roll by—places that had ignited young Aldo Leopold's imagination and made an environmentalist of him.

Abbey could hardly get his fill of the desert's beauty from a moving train. Hopping freights was not legal, however, and in Flagstaff the police jailed him overnight for vagrancy. Reflecting on it later, he averred that although he wasn't particularly proud of being arrested, "it's important for a writer to spend at least one night in jail." Then he added, getting jailed may be "even more important for lawyers and judges." On the road once again, Abbey continued riding freight cars across New Mexico, more careful now not to get caught. He saw "the sharp, red cliffs of Gallup. Mesas and mountains in the distance. Lava beds baking under the sun. Old volcanoes. Indian villages, cornfields, antique adobe churches, children splashing in a stream, an enchanted mesa. And over all a gold light, a gold stillness, a sweet but awesome loneliness—an old white horse browsing on a slope miles away from any sign of man."[8]

Elated by his sense of freedom and hobohood but hungry and worn out by his ramblings, Abbey finally gave in to homesickness. In Albuquerque he bought a bus ticket back to Pennsylvania, to the submarginal farm of his father, Paul Revere Abbey, who supported the family as a woodcutter and subsistence hunter. Even as he traveled home, Abbey knew he would return to the West. He had got a taste of the mountains. He savored their names on his tongue and could repeat them like the items on the menu of a fabulous diner: "the Calicos, the Chocolates, the Panamints, the Chuckawallas." He had learned that he was "the kind of person who cannot live comfortably, tolerably, on all-flat terrain. For the sake of inner equilibrium there has to be at least one mountain range on at least one of the four quarters of my horizon—and not more than a day's walk away."[9]

After Abbey graduated from high school, the army shipped him off to Italy for the remainder of the war. He arrived on the front just in time to be pressed into being a military policeman. "I was an eighteen-year-old acne-haunted draftee rifleman in the infantry," he recalled, "and on that particular day every replacement six feet tall or taller was being shunted, willing or not, into the military police." A budding anarchist and writer, Abbey was chagrined by this twist of fate. "My feelings were hurt at being assigned to the MP's," he remembered, "since my true military ambition was to become a clerk-typist like James Jones and Norman Mailer." While in Europe, Abbey took a railway tour of the Alps, sauntered into the countryside, and even climbed Vesuvius. "One could do worse than be an inspector of volcanoes," he remarked later, no doubt remembering Thoreau's claim to being an inspector of snow-storms.[10]

Discharged from the service in 1947, Abbey returned to the Southwest and enrolled on the GI Bill at the University of New Mexico as a philosophy major. He married a fellow student—the first of five marriages—and between classes he explored the deserts and canyons he had seen from rolling boxcars. He hiked into the dry backcountry, among mesas, and along the riverbeds and arroyos. During those four years as an undergraduate, he fell more than ever in love with the desert's freedom and the spiritual and physical pleasure it gave him—and the more he grew to love deserts and freedom, the more outraged he grew at the ruin that came with unenforced emigration laws, overpopulation, black-top highways, billboards, copper mining, and uncontrolled real estate development.

After graduation Abbey returned to Europe briefly as a Fulbright fellow in Edinburgh, then enrolled at Yale as a graduate student in philosophy. After two weeks in New Haven, however, he had a vision of himself as an East Coast academic, and recoiled at the horror and unsuitability of that role for him. He withdrew from school to go to work in New Jersey and New York, and the next fall he and his wife returned to the University of New Mexico. Two years later he received a master's degree; his thesis, "Anarchism and the Morality of Violence," contained the ideas that he would later enlarge upon and dramatize in his fiction, his nonfiction, and his life.

Abbey had long been pondering the public good that would come from sawing down billboards, closing roads, pulling up survey stakes, and disabling bulldozers; they seemed to him legitimate acts of civil disobedience if they would slow what he called "the second rape of the West." "My favorite melodramatic theme," he wrote in the journal he kept for many years, "is of the harried anarchist, a wounded wolf, struggling toward the green hills, or the black-white alpine mountains, or the purple-golden desert range, and liberty. Will he make it? Or will the FBI shoot him down on the very threshold of wilderness and freedom? Obviously."[11]

All during his early years at college, Abbey had been writing fiction. While still an undergraduate he had published his first novel, *Jonathan Troy*, which had quickly gone out of print; the *New York Times* called it "a symphony of disgust." Just as he was finishing his master's thesis, he published a second, more successful novel, *The Brave Cowboy*. Hollywood bought the rights to the book and, six years later, in 1962, made it into a successful movie, *Lonely Are the Brave*. Dalton Trumbo adapted the book for the screen, and Kirk Douglas played Abbey's anachronistic, freedom-loving hero. While this was encouraging to Abbey's ambitions to be a novelist, he received only $7,500 for the film rights and a bit part as a sheriff's deputy, which was cut in the final editing. It was hardly enough material reward to support himself and his wife.

So Abbey turned to an occupation that would suit his temperament and feed his writing. On and off for the next fifteen years he worked as a seasonal employee for the National Park Service, assigned to ranger posts and fire lookouts throughout the Southwest. His first summer stint was at Arches National Monument in Utah; later his assignments included Organ Pipe Cactus National Monument in Arizona, the North Rim of the Grand Canyon, and Glacier National Park in Montana. Six years into this new career, he published a third novel, *Fire on the Mountain*. Often preferring to be called a novelist rather than an essayist, Abbey published nine novels, including the posthumous *Hayduke Lives!* Abbey's controversial, lasting fame, however, was launched not by his novels but by his nonfiction.

Using material from notebooks and musings on several summers at Arches National Monument, at age thirty-nine Abbey produced his first and most highly regarded book of nonfiction, *Desert Solitaire: A Season in the Wilderness*.[12] This book, published four years after *Fire on the Mountain*, changed Abbey's life. It made

him famous, or what some called notorious, for his high-spirited
writing and iconoclastic ideas. Across America, his outrageous,
anarchistic, and unpredictable opinions on nature and landscape—in the form of articles, travel journalism, interviews, and
occasional essays for magazines like *Audubon*, *National Geo-
graphic*, *Harper's*, *Rolling Stone*, *Architectural Digest*, and *Play-
boy*—were suddenly in high demand, and Abbey kept up a steady
stream of work to satisfy his readers.

Appropriate to its function as a wake-up alarm, *Desert Solitaire*
begins at dawn as the narrator, a summer employee posted to a
one-man station twenty miles in the interior, steps out of his Park
Service house trailer for his first sunrise in Arches National Monument. "Suddenly it comes, the flaming globe, blazing on the pinnacles and minarets and balanced rocks, on the canyon walls and
through the windows in the sandstone fins," the narrator says.
"We greet each other, sun and I, across the black void of ninety-
three million miles . . . Three ravens are wheeling near the balanced rock, squawking at each other and at the dawn. I'm sure
they're as delighted by the return of the sun as I am and I wish I
knew the language. I'd sooner exchange ideas with the birds on
earth than learn to carry on intergalactic communications with
some obscure race of humanoids on a satellite planet from the
world of Betelgeuse."

   Readers of *Desert Solitaire* might assume that this Ranger Abbey who greets the sun and wants to know the language of ravens
is Edward Abbey, the book's author. But the lines between fiction
and nonfiction are blurred in *Desert Solitaire* just as they were in
The Natural History of Selborne when Gilbert White fabricated certain of the letters that constituted chapters in his book, and as they
were in *Walden* when Thoreau created a narrating observer who
speaks of growing beans, fishing in the air, and chasing parabolic
doves, but says little about the biographical facts of his life, except
to turn them into myth and evasion.[13]

Putting disguise upon disguise, as Abbey stated in the introduction to one of his later collections of essays, "the author as seen in the pages of his own book is largely a fictional creation. Often the author's best creation. The 'Edward Abbey' of my own books, for example, bears only the dimmest resemblance to the shy, timid, reclusive, rather dapper little gentleman who, always correctly attired for his labors in coat and tie and starched detachable cuffs, sits down each night for precisely four hours to type out the further adventures of that arrogant blustering macho fraud who counterfeits his name . . . Writers are shameless liars. In fact, we pride ourselves on the subtlety and grandeur of our lies. Salome had only seven veils; the author has a thousand."[14]

Like Thoreau's narrator in *Walden*, Abbey's narrator in *Desert Solitaire* would have readers believe that his words were pulled unchanged and artless from his journal—which is what Abbey sometimes claimed. His creation, Ranger Abbey, is contradictory, offhand, cantankerous, funny, punning, self-deprecatory, saying the opposite of what he means, speaking the unvarnished truth. He is passionately in love with the outdoors and with solitude, and at the same time fervently in favor of friendship and sociability. But all of these attributes, his careful readers soon discover, are part of a conscious literary design—part of that nature-writing tradition in which the author is authentically present in the work and respectful of "facts," but willing to use the guises and devices of fiction when necessary to direct readers toward spiritual, moral, and aesthetic truths.

Desert Solitaire's first dawn breaks on All Fools' Day, and the prankish, unsanctioned, sometimes moving and sometimes antic occurrences that follow are the children of this day. "I quite agree that much of the book will seem coarse, rude, bad-tempered, violently prejudiced, unconstructive—even frankly antisocial in its point of view," the author/narrator confesses in his introduction. "Serious critics, serious librarians, serious associate professors of English will if they read this work dislike it intensely; at least I

hope so. To others I can only say that if the book has virtues they
cannot be disentangled from the faults; that there is a way of being
wrong which is also sometimes necessarily right."

Daring to be wrong in order to be right appealed as much to Abbey as to Thoreau, and he regarded it as a risk necessary to reaching the underlying mysteries in the world. At the same time, Abbey
disavowed knowing anything about mystery or any "underlying
reality." "For my own part I am pleased enough with surfaces," he
wrote; "in fact they alone seem to me to be of much importance.
Such things for example as the grasp of a child's hand in your own,
the flavor of an apple, the embrace of friend or lover, the silk of a
girl's thigh, the sunlight on rock and leaves, the feel of music, the
bark of a tree, the abrasion of granite and sand, the plunge of clear
water into a pool, the face of the wind—what else is there? What
else do we need?"

Such things, of course, are not mere surfaces. They constitute
the glory of human experience, the mystery and certitude inherent in concrete phenomena, and the rapture and privilege in being
alive. In this passage—presented as "no more than" a list of surfaces—Abbey shows his understanding of the dual and even emblematic qualities of the physical world. Qualities mythic, extravagant, and fabulous arise so naturally out of the "real" and
"bedrock" narrative in *Desert Solitaire* that the reader is finally
startled into a new attentiveness.

From the beginning, Abbey's iconoclastic narrator confronts
the reader's expectations of who is speaking and what the speaker
believes. Ranger Abbey, for example, is introduced to the reader as
full of sympathy for living creatures; in the third chapter, although
he keeps his .45 close at hand, he declines to kill a rattlesnake that
takes up residence under the doorstep of his trailer. "It's my duty
as a park ranger to protect, preserve and defend all living things
within the park boundaries, making no exceptions," he proclaims.
The reader has come to expect such sentiments from a nature
writer, and even to expect the sentiments to be phrased in that

way. The surprise comes when, with an unsettling ambiguity, the ranger adds: "Even if this were not the case I have personal convictions to uphold. Ideals, you might say. I prefer not to kill animals. I'm a humanist; I'd rather kill a *man* than a snake."[15]

Ranger Abbey has other surprising beliefs. In the chapter that follows, he appears to violate both his recently declared duty as park ranger and his personal convictions as humanist when, for no apparent reason, he hurls a rock at a young cottontail rabbit he stalks on the trail. "Should I give the rabbit a sporting chance . . . or brain the little bastard where he is?" the narrator wonders, rearing back to throw. "To my amazement," he reports, "the stone flies true (as if guided by a Higher Power) and knocks the cottontail head over tincups, clear out from under the budding blackbush. He crumples, there's the usual gushing of blood, etc., a brief spasm, and then no more. The wicked rabbit is dead." Not only is the act senseless, but Ranger Abbey apparently feels no remorse. "I continue to walk with a new, augmented cheerfulness which is hard to understand but unmistakable . . . I try but cannot feel any sense of guilt. I examine my soul: white as snow."

This random violence would have shocked Rachel Carson and John Muir, and it initially shocks the reader. The shock is compounded by the comic irony with which Abbey describes the action. And once the rabbit is dead, Ranger Abbey's heretical behavior (he also leaves the rabbit's corpse to rot) leads him not to a sense of remorse or separation from nature but to what he claims is a more intimate kinship. Using the high (and familiar) rhetoric of a more genteel and self-congratulatory nature writing, his pronouncement of kinship becomes increasingly exaggerated as he works himself up into a mock rhapsody. "We are kindred all of us, killer and victim, predator and prey, me and the sly coyote, the soaring buzzard, the elegant gopher snake, the trembling cottontail, the foul worms that feed on our entrails, all of them, all of us," he declaims. "Long live diversity, long live the earth!"

After some moments of reflection, we realize that not only has the wicked rabbit been attacked, but so also have our sentimentalism about cute and cuddly wildlife and our assumptions that "merging" with or going back to nature is somehow a simple feat. The reader's trust in Ranger Abbey's predictability (or stability) has also been slain. In the company of a wilderness guide like Ranger Abbey, the reader must brace for an off-trail journey that sometimes upsets and annoys, and often thumps nature writing's sacred cows as soundly as Ranger Abbey has thumped the wicked rabbit. "I have no desire to simply soothe or please," Abbey once stated in an interview. "I would rather risk making people angry than putting them to sleep."[16]

Even though he shocks us, Abbey's rabbit-slaying narrator is not unique in the nature-writing tradition. Abbey expected that his most careful readers would remember the encounter of Thoreau's narrator with a woodchuck, in the chapter in *Walden* titled "Higher Laws." After catching a glimpse of the little creature in the forest, Thoreau's narrator was overcome with "a strange thrill of savage delight, and was strongly tempted to seize and devour him raw." No morsel, whether cottontail or woodchuck, would be wild enough to feed that narrator's primitive hunger. Abbey's careful readers would also remember young Aldo Leopold's gunning down the old she-wolf in the Arizona desert, and that the killing had no moral content for Leopold at the time. Both events are reenacted in Abbey's assault on the cottontail—just as the lengthy history of hunting and killing of wildlife in America, its senselessness and atavism, is reenacted in Ranger Abbey's justification of his conduct.

In such subtle and not so subtle ways, Abbey frequently invoked Thoreau, Leopold, and other nature writers.[17] His actions and statements often functioned as a critique of past nature writing and of the form itself. Like the best writers before him, he served the tradition by shining a critical light on his own assumptions, and especially on responses to nature that are so mannered and automatic that they lull readers to sleep with their familiarity

rather than waking them up. Abbey's strategy was to counter sentimentality and cliché with what he called "hard and brutal mys-
ticism," and with an ornery, present-tense spontaneity.[18]

Among Abbey's most effective narrative methods was the creation
of parables in the midst of the accounts of his hardscrabble, slickrock desert adventures. In one of these metaphoric tales, he illuminated some of the fundamental paradoxes of the nature-writing
tradition by evoking a central parable in *Walden*, and by examining a familiar nature-writing theme: the love of wilderness contrasted to a life of domestication.

In the eleventh chapter of *Desert Solitaire*, the reader discovers that, like *Walden*'s narrator, Ranger Abbey has been haunted
by a natural-supernatural horse that has been lost and pursued.
Though not accompanied by a hound and a dove, the animal had
been seen occasionally by neighbors, who reported it sometimes
as real and sometimes as a phantom disappearing among the trees.
Turning Thoreau's story on its head, Abbey's comic narrator not
only seeks out the lost horse but finds it and attempts to drag it
back to its stable.

In this chapter, Ranger Abbey is driving cattle down a canyon
wash along Salt Creek, outside of Arches National Monument. On
a break from his regular ranger job, he is working cattle "for fun,"
a relief from having to answer the mind-numbing questions of
simpleminded tourists. The air swarms with thirsty deerflies and
gnats, and the sun is unrelenting as Abbey and his cowboy companion, Mackie, round up the herd and urge the skinny strays toward the corrals in Moab.

Pausing by an alkali-encrusted streambed to water his mount,
Abbey notices the trail of a horse. He assumes that it must be wild,
living in a side canyon and occasionally coming down to the
stream to drink. Mackie, who knows the country far better than
Ranger Abbey, informs him that the tracks belong not to a wild
horse but to Old Moon-Eye, a runaway.

"Old Moon-Eye is what you might call an independent horse," Mackie says. Then Mackie adds a description that might have been composed to fit Abbey himself: "He don't belong to anybody. But he ain't wild."

Mackie goes on to tell what he knows of the horse's history. Moon-Eye got his name from an inflammation in one of his eyes. Called "moon blindness," it had made the animal irritable and temperamental.[19] He had been used as a horse-for-hire on a dude ranch; but the work did not suit his nature, and his irritation grew until "one day on a sight-seeing tour through the Arches . . . all his angers came to a boil and he bucked off a middle-aged lady from Salt Lake City." The cowboy leading the group caught up with the animal and gave him a vicious beating. Moon-Eye broke away and escaped to the canyons, where he had been living alone for ten years. People had seen him and his tracks, but no one had been able to catch the horse and bring him back to civilization.

As Ranger Abbey listens to Mackie's story, he becomes determined, out of sympathy and identification with the lost horse, to search for him. Abbey cannot explain his reasons to Mackie, who thinks the idea ridiculous. He can only express his empathy for Moon-Eye. "The horse is a gregarious beast," Abbey tells the cowboy, "a herd animal, like the cow, like the human. It's not natural for a horse to live alone."

"Moon-Eye is not a natural horse," Mackie replies.

"He's supernatural?" Abbey asks.

"He's crazy," the impatient cowboy says. "How should I know? Go ask the horse."

A month after hearing the story, Range Abbey heads back alone to the canyon near Salt Creek, determined to find the horse who has revolted against his life of quiet desperation and has embraced solitude and wildness.

At noon in the canyon, the dry summer sun is so intense that nothing stirs but heat waves. Almost at once the landscape becomes mythic. "Out of the heat and stillness came an inaudible whisper," Abbey writes, "a sort of telepathic intimation that perhaps the horse did not exist at all—only his tracks." Throughout the following account the horse is called "a specter," "a creature out of a bad dream," "a scarecrow," "like a part of the burnt-out landscape," like "the steed of Don Quixote carved out of wood by Giacometti." Is Abbey making a fool of himself, as Mackie believes, chasing a symbol that exists only in his mind?

Ranger Abbey ties his saddlehorse to a tree and advances into the narrow side canyon on foot, acting against common sense and reason. With a rope and hackamore hidden inside his shirt, he stumbles over boulders and around spiny cactus. At the far end of the box canyon, he finally spies Moon-Eye, hidden behind a massive old juniper with a twisted trunk.

Until Abbey makes sense of what he is seeing, the horse seems to be like a man, then like the tree itself, with a gleaming eyeball peering through the branches. "Hanging from one of the limbs was what looked at first glance like a pair of trousers that reached to the ground," Abbey says. "Blinking the sweat out of my eyes I looked harder and saw the trousers transform themselves into the legs of a large animal, focused my attention and distinguished through the obscurity of the branches and foliage the outline of a tall horse. A very tall horse."

Ranger Abbey speaks gently to the animal. "I've come to take you home, old horse," he says. "You've been out here in the wilderness long enough."

But the closer he gets to Moon-Eye, the more he notices the horse's monstrous size and gaunt condition. The ribs jut out, the hide is "faded as an old rug," the tail is a ragged broom, and the ugly oversized head is shaped like a coffin. "If that animal was breathing I couldn't hear it," Abbey says; "the silence seemed absolute."

Cautiously Ranger Abbey moves in, speaking softly to the horse, one hand on the rope inside his shirt. His gaze is fixed on the animal's one good eye, glaring at him like a bloodshot cueball. Backed up against the canyon wall, Moon-Eye is cut off from escape. But as Abbey steps nearer, Moon-Eye suddenly leaps through the tree, and Abbey dives for cover. "Dry wood snapped and popped, dust filled the air and as I dove for the ground I had a glimpse of a lunatic horse expanding suddenly, growing bigger than all the world and soaring over me on wings that flapped like a bat's and nearly tore the tree out of the earth."

Shaking the dirt off himself, Ranger Abbey sees that there will be no sneaking up on this horse. He resorts to reasoning with Moon-Eye, who is now on open ground. He encourages the horse to remember the sweet taste of alfalfa and barley back in the corral, and the fields of fresh grass. When this has no effect, he tells the horse to consider what it will be like to die all alone, an old hermit, out in the desert.

"The turkey buzzards will get you, Moon-Eye. They'll smell you dying, they'll come flapping down on you like foul and dirty kites and roost on your neck and drink your eyeballs while you're still alive. Yes, they do that. And just before that good eye is punctured you'll see those black wings shutting off the sky, shutting out the sun, you'll see a crooked yellow beak and a red neck crawling with lice and a pair of insane eyes looking into yours. You won't like that, old horse." After the buzzards, the coyotes will come, he says. In a few months there will be nothing left of the hermit horse but dry bones and tattered scraps of hide.

In the quavering heat, Moon-Eye stands, unmoved by the sermon. He looks like only "the idea—without the substance—of a horse." The sun goes below the canyon walls. The standoff is nearly finished. Exhausted, dehydrated, with all of his persuasive powers gone, Ranger Abbey can only croak his farewell. He turns and walks out of the canyon alone, throwing the hackamore at Moon-Eye in disgust. "One or twice," he says, "I thought I heard footsteps following me but when I looked back I saw nothing."

Like every good parable, this one does not yield its meaning in its parts but all at once; it is a "parallel" or similitude—as the ety-

mology of "parable" implies—rather than an allegory.[20] The story
of Moon-Eye questions, for example, the relationship of solitude
to freedom and wilderness, and whether humans (being gregarious) can ever achieve union with the nonhuman landscape. The
parable of Old Moon-Eye asks whether a love for wilderness and
solitude isn't in some way "unnatural" for humans (and other gregarious beasts), turning them into grotesque versions of themselves, and whether, as Abbey asks often in his later books, the
price of freedom is a particular sort of madness and a horrible,
lonely death.[21]

Similar questions troubled the narrator in *Walden*. Asking
them again, using the runaway horse—which appears over and
over in Abbey's work—Abbey made Thoreau's concerns contemporary and part of his own. In the chapter in *Walden* titled "Solitude," Thoreau's narrator expressed a love for isolation so complete he seemed irredeemably misanthropic, like Old Moon-Eye,
and, in another way, like Ranger Abbey. "I have never felt lonesome, or in the least oppressed by a sense of solitude," Thoreau
wrote, "but once, and that was a few weeks after I came to the
woods." But even in that moment, he continued, he felt that his
loneliness was an indication of a "slight insanity" from which he
would recover. "I love to be alone," he continued; "I never found
the companion that was so companionable as solitude."

Just a few pages beyond, however, Thoreau's narrator confessed equally fervently his love for society. In the chapter called
"Visitors," he declared himself ready to fasten "like a bloodsucker
for the time to any full-blooded man that comes in my way. I am
naturally no hermit, but might possibly sit out the sturdiest fre-
quenter of the bar-room, if my business called me thither."

This narrator is obviously as contradictory as Abbey's, and as
paradoxical. While *Walden* is about rapture in the natural world
and rage at the social one, it is also about rage at the natural world's
resistance to human approach, and rapture in society's comforting

friendships.[22] Although in *Desert Solitaire* the jokes are broader and some situations more farfetched, Abbey's paradoxical narrator feels the same ecstasy and fury.

There is a sense, at the beginning of *Desert Solitaire*, that Ranger Abbey loves the desert because, as Abbey wrote elsewhere, "there was nothing out there. Nothing at all. Nothing but the desert. Nothing but the silent world."[23] But by the end of the book he admits that the loneliness of the desert has driven him a little crazy, and he is ready to leave it voluntarily for "the jolly, rosy faces on 42nd Street and the cheerful throngs on the sidewalks of Atlantic Avenue. Enough of Land's End, Dead Horse Point, Tukuhnikivats and other high resolves," he rhapsodizes. "I grow weary of nobody's company but my own—let me hear the wit and wisdom of the subway crowds again, the cabdriver's shrewd aphorisms, the genial chuckle of a Jersey City cop, the happy laughter of Greater New York's one million illegitimate children."

Like Thoreau, Abbey is an extremist who embraces his extremism by testing its limits. Old Moon-Eye is at one end of the spectrum. The dull, gregarious tourists who live moderate lives and whom the ranger meets in the park—their brains sucked out by television, whose blue glow they carry along on their motorized "visitations" to the desert—are at the other end. Abbey's solution is to transcend the dilemma, to leap ahead into paradox, into what he calls "moderate extremism." That's the secret, he says at the end of *Desert Solitaire*, "the best of both worlds. Unlike Thoreau who insisted on one world at a time I am attempting to make the best of two."

True to this philosophy of paradox, Abbey follows the chapter on Old Moon-Eye with a chapter that seems to refute many of the elements in his parable. In late August, near the end of his stay in Arches National Monument, Ranger Abbey is required to join a manhunt for an elderly tourist who has been missing for two days on a hot, dry mesa called, interestingly enough, Dead Horse. Ap-

parently the man, an amateur photographer, left his car and became disoriented away from the trail. The rescue party fans out as
the blazing sun reaches its zenith.

After several hours of searching, Ranger Abbey discovers the
old man's body slumped under a lone juniper—perhaps not unlike that juniper in Moon-Eye's parable—at a place named Grandview Point. "Coming close we see that he lies on his back, limbs extended rigidly from a body bloated like a balloon," the ranger says.
"A large stain discolors the crotch of his trousers. The smell of decay is rich and sickening. Although the buzzards for some reason
have not discovered him two other scavengers, ravens, rise heavily
and awkwardly from the corpse as we approach. No canteen or
water bag in sight."

From all appearances, the man met the fate Ranger Abbey predicted for Old Moon-Eye—a horrible death alone in the desert.
But no. Looking around him, Ranger Abbey finds the death to have
been good. The landscape is isolated and spectacular. The gorge of
the Colorado runs below. Nearby is the deep cut made by Green
River, then more wilderness labyrinths, canyons, and pinnacles.
Glorious mesas and the Henry and Abajo mountains rise in the
distance, and for miles virtually no human settlements mar the
landscape.

"I am inclined to congratulate the dead man on his choice of
jumping-off place," Abbey says. "He had good taste. He had good
luck—I envy him the manner of his going; to die alone, on rock
under sun at the brink of the unknown, like a wolf, like a great bird,
seems to me very good fortune indeed. To die in the open, under
the sky, far from the insolent interference of leech and priest, before this desert vastness opening like a window onto eternity—
that surely was an overwhelming stroke of rare good luck."

Lest the reader be inclined to think Ranger Abbey is sentimen-
talizing this death, he and the other rescuers joke about the putrid
mass stuffed into the black body bag as they lug it laboriously up
the trail to the road. "I wonder if the old fart would walk part way

if we let him out of that bag?" one of them wonders aloud. The dead man is a stranger to the rescuers, and so they have nothing to mourn. The abiding feeling that Ranger Abbey registers finally is "satisfaction."

"Each man's death diminishes me? Not necessarily," he says. "Given this man's age, the inevitability and suitability of his death, and the essential nature of life on earth, there is in each of us the unspeakable conviction that we are well rid of him. His departure makes room for the living. Away with the old, in with the new. He is gone—we remain, others come. The plot of mortality drives through the stubble, turns over rocks and sod and weeds to cover the old, the worn-out, the husks, shells, empty seedpods and sapless roots, clearing the field for the next crop. A ruthless, brutal process—but clean and beautiful."

Days later, Ranger Abbey watches from the back of his trailer in Arches as the sun goes down and Venus rises in the clear desert sky. He looks southwest toward Grandview Point and thinks of the dead man under the juniper. He sees the shape of black wings soaring above the Point and suddenly imagines the man as the grim vulture would have seen him, "far below and from a great distance." Then, "with the wings of imagination," Abbey ascends and looks down at his own body, "through the eyes of the bird, watching a human figure that becomes smaller, smaller in the receding landscape as the bird rises into the evening—a man at a table near a twinkling campfire." And he imagines the vast, rolling wasteland around himself seen from that height, the monumental canyons and plateaus, the great mountain ranges carved by time, the curve of the earth, and finally the arc of everlasting stars and darkness. The horse and the bird, the human and nonhuman, comedy and tragedy, merge all at once in the freedom and wilderness of Abbey's world.[24]

Desert Solitaire became a best-seller, and its success brought Abbey a scattering of book contracts. He presently wrote the text for several volumes of what he self-deprecatingly called "scenic-photographic coffee-table compendiums, which I do not count as legitimate books and which in any case nobody reads."[25] In the first of these, Abbey teamed up with photographer Eliot Porter to produce *Appalachian Wilderness: The Great Smoky Mountains*. Researching the book, Abbey and Porter drove through the Appalachian mountains, noting with dismay the effects of industrialization and tourism on a region once wild and beautiful. Abbey responded with the same outrage, wonder, and misanthropic humor he had marshaled to protest the rape of his glorious Southwest.

"How strange and wonderful is our home, our earth, with its swirling vaporous atmosphere, its flowing and frozen liquids, its trembling plants, its creeping, crawling, climbing creatures, the croaking things with wings that hang on rocks and soar through fog, the furry grass, the scaly seas," he wrote of Appalachia. "To see our world as a space traveler might see it for the first time, through Venusian eyes or Martian antennae, how utterly rich and wild it would seem, how far beyond the power of the craziest, spaced-out, acid-headed imagination, even a god's, to conjure up from nothing.

"Yet some among us have the nerve, the insolence, the brass, the gall to whine about the limitations of our earthbound fate and yearn for some more perfect world beyond the sky. We are none of us good enough for the world we have and yet we dream of Heaven."[26]

Appalachian Wilderness was followed by *Slickrock: Endangered Canyons of the Southwest*, with photographs by Philip Hyde. Two years later Abbey wrote the text for *Cactus Country*. In 1977 he collaborated with John Blaustein on *The Hidden Canyon: A River Journey* and in 1979 with David Muench on *Desert Images*.

These commercial works may have reminded Abbey too much of what he had already said in *Desert Solitaire*. In an interview about them in *Publishers Weekly* he remarked, "I don't find it dif-

ficult to dredge up the appropriate emotions, but I do find it difficult making it sound different each time around." But the subjects
Abbey had raised in *Desert Solitaire* were large enough and important enough to warrant elaboration and repetition. He undertook
that elaboration in the many essays and books of essays that
ensued—using essentially the same impassioned, unpredictable
voice crying in the wilderness.

Following the picture books, Abbey published five collections
of the essays he had written for magazines and newspapers, as well
as a book of excerpts from most of what he had written before
1984, including the novels. In each of his collections, Abbey felt it
necessary to explain the kind of writing he had undertaken, a nature writing quite different from the usual, and yet an extension of
the wild and uninhibited spirit at the heart of the nature-writing
tradition.

In *The Journey Home*, the first of his collections of essays following *Desert Solitaire*, Abbey stressed that his stance was not that of
a naturalist, and that he had no training in biology.[27] Unlike Carson or Leopold, he was no scientist and had none of the limitations
of dignified restraint, collegiality, or judiciousness imposed by the
scientist's profession. In almost a parody of mass-market nature
writing, he claimed his books were mainly "personal history
rather than natural history," with technical information stolen
from other sources. "In the main," he said, they were "simple narrative accounts of travel and adventure, with philosophical com-
mentary added here and there to give the prose a high-toned surface gleam." But call them what you like, he said, becoming more
serious, they shared a common theme with Thoreau, Muir, and
other nature writers: "the need to make sense of private experience
by exploring the connections and contradictions among wildness
and wilderness, community and anarchy; between civilization
and human freedom."[28]

He shared other themes with previous nature writers. Like
most of his predecessors and peers who wrote on nature subjects,

Abbey believed the Earth to be a living being in need of protection. In the Southwest, this meant protection from greedy developers, hustlers, and soulless politicians.

Abbey's assertion that the Earth was alive—which might seem like nonsense to the hardheaded, he conceded—could be examined by writers like himself better than it could be tested by scientists. "Such verification requires a more sophisticated science than we possess at present. It requires a science with room for more than data and information, a science that includes sympathy for the object under study, and more than sympathy, love. A love based on prolonged contact and interaction. Intercourse, if possible. Observation informed by sympathy, love, intuition. Numbers, charts, diagrams, and formulas are not in themselves sufficient. The face of science as currently construed is a face that only a mathematician could love. The root meaning of 'science' is 'knowledge'; to see and to see truly, a qualitative, not merely quantitative, understanding."[9]

In his second collection of essays, *Abbey's Road*, Abbey reasserted his place among the other "literary hobos" who had been dubbed "nature writers." It was a label he could feel comfortable with provided it was used for the authors he most admired: fiction writers, essayists, or muckraking gonzo journalists—most of them despised and misunderstood, like himself, by East Coast book reviewers and critics. Among the common motivations of these writers, he said, was to communicate the unbearable, to share with others "what would be intolerable to bear alone." Nature writers like himself wrote "to defend the diversity and freedom of humankind from those forces in our modern techno-industrial culture that would reduce us all, if we let them, to the status of things, objects, raw material, personnel; to the rank of subjects." He wondered in the book why "so many want to read about the world out-of-doors, when it's more interesting simply to go for a walk into the heart of it." His answer was that the natural world seems to urban and suburban people to be slipping away.

But that world "can still be rescued," he asserted. "That is one reason why I myself am still willing to write about it. That is my main
excuse for this book."[30]

Despite this mixture of hope and anger, by his last book of nonfiction, *Beyond the Wall*, Abbey seemed to despair—in print at
least—of saving the Western desert, or much else, with words. In
the preface to the book, which came out six years before his death
in 1989, Abbey wrote, "We need no more words on the matter.
What we need now are heroes. And heroines. About a million of
them. One brave deed is worth a thousand books. Sentiment without action is the ruin of the soul." And again, as so often in his
writing, he invoked Thoreau, who had also been moved to civil
disobedience from time to time, harboring fugitive slaves, for example, and arguing in defense of John Brown's armed insurrection
at Harper's Ferry. He quoted Thoreau's self-criticism: "If I regret
anything, it is my good behavior. What demon possessed me that
I behaved so well?"

In this final book of essays, Abbey had an imperative for those
readers who loved the wilderness and embraced the need in the
human soul for independence: "Go there. Be there. Walk gently
and quietly deep within it. And then—."[31] He left unspoken the
course of action he was suggesting. Elsewhere, however, he had
said, "the idea of wilderness needs no defense, it only needs more
defenders."[32] Abbey was implying that people ought to consider as
many forms of defending the West as seemed necessary, including
"monkey wrenching," the extralegal direct action dramatized in
his enormously successful 1975 novel, *The Monkey Wrench Gang*.
In that hilarious-serious fiction, a small band of anarchistic heroes
take to blowing up bridges with dynamite, plotting the destruction of Glen Canyon Dam, and sabotaging earthmoving equip-
ment by pouring sand in crankcases—anything to stop what Abbey once called the Californication of the Southwest. Or, as he had
George Hayduke, his most fervent and comic monkey wrencher

and "a saboteur of much wrath but little brain," proclaim: "My job is to save the fucking wilderness. I don't know anything else worth saving. That's simple, right?"[33] The principles and strategies of Abbey's monkey wrenchers, though comic and exaggerated in his novel, inspired the formation of, among other groups, the eco-guerrilla organization Earth First!. Abbey had more than a little sympathy for such bands of anarchists.[34]

Abbey's principles in his writing were never a literary pose, words unsupported by deeds. His thunderous rage was as genuine as his bounding love. Speaking of that passion and its importance in our time, essayist Edward Hoagland writes in Abbey's defense: "what is needed is honesty, a pair of eyes and a dollop of fortitude to spit the truth out, not genuflecting to Emersonian optimism, or journalistic traditions of staying deadpan, or the saccharine pressures of magazine editors who want their readers to feel good. Emerson would be roaring with heartbreak and Thoreau would be raging with grief in these 1980s. *Where were you when the world burned? Get mad, for a change, for heaven's sake!*"[35]

Abbey moved his readers because he expressed the ardor and grief that so many of them felt and because he understood the redemptive role of his art when leavened with humor and grace. "We write in order to record the truth," he said, "to unfold the folded lie, to bear witness to the future of what we have known in the present, to keep the record straight . . . It is this transient moment of bliss, which is for the artist, as it is for other lovers, the one ultimate, indescribable, perfectly sufficient justification for the sweat and pain and misery and humiliation and doubt that lead, if lucky, to the consummation we desire. That is the reason men and women write books, and of it—the mystery—there is no more to be said."[36]

In early 1989, just as Abbey turned a robust and scruffy sixty-two, he developed internal bleeding from a circulatory disorder. Several years earlier, disabled by another illness, he had been informed that he had only months to live. This time, however, the diagnosis was correct, and he died within weeks of being told the news.

In an obituary in the *New York Times Book Review*, Edward Hoagland recounted the circumstances just two days before Abbey's death: "he decided to leave the hospital, wishing to die in the desert; at sunup he had himself disconnected from the tubes and machinery. His wife Clarke and three friends drove him as far out of town as his condition allowed. They built a campfire for him to look at, until, feeling death at hand, he crawled into his sleeping bag with Clarke. But by noon, finding he was still alive and possibly better, he asked to be taken home and placed on the mattress on the floor of his writing cabin. There he said his gentle good-byes."

Following Abbey's instructions after his death, his close friends packed his body with ice, put it in the back of a pickup truck, and drove his remains into the desert wilderness. As he had wished, he was buried anonymously. Hoagland wrote that he was "wrapped in his sleeping bag, in the beautiful spot where his grave would never be found," covered with "lots of rocks" to keep away the coyotes and buzzards. "First seven, then ten buzzards gathered while the grave was being dug," Hoagland added. "One man jumped into the hole to be sure it felt O.K. before laying Abbey in, and afterward in a kind of reprise of the antic spirit that animates *The Monkey Wrench Gang* . . . went around heaping up false rockpiles at ideal gravesites throughout the Southwest."[37]

Abbey elicited great devotion from those who knew him well, adulation, and even something of cult worship from the many who knew him only from his calls for action and the uncompromising honesty of his books. He altered stereotyped notions of the West as a wasteland, of Western writers as regional hicks, and of nature writing as humorless and self-important. While for most of America the changes in attitude he advocated so fervently are yet to be adopted, "almost everyone doing creative work in the American

West today owes Ed a debt," his friends James Hepworth and Gregory McNamee wrote in their eulogy to him. "He left a hole in our hearts, in the heart of the American West, in the heart of modern American writing."[38]

In his final book of nonfiction Abbey offered a benediction. "May your trails be dim, lonesome, stony, narrow, winding and only slightly uphill," he wrote to his readers. "May the wind bring rain for the slickrock potholes fourteen miles on the other side of yonder blue ridge. May God's dog serenade your campfire, may the rattlesnake and the screech owl amuse your reverie, may the Great Sun dazzle your eyes by day and the Great Bear watch over you by night."[39]

Abbey also gave two clear admonitions that are as good for today and tomorrow as they were for yesterday. And these directives are good for nature writing, too. Always pull up survey stakes, he said, and make your own road.

Chapter Ten

WRITING THE WILD

I n *The End of Nature*, published the year of Edward Abbey's death, essayist Bill McKibben argued that in the decades since the Industrial Revolution began humans have fundamentally altered all of nature—worldwide, land and sea, to the farthest reaches of the polar icecaps, to the heart of formerly pristine rainforests, and to the upper atmosphere of the planet.[1] Overpopulation, hydrocarbon emissions, and industrial waste have accelerated the despoiling of rivers, prairies, and oceans; civilization's poisonous by-products and toxic pollution have damaged the once-sweet rain and snow; even the vast and intricate climate of the globe has been sickened.

The degradation and contamination of land, sea, and sky—of life itself—has been caused not only by exploiters of the Earth, McKibben lamented, but by the planetary managers, the "imperial" ecologists, as historian Donald Worster calls them, who have attempted to control nature with enormous hydroelectric dams, nuclear power generators, biocides, and genetic engineering meant to maintain the wasteful, high-consumption behavior of the large minority of humans living in developed societies. In short, McKibben asserted, those who subdue nature in order to advance the social good have been as hurtful and unwise as those who have pillaged natural resources out of greed and short-term interest. Nature, defined by McKibben as a category of processes and forms uninfluenced by human tampering, is coming to an end, he concluded. Indeed, by his definition, nature may have already passed from our lives. Because of manmade global disruptions in climate, "a child born now will never know a natural summer, a natural autumn, winter, or spring," McKibben wrote.

Responding to *The End of Nature*, whose thesis contained no new facts yet exemplified the most recent environmental concerns reaching a large reading audience, many prominent biologists called McKibben's claims overheated, preposterous, hysterical.[2] Taking the evolutionary perspective of deep time, they argued that not even humans can kill the dynamic forces that forged the planet, created living organisms, and precipitated the unfailing cycles that have maintained life's diverse, evolving forms for almost 4 billion years. Nature will endure, they asserted, with or without *Homo sapiens*, and all human activities are, in a relative sense, insignificant when seen from a great distance and across the whole of nature's evolutionary expanse.

Scientists taking this long-range perspective were right. Paleobiologists tell us that for millennia organisms have been evolving on Earth, altering their environments in ways large and small; in turn, the environments have been modified by them. And despite all the present biodiversity—perhaps over 30 million species—99 percent of the life forms that have ever lived are now extinct. Nature, in this sense at least, is not about to end.[3]

But purely scientific criticism of McKibben's book missed an important message of his argument, the one obscured by his scenario of a world in which biological processes independent of human tampering no longer survive. Altering the physical world to the radical extent now occurring, McKibben emphasized, also means fundamentally altering *the idea of nature*, including all that descends from that idea. The consequences of that alteration may be as calamitous as the holocaust of extinction we have recklessly brought about.

The speed at which our idea of nature changes still lags behind the breathtaking pace with which the global environment is transforming. Some estimates predict, for example, that at current rates of destruction all of the Earth's tropical, species-rich rainforests will be either clearcut or seriously disturbed by the year 2100. Similarly, the current pace of species extinction may well eliminate one-third to one-half of all living species by the end of this century. This is a biological catastrophe on a scale not seen on Earth since the mass extinctions following large meteorite strikes 65 million years ago.[4]

Even though our culture-specific ideas of nature have not caught up with the reality of these transformations in the natural environment, our ideas are indeed changing swiftly.

No one knows what ideas of nature will emerge on such an ecologically ravaged globe as the one many biologists envision: what concept of nature will arise from a world that no longer contains a diversity of wild animals except in zoos and gene banks—a world with drastically fewer songbirds, small amphibians, or wildflowers? What will the word "wilderness" mean, or the word "freedom" when every tract of land is owned and its use proscribed? What will we mean by "nature" when a large part of the Earth is—or appears to be—entirely under human dominion, from huge monoculture farms to the patterning and recombining of DNA; and when the other part has been eroded, stripped of its fertility, and poisoned beyond repair in a desperate attempt to support 9 billion humans?

Writing as if undespoiled nature were already in the past tense, McKibben noted, "Though Thoreau's writings grew in value and importance the closer we drew to the end of nature, the time fast approaches when Thoreau will be inexplicable, his notions less sensible to future men than the cave paintings are to us."

Thoreau will be inexplicable, in McKibben's opinion, when nature is no longer regarded as something separate from humankind, something wild, free of our manipulation. When nature has become merely a place we drive to in an RV for a weekend hobby, a spectacle viewed from a speeding car or airplane, a warehouse of vanishing resources, or a dumping ground for poisonous waste, then the end of nature—not the biological end but the psychic and spiritual end to nature as civilization has understood it—will truly have come. That time, McKibben lamented, is not only fast approaching, but has already arrived—if not universally, then certainly on a local scale and among the throngs of people in urban centers and in environmentally depleted parts of the globe.

Concerns over our changing ideas about the natural world—usually stated in terms less alarming and more indirect than McKibben's—have been at the heart of nature writing from the outset. Writer and naturalist Joseph Wood Krutch characterized nature writing's perspective as *experience with* the natural world, as opposed, for example, to science writing, which is *knowledge about* natural phenomena. Thoreau, as Krutch observed, expressed his concern by making his experience with nature immediate and personal. Through literary imagination, those who have come after him have taken readers into forests and deserts, to the tops of mountains, and out among coral reefs. Through experiential knowledge they have demonstrated the importance to our psychic and spiritual health of living in contact with—or, at the very least, of living with a consciousness of—environments as yet rich in biodiversity, wilderness, and geological beauty.

Nature writers past and present help us to understand in the most intimate fashion how our ideas about nature and our beliefs concerning the physical facts of science configure and disfigure the world that is not us—how our minds and hearts determine what we see and what we are blind to, how our perceptions determine what we value and therefore preserve, and, by the same token, what we enslave, desecrate, or plunder.

In the previous chapters of this book I have defined nature writing as a conversation through literature that specifically pursues such vitally important issues by using the powerful instrument of expressive language. While remaining true to empirical facts, nature writers juxtapose disparate parts of experience and the vocabulary of disparate disciplines to pose moral and ethical questions.

I have avoided a definition that goes much beyond this because nature writing's openness to a range of utterances is to me more of a virtue than a flaw. Much experimentation is taking place. As a consequence of the difficult and urgent questions still emerging, along with the willingness of contemporary nature writers to take risks in their work to answer them, the borders of this broad category of writing remain generous. In one sense nature writing is about nature's "laws," and in another its style and perspective have the potential—as with great science and great art—to be wild and unbounded.

Today, nature writing's language and forms span the range from the precise, technical prose of an entomologist in the tropical rainforests to the lyrical, allegorical reflections of a native American artist in the Southwest; from the field notes of an Arctic anthropologist to the personal diaries of a desert backpacker. Although nature writing might justifiably include the hardscrabble narratives of a Texas novelist or the verses of a Kentucky farmer, in general it is the literary essayists who have been most willing to address the difficult and profound questions presented by our relation to the natural world. Whether motivated by justice, ethics, religion, or conservation biology, these nature essayists have engaged us deeply in seeking a responsible stance with respect to the Earth and to its human and nonhuman inhabitants.

When Thoreau expressed his observations as a literary discipline, poets and fiction writers contributed to the genre as much as did essayists. Well into the twentieth century, all were writing for an avid general public, for it was still believed by authors and readers that knowledge about nature was the common concern of everyone.

But with a few notable exceptions, somewhere in midcentury

American poets and fiction writers gradually withdrew from the conversation. Whether this withdrawal was the result of urban critics' demanding urban subjects from these writers; the labeling of writers who portrayed the land and landscape as regional, quaint, or parochial; or simply the reading public's preference for novels about cities, suburbs, and bedrooms, it's hard to say. Whatever the cause, mainstream fiction writers and poets stopped writing about the natural sciences or situating their work in living, complex landscapes. As a result they are no longer among the writers most readers now turn to for an understanding of our relation to the nonhuman environment.

Even as concerns for the environment mount—in the face of global biodiversity disasters and international competition for scarce resources—literary theorists and academics continue to distance the humanities and the literary arts from the natural world outside their offices. This defoliated and desacralized world doesn't really count as a subject in our literature, I have been informed by poets and critics who argue the point in person and in their books. Like it or not, we live in a postcapitalistic, postindustrial, postmodern urban world from which the gods have departed. The only real and important theme to write about in such a world, they have concluded, is the indeterminacy of language.

Well-respected poets and writers not only articulate this characterization of the literary world of postnature, but cheerfully approve of it. With Nature and God both finally dead for them, they can get on with what they assert are the central issues of contemporary literature—theorizing as a transitive verb, linguistic deconstruction, and politics as the formulation of ideological agendas.

McKibben, following Thoreau, would probably call this condition a loss of the memory and meaning of the wild, and would argue that we inhabit a planet that contains far more than linguistic predicaments. In *The End of Nature* he recalled how it pleased Thoreau that, within a half-hour walk from Concord, he could still reach "some portion of the earth's surface where man does not stand from one year's end to another, and there, consequently, politics are not, for they are but the cigar-smoke of a man." Politics, like industrial pollution, McKibben added ruefully, "now blows its smoke over every inch of the globe."

I have read arguments concerning serious fiction similar to the one the poets were making. Urban realities require novels free of old-fashioned plot, character, and mere story telling, the novelists and their critics have argued. Today they should be composed with a sense of detached irony and with an emphasis on formal innovation, stripped of naive notions that stories, even when they are disturbing, illuminate and heal our lives. For many fiction writers, as for many poets, the world has become happily postnatural and posttranscendent. At least this would seem to be true if we looked only at their novels.[5]

On a morning several summers ago, as I glanced up from rereading the postmodern poets and critics, through the narrow window above my head I saw that the brightening dawn had made my reading lamp unnecessary. A pale mist hung like a veil over the deep meadow outside, and the violet morning colors were tinting the ends of the long grasses. At the time, I was living on a plain about 3,000 feet above sea level in a friend's cabin on the northeastern end of the island of Hawai'i. The air is satiny and cool there. At night the moon is clear and white as porcelain and you can see the Southern Cross as a small x low on the horizon. The nearest village is a cowboy town called Kamuela—the Hawaiian word for Samuel—with narrow streets lined by towering jacaranda, acacia, and eucalyptus. The people in town were in a fuss, I recall, because Kamuela was about to get its first traffic light, the only one for miles around. In the town, situated on a 200,000-acre range called Parker Ranch, there had been a courtesy practiced at the intersection that people feared would be lost. The change from a stop sign to an electric signal seemed an ominous indication of growth, and therefore the end of certain courtesies the townspeople cherished.

Beyond the fence behind the cabin stretched thousands of acres of pasture, marked by old volcanic cinder cones sprouting from the land like haystacks 50 to 600 feet high, rounded and softened by vegetation. Beyond the pastures and green cones, the land slanted gradually upward toward the base of Mauna Kea, a broad, shield volcano that dominates the horizon. On this particular morning a blue smear of snow, deposited the night before, brightened the mountain's 14,000-foot crest.

Mauna Kea hasn't erupted in historical times, but its companion to the southwest, Mauna Loa—looming just as large and snowcapped on the horizon—erupted in March 1984. For three weeks, at the summit and along Mauna Loa's flanks, lava vented at an average rate of 2 million cubic yards per hour. A third volcano, Kīlauea, adjacent to the others, has been erupting continuously since 1983, producing about 650,000 cubic yards of lava daily. You can stand by the ocean and watch the lava cascade for miles down Kīlauea's flanks, spilling over cliffs, covering roads and houses under 15 feet of molten rock, creating acres of new black coastline. The lava explodes into the sea in clouds of dense steam and hydrochloric acid. Because the eruptive process is so slow most of the time, however, you can also walk relatively safely across the floor of Kīlauea's summit caldera—over two miles wide and 400 feet below ground level—through venting sulfurous fumes, on lava only recently cooled and solidified.

Stepping out of the rear of the cabin, turning my back to Mauna Kea, I watched a white Hawaiian owl hover almost motionlessly above the meadow to the north, hunting for mice in the tall grasses. Beyond the meadow, I could see the Pacific Ocean as it stretched northward for 2,000 miles, virtually uninterrupted by landforms, from the black lava shore below me all the way to the monumental glaciers and bays of the Arctic.

The day before, I had driven up the coast to the ruins of an ancient Hawaiian temple, or *heiau*. Many throughout the islands are still standing, in urgent need of care and conservation. Commonly they are terraced structures, often oriented toward the ocean or located deep in the fertile valleys. Some stand in nearly inaccessible places, comprising networks of stone walls enclosing massive platforms and ritual structures. The particular *heiau* I visited, Mo'okini, was built about 500 A.D. Later, legend says, it was enlarged under the direction of a powerful priest from Tahiti. The main walls—lava rocks stacked twenty feet high, thirty-three feet wide at the base—were raised without mortar, beautifully engineered on a slanted plain looking toward the Pacific. The traditional poems that describe the temple's construction tell of its being completed in a single night from boulders brought from a valley ten miles down the coast—15,000 workers standing in line and passing the rocks from hand to hand, finishing the construction at sunrise.

Mo'okini is a type of *heiau* called *luakini*, dedicated to the powerful god Ku. Nearby is a stone eight feet long and six feet wide called *pohaku-holehole-kanaka*: a stone for stripping away human flesh. To consecrate the temple and to carry out its functions required human sacrifice. The flesh was often removed from the victims after they were beheaded. Their bones were sometimes made into fish hooks, their teeth and hair into ornaments.

The Hawaiian religion that sanctified these temples was officially banned shortly after Western contact, but the spiritual otherness and feelings of sacredness coming from the landscape in and around Mo'okini are still intact and intense. Entering this *heiau*, many people—Hawaiian and non-Hawaiian—experience a distinct, chilling sensation along the spine and across the scalp. No law could abolish these feelings, regardless of the changing reasons people have given to explain them. Even today, no one with good sense will move any of the stones within a *heiau*, much less carry any away—just as most people wouldn't think of entering a church and carrying away pieces of the altar. Numerous stories persist of misfortunes befalling travelers foolish enough to have removed rocks from the sacred structures. Local residents know the stories and respect the sacredness of these sites. It is common to find in the *heiau* bundles of ti leaves containing offerings, *ho'okupu*, left as gestures to the palpable spirit of the place. Clearly, among these residents—and particularly among some native Hawaiians—that spirit has not left but resides in its original grace, even though the structures that have housed it are no longer intact.

For the most part it is not superstition that compels our respect here. Instead, a powerful, undeniable sense of the sacred forces itself on us physically as well as psychologically. A sensation brushes against the skin like a cold wind while you stand in the warm sunlight, or it may seem to enter your bloodstream and resonate like a dark bell in your ears. Throughout Hawai'i similar locations and structures are touched by such an invisible atmosphere. You might come across numinous sites in the rainforests or on the seacoast, in the volcanic deserts, beside fountaining eruptions, or looking down into ancient rifts that have opened up the Earth, exposing deep lava caves

Wherever it is found, this aura is not dissimilar to experiences in great cathedrals or on particularly holy sites in any other country. As in all such landscapes and situations, you might wonder if the source of your sensations is external or internal, but you cannot doubt that these responses are common to many people whose senses are alert to them.

I am not referring to the respectfulness that books tell us is appropriate in the presence of past glory. I mean to suggest a living, phenomenological fact, as difficult to account for as the visions that so excited John Muir on the steep trails of the Sierra Nevada; or the aesthetic and moral insights that, in combination with his scientific training, transformed Aldo Leopold as he stood in the sandhill marshes of Wisconsin when the cranes rose up in front of him; or the courage and compassion that came to Rachel Carson in the tidal pools of Maine. We have not really understood the work of any of these writers unless we allow for the authenticity of certain deeply transforming moments in their experiences, located in specific environments.

The eminent art historian Vincent Scully made relevant observations about landscapes and sacred sites in his book *The Earth, the Temple, and the Gods.* Having surveyed the sacred sanctuaries of ancient Greece, Scully argued that the archaic structures he documented should be understood not merely as "architecture" but as emotional and spiritual responses to the specific landscapes in which they were built. The conventional approach of archaeologists and art historians to these sacred buildings had been in terms of their linear dimensions, their technical problems of design and engineering, and the relation of their floor plans to the rituals enacted within their walls. The surrounding landscapes, if noticed at all by scholars, were hardly commented on, and the sites themselves were discussed only in relation to their steepness or flatness, and the engineering required to build on them.

Scully, however, asserted that, for the early Greeks, landscapes and sacred structures were inseparable features. Sacred buildings, he attempted to show, were conceived of as the physical forms of qualities that the builders sensed were already present in the locations where they were placed; they did not, as in the case of Christian churches, sanctify a neutral or heathen environment. The Greeks, Scully wrote, "partly inherited and partly developed an eye for certain surprisingly specific combinations of landscape features as expressive of particular holiness. This came about because of a religious tradition in which the land was not a picture but a true force which physically embodied the powers that ruled the world." Sites were deemed holy because of combinations of visual, atmospheric, and biological elements in the location and because of shapes on the horizon that resonated in the psyches of the people coming upon the sites. To them, as they scanned the matrix of phenomena and topography, the sacredness of the location was obvious.[6]

In reuniting the Greek structures with their environments, in pointing out a larger organizational whole that included the human and nonhuman, Scully's work makes present again a knowledge of the world that Western culture has forgotten but that nature writing, in parallel with the environmental sciences, has attempted to revive. The linking of certain human structures with their environs is not dissimilar to the way ecologists over the last century have reunited all "biological structures" with their natural habitats. While measurements and schematic renderings may be unquestionably helpful in systematics and taxonomic analysis, nature writing, hand-in-hand with developments in contemporary biology, suggests that an organism must be seen as part of an exceedingly complex system if it is to be understood comprehensively. Attesting to an idea of nature that transformed him and his writing, Aldo Leopold wrote in A Sand County Almanac, "The outstanding scientific discovery of the twentieth century is . . . the complexity of the land organism." He learned to include within that complexity the eye that is trained to see such a profoundly successful yet vulnerable organism, and a mind capable of ethical reflection.

Nothing is strange, Scully wrote, about the fact that modern culture is blind to the sculptural, aesthetic, and spiritual manner in which the Greeks perceived landscape, or that modern people are blind to the land itself. "Human beings perceive programmatically and within a framework of pragmatic prefiguration," he wrote. "For this reason, the human eye always needs to be trained and released to see the meaning of things. It can usually focus intelligently only upon what the brain has already imagined for it, and it faithfully reflects the timidity of that culture-bound, sometimes occluded, organ."[7]

Part of McKibben's concern in his book was that nature and human society have been separate in the past and that we have foolishly ended their distinction by tampering with the natural world
on a global scale. Late in *The End of Nature* he declared, "*We have
ended the thing that has, at least in modern times, defined nature for
us—its separation from human society.*" I am suggesting, in contrast, that our tampering is rapidly bringing home to us the real-
ization—one that is our best hope—that we have never been separate from nature at all. Evolutionary biology has long proved this
about our physical existence; and the wisest part of every world
culture has asserted the same fact about our spiritual selves. Nowhere is the latter more apparent than at sacred sites such as
the ones I have described in Hawai'i or the ones Scully visited
in Greece. They demonstrate that from ancient times human
thought and human culture have been part of the single "land organism" Leopold conceptualized.

The sacred structures of ancient Greece and Polynesia arose
from a direct understanding that the land is continuous with humanity and humanity is continuous with the land—an idea of nature and humankind so deep in the cultural understanding of their
builders as to be self-evident to them. Their structures were as
much a part of nature as the animals and plants that shared their
environment. And even now, once the eye is trained and released,
they cannot be understood by reduction to structural diagrams removed from an integrated landscape—a landscape that includes
life forms, atmosphere, wind, colors, sounds, smells, exposure to
the elements, danger, and how these and a myriad of other elements change in relation to time of day or season—any more than
an owl or a hawk can be understood separate from the complex
habitat that shaped it over millennia and makes its comprehensi-
ble to the human heart and mind on a bright tropical morning at
the end of the twentieth century. Only by recovering such a wise,
essentially religious sympathy for the continuity between the hu-

man and nonhuman can our modern structures and our changes to the Earth be benign and even life-enhancing for other biological communities.

Nature writing, in its most thoughtful, responsible expression, is an exploration of these important ideas about nature, including the assumption that nature is separate from us neither biologically nor culturally—an idea reinforced by such academic disciplines as behavioral ecology. Indeed, as these disciplines would strongly aver, nature writing, as part of human culture, is itself one of those natural forms. It is up to our nature writers, with their vivifying gift for narration, to clarify and personalize the moral implications of this notion.

We yearn to understand a state of being in which our modern separation from the nonhuman world does not loom as certain or final. By combining all our cognitive resources—imagination as well as logic—nature writing explores how we might restore balance in our paradoxical selves, a restoration achievable only by awakening our kinship with all the other parts and processes in nature. "The ruin or the blank that we see when we look at nature is in our own eye," Thoreau proclaimed in *Walden*. When our eyes are restored, as in nature writing at its best, we are not separate from the world but become, as Thoreau added, "nature looking into nature," not an abstracted intellect examining and coolly manipulating the alien "other."

What we always see when we look at nature is our own eyes looking back at us, filtering and altering what we choose to perceive, what we emphasize or ignore, what questions we ask and pursue. It may be necessary to investigate more ways of knowing and seeing, and more approaches to nature than have been employed in the past, to answer how the human and nonhuman can survive together in a tolerant and dignified way, particularly as the Earth grows more crowded with humans and its resources are exhausted. The new openness in science and literature to a pluralism of ideas, to respect for local forms of knowledge, and to the coordination of the entire range of our cognitive capabilities—as expressed in part through nature writing—is a sign of hope that humans can survive without continuing to annihilate other life forms at an insane pace, and can even invent responsible methods for ecological restoration of the planet.

Several years ago, in the volcano country near Kīlauea Crater, I hiked with a friend into one of the region's most remote and unstable areas. We wanted to camp as near as possible to a newly emergent volcanic cone, still in the midst of eruption, expanding and thrusting higher day by day. For ten years this mound called Puʻu Oʻo, now 900 feet high, had churned and roared, rising out of the midst of an old forest and flooding the scorched land with molten rock. Its fountaining created a steaming world of glassy slag, shifting scrabble, and glowing flues. Deformed by heat and pressure, acres of land expelled from its vents were on the move. Chunks of brittle rock skittered down the crater's slopes and were swallowed by a hissing lava lake. Sulfurous crevasses split the surrounding land, and unstoppable black glaciers; their interiors glowed redhot as they inched toward the sea.

All day as we hiked we could see Puʻu Oʻo looming above the forest in front of us. Its eruptions had slowed considerably over the past months, but even from three miles upland, where we finally set up camp, it looked decidedly dangerous. As night fell, rainclouds descended over the active cone. In the dusky light the summit's colors flashed from ashen white to orange, from pale reds to bronze. Hot gases rose through the porous sides of the summit, and tephra and debris were ejected high into the air.

We camped on a small clearing of solid lava, no more than twelve feet square, hemmed in by thickly tangled fields of a fern called uluhe. An aggressive lava colonizer, the wiry uluhe is nearly as tough as the rock from which it grows. In the darkness and rain that night, the faint light of stars illuminated the twisted ferns and created the impression that we were surrounded by an impenetrable, waist-deep meadow of dark thorns. The volcano poured out a vermilion light that shifted and flickered on the belly of the low clouds. And when the moon finally broke through the overcast, we saw around us, standing on five-foot stalks above the fierce uluhe, a constellation of delicate wild orchids thriving among the ferns and sulfurous gases. The tall, elegant flowers glittered and waved in the broken moonlight.

"Every sunset which I witness inspires me with the desire to go to a West as distant and as fair as that into which the sun goes down," Thoreau wrote in "Walking." Go west far enough, and you'll find "a wildness whose glance no civilization can endure," containing not only the "strength, the marrow, of Nature," but also the strength and marrow of the human heart.[8] In this rainy, steaming mix of volcanic processes, I knew I was seeing part of that very wildness in which, according to Thoreau, the preservation of the world is contained.

Thoreau never observed a physical wildness as dramatic and extreme as the volcano country's geological fury and biological gentleness. Nevertheless he translated for us an important essence found in every wilderness: its capacity to contain enormous diversity out of which might emerge a cosmos of beauty and a disorderly order, unforgiving and yet joyous. He gave us a vision of nature as an inner as well as an outer phenomenon—a *conceptual* wildness as important as the material one.

Thoreau claimed that he wanted to understand nature by being as much as possible in the experience of the land. To do this, he asserted, sometimes it is necessary to "let science slide," at least for a while, to rejoice in the knowledge that "the woods are not tenantless, but chock full of honest spirits" as good as ourselves. He would have agreed, along with many of the other nature writers presented in this book, that the ferns and orchids, and even the fictile rocks—which at times are as warm and mobile as living creatures—contain such spirits.

Thoreau's writing set the stage for a momentous change in

American thought, an evolution of what Aldo Leopold would later call "the mental eye." He and the nature writers after him have continued to transform our perception of what we find irreplaceably beautiful, rapturous, and essential in nature—that which is *in us* as well as in the nonhuman world. In doing so, nature writers have gradually extended our sense of community, what we hold ourselves responsible for, and what we must do to preserve this sweet, vulnerable biosphere in which we are embedded, this harmonious and fertile web of living tissue that we have ravaged.

The vision at the heart of nature writing is a sober and attentive rhapsody that we cannot help but be obligated by. Out of their delight and outrage, their observations and measurements, Thoreau, Burroughs, Muir, Austin, Leopold, Carson, Abbey, and many others have reiterated the injunction they felt coming from nature. And like Coleridge's ancient mariner, they pull on our sleeves with something urgent to say, compelling us to action.

This injunction is felt by scientists as much as by nonscientists attempting to see nature comprehensively. Robert S. Root-Bernstein, one of the first MacArthur Fellows and a professor of natural science and physiology, writes, "In the search for universal truth, a scientist is wise to know intimately, even to identify with, the things or creatures he studies . . . but intimacy means more than mere knowledge." He quotes geneticist Barbara McClintock, winner of the 1983 Nobel Prize in medicine, who, speaking of her work on the chromosomes of the *Neurospora* fungus, said: "When I was really working with them, I wasn't outside. I was down there. I was part of the system . . . As you look at these things, they become part of you. And you forget yourself. The main thing about it is you forget yourself." Peter Debye, winner of the Nobel Prize in chemistry, said he would ask himself during his work on molecular structures, "What did the carbon atom *want* to do?" Similarly, Jonas Salk wrote concerning his method of working, "I would picture myself as a virus, or as a cancer cell, for example, and try to sense what it would be like to be either. I would imagine myself as the immune system." This "internalization of subject matter," according to Root-Bernstein, the power to bring imagination into partnership with reason, is common in great discoveries because it results in "the ability to sense an underlying order in things," to apprehend deep forms and relationships unavailable through what he calls "impersonal knowledge" and propositions.[9]

Nature writing, I suggest, through its emphasis on personal knowledge, is another way for nature to understand itself, to articulate its unexpected configurations, its mysteries, and its requirements of us. Thoreau noted in his journal, in a moment of bliss, "A writer is the scribe of all nature—he is the corn & the grass & the atmosphere writing."[10] This definition, too, is an essential part of what we mean by "nature writing."

NOTES

Notes to Chapter One

1. Henry Seidel Canby, *Thoreau: The Biography of a Man Who Believed in Doing What He Wanted* (Boston: Beacon Press, 1939), p. 294.

2. William Howarth, *The Book of Concord: Thoreau's Life as a Writer* (New York: Viking Press, 1982), p. 61.

3. Edith Peairs, "The Hound, the Bay Horse, and the Turtle Dove: A Study of Thoreau and Voltaire," *PMLA* 52, no. 3 (Sept. 1937): 863–69.

4. Henry David Thoreau, *The Journal of Henry D. Thoreau*, ed. Bradford Torrey and Francis H. Allen, 14 vols. (Boston: Houghton Mifflin, 1906; reprint, Salt Lake City: Peregrine Smith, 1984), May 31, 1853.

5. Henry Thoreau, "The Natural History of Massachusetts," in *The Natural History Essays* (Salt Lake City: Peregrine Smith, 1980), p. 29.

6. Thoreau, *Journal*, Aug. 19, 1851.

7. Ibid.

8. Ibid., June 6, 1851.

9. Ibid., May 31, 1853.

10. Quoted in Robert D. Richardson, Jr., *Henry Thoreau: A Life of the Mind* (Berkeley: University of California Press, 1986), p. 247.

11. Quoted in ibid., p. 250.

12. Thoreau, *Journal*, June 7, 1851.

13. Ibid., July 23, 1851.

14. William C. Johnson, Jr., *What Thoreau Said: Walden and the Unsayable* (Moscow: University of Idaho Press, 1991), p. xvi.

15. Thoreau, *Journal*, Dec. 20, 1851, quoted in Johnson, *What Thoreau Said*, p. 64.

16. Thoreau, *Journal*, Sept. 2, 1851.

17. Henry D. Thoreau, *The Correspondence of Henry David Thoreau*, ed. Walter Harding and Carl Bode (New York: New York University Press, 1985), p. 125. See also Henry Golemba, *Thoreau's Wild Rhetoric* (New York: New York University Press, 1990), p. 106.

18. Thoreau, *Journal*, June 23, 1840.

19. Johnson, *What Thoreau Said*, p. 151.

Notes to Chapter Two

1. Gilbert White, *The Natural History and Antiquities of Selborne, in the County of Southampton* (London: Benjamin White & Son, 1789); reprint, ed. Richard Mabey (New York: Penguin, 1987), p. 140.

2. Quoted in Walter S. Scott, *White of Selborne and His Times* (London: John Westhouse, 1946), pp. 125–28.

3. White, *Natural History*, p. 139.

4. Ibid., p. 122.

5. Quoted in Paul G. M. Foster, *Gilbert White and His Records: A Scientific Biography* (London: Christopher Helm, 1988), p. 130.

6. See Donald Worster, *Nature's Economy: A History of Ecological Ideas* (New York: Cambridge University Press, 1977), pp. 3–25. See also Roderick Frazier Nash, *The Rights of Nature* (Madison: University of Wisconsin Press, 1989), pp. 22–24.

7. Foster, *Gilbert White*, p. 159.

8. Quoted in John Hildebidle, *Thoreau: A Naturalist's Liberty* (Cambridge, Mass.: Harvard University Press, 1983), p. 33.

9. Virginia Woolf, "White's Selborne," in *The Captain's Death Bed* (London: Hogarth Press, 1950), p. 23; quoted in W. J. Keith, *The Rural Tradition: A Study of the Non-fiction Prose Writers of the English Countryside* (Toronto: University of Toronto Press, 1974), p. 56.

10. White, *Natural History*, p. 136.

11. Ibid., pp. 65, 81.

12. Quoted in Keith, *The Rural Tradition*, p. 55.

13. Hildebidle, *Thoreau*, pp. 24–39.

14. Woolf, "White's Selborne," p. 20; quoted in Keith, *The Rural Tradition*, p. 52.

15. White, *Natural History*, p. 93.

16. Charles Darwin, *The Voyage of the Beagle*, ed. Leonard Engel (Garden City, N.Y.: Doubleday, 1962), p. xxiii; quoted in Hildebidle, *Thoreau*, pp. 30–31.

17. Hildebidle, *Thoreau*, pp. 24–31.
18. Worster, *Nature's Economy*, p. 5.
19. David Elliston Allen, *The Naturalist in Britain: A Social History* (London: Allen Lane, 1976), p. 99.
20. Ibid., p. 50.
21. Ibid., pp. 50–51.
22. Worster, *Nature's Economy*, p. 16.
23. Thoreau, *Correspondence*, pp. 309–10.
24. MS, New York Public Library, quoted in Walter Harding, *The Days of Henry Thoreau: A Biography* (New York: Dover, 1982), pp. 243–44; Thoreau, *Correspondence*, p. 453; MS, Concord Library, quoted in Henry Seidel Canby, *Thoreau* (Boston: Beacon Press, 1939), p. 433.
25. Richardson, *Henry Thoreau*, p. 309.
26. White, *Natural History*, p. 125.
27. Thoreau, *Journal*, Nov. 12, 1853.
28. Richardson, *Henry Thoreau*, p. 309.
29. Thoreau, *Journal*, April 19 and May 6, 1854. See Richardson, *Henry Thoreau*, pp. 309–10.
30. Quoted in Worster, *Nature's Economy*, p. 64
31. Quoted in Fritz Oehlschlaeger and George Hendrick, eds., *Toward the Making of Thoreau's Modern Reputation* (Urbana: University of Illinois Press, 1979), p. 111.
32. Hildebidle, *Thoreau*, p. 46.
33. See ibid., p. 47.
34. Thoreau, *Journal*, Nov. 9, 1851; quoted in Golemba, *Thoreau's Wild Rhetoric*, p. 2.
35. Thoreau, *Journal*, Nov. 5, 1857.
36. See Golemba, *Thoreau's Wild Rhetoric*, pp. 198–99.

Notes to Chapter Three
1. Thoreau, *Journal*, Nov. 30, 1858.
2. Ibid.
3. See H. Daniel Peck, *Thoreau's Morning Work: Memory and Perception in A Week on the Concord and Merrimack River, the Journal, and Walden* (New Haven: Yale University Press, 1990), p. 50.
4. Thoreau, *Journal*, Dec. 25, 1851.
5. Ibid., Nov. 30, 1858.
6. Peck, *Thoreau's Morning Work*, pp. 65–66.
7. Ibid., p. 53.

8. See ibid., passim.

9. Thoreau, *Journal*, Nov. 1, 1851.

10. See F. O. Matthiessen, *American Renaissance: Art and Expression in the Age of Emerson and Whitman* (New York: Oxford University Press, 1941), for a discussion of "seeing" among nineteenth-century American writers.

11. Thoreau, *Journal*, March 15, 1842.

12. Ibid., April 10, 1841.

13. Ibid., Nov. 1, 1851.

14. Ibid., Sept. 13, 1852. See also Naomi J. Miller, "Seer and Seen: Aspects of Vision in Thoreau's *Cape Cod*," *ESQ* 29 (1983):190–91.

15. See Joel Porte, *Emerson and Thoreau: Transcendentalists in Conflict* (Middletown, Conn.: Wesleyan University Press, 1966); idem, "Emerson, Thoreau, and the Double Consciousness," *NEQ* 41 (1968):40–50; and Edward Wagenknecht, *Henry David Thoreau: What Manner of Man?* (Amherst: University of Massachusetts Press, 1981), pp. 123–54.

16. Thoreau, *Journal*, Oct. 27, 1858.

17. Ibid.

18. John Ruskin, *Modern Painters, Volume Two* (1846; New York: John Wiley and Sons, 1884); pt. 3, sec. 1, chap. 1, p. 5; quoted in Richardson, *Henry Thoreau*, p. 359.

19. Thoreau, *Journal*, Aug. 22, 1851.

20. John Ruskin, *The Elements of Drawing & The Elements of Perspective* (London: Dutton, 1907; first published 1857), p. 103.

21. Originally in Thoreau, *Journal*, March 15, 1842.

22. Ruskin, *The Elements of Drawing*, p. 100.

23. Thoreau, *Journal*, Oct. 6, 1857; see Wagenknecht, *Henry David Thoreau*, pp. 34, 151–54.

24. Thoreau, *Journal*, Oct. 6, 1858.

25. Henry David Thoreau, "Autumnal Tints," in *The Natural History Essays* (Salt Lake City: Peregrine Smith, 1980), pp. 137–77. The other essays were "Life without Principles," "Walking," and "Wild Apples."

26. Thoreau, "Autumnal Tints," p. 174.

27. See Wagenknecht, *Henry David Thoreau*, p. 153; and Peck, *Thoreau's Morning Work*, p. 97.

28. William Gilpin, *Observations on the River Wye . . . 1770*, quoted in Hans Huth, *Nature and the American: Three Centuries of Changing Attitudes* (Lincoln: University of Nebraska Press, 1957), p. 12.

29. Thoreau read eleven volumes of Gilpin's work over the next two years and made more notes in his journal about Gilpin than he did about nearly any other writer. See William D. Templeman, "Thoreau, Moralist of the Picturesque," *PMLA* 47 (1932):864–89; Gordon V. Boudreau, "Henry David Thoreau, William Gilpin, and the Metaphysical Ground of the Picturesque," *American Literature* 45 (1973):357–69; and Norman Foerster, "Thoreau as Artist," *Sewanee Review* 29, no. 1 (1921):2–13.

30. See William D. Templeman, "The Life and Work of William Gilpin," *Studies in Language and Literature* 24 (1939): 9–336.

31. Although Gilpin apparently never knew of Gilbert White, it is likely that White knew Gilpin's work. White's friend Robert Marsham wrote to him on Feb. 12, 1792, "I presume you have seen Gilpin's Book of the views in the new Forest." Many writers since have compared Gilpin and White.

32. Templeman, "Life of Gilpin," p. 243.

33. Ibid., p. 118.

34. Walter John Hipple, Jr., *The Beautiful, the Sublime, and the Picturesque in Eighteenth-Century British Aesthetic Theory* (Carbondale: Southern Illinois University Press, 1957), p. 186.

35. See Allen, *The Naturalist in Britain*, p. 53.

36. Quoted in Carl Paul Barbier, *William Gilpin: His Drawings, Teaching, and Theory of the Picturesque* (Oxford: Oxford University Press, 1963), p. 103.

37. Quoted in Huth, *Nature and the American*, p. 89.

38. Barbier, *William Gilpin*, p. 99.

39. Thoreau, *Journal*, March 31, 1852; quoted in Templeman, "Thoreau, Moralist of the Picturesque," p. 872.

40. Thoreau, *Journal*, June 21, 1852.

41. Richardson, *Henry Thoreau*, p. 266.

42. Gary Paul Nabhan, Foreword to Henry D. Thoreau, *Faith in a Seed: The Dispersion of Seeds and Other Late Natural History Writings*, ed. Bradley P. Dean (Washington, D.C.: Island/Shearwater, 1993), p. xiv.

43. Thoreau, *Journal*, Nov. 10, 1851.

44. Ibid., Oct. 4, 1859.

45. Henry David Thoreau, "Walking," in *The Natural History Essays*, p. 130.

Notes to Chapter Four

1. Thoreau, *Journal*, Dec. 31, 1841.

2. Ibid., Aug. 19, 1851.

3. Edward Hoagland, "Bragging for Humanity," *American Heritage* 38, no. 5 (July/Aug. 1988):74.

4. George Perkins Marsh, *Man and Nature; Or, Physical Geography as Modified by Human Action* (Cambridge, Mass.: Harvard University Press, 1965; first published 1864), p. 43.

5. Ibid., p. 44. See also Roderick Frazier Nash, *The Rights of Nature: A History of Environmental Ethics* (Madison: University of Wisconsin Press, 1989), p. 38.

6. Hans Huth, *Nature and the American: Three Centuries of Changing Attitudes* (Lincoln: University of Nebraska Press, 1972), p. 169; also see Roderick Nash, *Wilderness and the American Mind* (New Haven: Yale University Press, 1973), p. 104.

7. George Perkins Marsh, *The Earth as Modified by Human Action* (New York: Scribner's, 1874), p. 327; quoted in Huth, *Nature and the American*, p. 169.

8. Worster, *Nature's Economy*, p. 16.

9. Frances Halsey, "The Rise of Nature Writers," *American Monthly Review of the Reviews* 26 (Nov. 1902):567–71; quoted in Worster, *Nature's Economy*, p. 16.

10. Fritz Oehlschlaeger and George Hendrick, eds., *Toward the Making of Thoreau's Modern Reputation* (Urbana: University of Illinois Press, 1979), p. 15.

11. James Russell Lowell, Review of Thoreau, *Letters to Various Persons*, *North American Review* 101 (Oct. 1865):597–608.

12. Walter Harding, *The Days of Henry Thoreau* (New York: Dover, 1982), p. 395; see also Oehlschlaeger and Hendrick, *Toward Making Thoreau's Reputation*, pp. 12–20.

13. Clara Barrus, *Our Friend John Burroughs* (Boston: Houghton Mifflin, 1914), pp. 129–30.

14. In 1868 Whitman recalled that he talked to Thoreau "several times" and took walks with him in Brooklyn. He may have been misremembering the number of their meetings. See Horace L. Traubel, *With Walt Whitman in Camden*, vol. 1 (New York: Kennerly, 1915), pp. 212–13. Odell Shepard, ed., *The Journals of Bronson Alcott* (Boston: Little, Brown, 1938), pp. 286–91. For contemporaneous remembrances see also Herbert Gilchrist, ed., *Anne Gilchrist: Her Life and Writings* (London: Unwin, 1887).

15. Quoted in Justin Kaplan, *Walt Whitman: A Life* (New York: Simon and Schuster, 1980), p. 218.

16. See ibid., p. 219.

17. Thoreau, *Correspondence*, p. 445.

18. Henry Thoreau, *Familiar Letters of Henry David Thoreau* (Boston: Houghton Mifflin, 1906), pp. 295–96.

19. Thoreau, *Correspondence*, pp. 444–45.

20. Traubel, *With Walt Whitman in Camden*, vol. 3, pp. 318–19.

21. Ibid., p. 375.

22. Richardson, *Henry Thoreau*, p. 349; quoted in Kaplan, *Walt Whitman*, pp. 303–06.

23. Edward J. Renehan, Jr., *John Burroughs: An American Naturalist* (Post Mills, Vt.: Chelsea Green, 1992), p. 70.

24. Quoted in Kaplan, *Walt Whitman*, p. 307.

25. Quoted in Clara Barrus, *John Burroughs, Boy and Man* (Boston: Houghton Mifflin, 1928), p. 238.

26. Renehan, *John Burroughs*, p. 74.

27. Ibid., p. 85.

28. Kaplan, *Walt Whitman*, p. 307.

29. *Wake-Robin*, in *The Writings of John Burroughs*, 23 vols., vol. 1 (Boston: Houghton Mifflin, 1904).

30. Quoted in Renehan, *John Burroughs*, p. 95.

31. Clara Barrus, ed., *The Life and Letters of John Burroughs*, 2 vols. (Boston: Houghton Mifflin, 1925), vol. 1, pp. 145–46.

32. Clara Barrus, ed., *The Heart of Burroughs's Journals* (Boston: Houghton Mifflin, 1928), pp. 40–41.

33. Ibid., p. 41.

34. Renehan, *John Burroughs*, p. 77.

35. Barrus, *Burroughs's Journals*, pp. 47–48.

36. Barrus, *Burroughs, Boy and Man*, p. 273.

37. Renehan, *John Burroughs*, p. 121.

38. Quoted in ibid., pp. 121–22. See also Joseph Wood Krutch, *Great American Nature Writing* (New York: William Sloane, 1950), p. 71.

39. John Burroughs, "Henry D. Thoreau," in *Writings of Burroughs*, vol. 8, p. 45.

40. Clifton Johnson, ed., *Burroughs Talks* (Boston: Houghton Mifflin, 1922), p. 188.

41. John Burroughs, "Another Word on Thoreau," in *The Last Harvest* (Boston: Houghton Mifflin, 1922), p. 110.

42. Burroughs, "Henry D. Thoreau," p. 39.

43. Burroughs, "Another Word on Thoreau," p. 120.

44. Ibid., p. 121.

45. Barrus, *Life and Letters of Burroughs*, vol. 2, p. 336.

46. Krutch, *Great American Nature Writing*, p. 78.

47. Renehan, *John Burroughs*, p. 23.

48. Barrus, *Life and Letters of Burroughs*, vol. 2, pp. 185–86.

49. Quoted in Renehan, *John Burroughs*, p. 130.

50. Dallas Lore Sharp, "John Burroughs," in *The Face of the Fields* (1911; reprint, Freeport, N.Y.: Books for Libraries Press, 1967), pp. 163–65. Also quoted in Paul Brooks, *Speaking for Nature* (Boston: Houghton Mifflin, 1980), pp. 12–13.

51. In his letters, at least, Burroughs disowned Sharp's comparison of him with Thoreau. He wrote: "Why compare *me* to the disadvantage of Thoreau? Thoreau is my master in many ways—much nearer the stars than I am—less human, maybe, but more divine—more heroic"; Barrus, *Life and Letters of Burroughs*, vol. 2, p. 147.

52. Dallas Lore Sharp, "The Nature-Writer," in *The Face of the Fields*, p. 122.

Notes to Chapter Five

1. Barrus, *Our Friend John Burroughs*, p. 3.

2. Quoted in Peter J. Schmitt, *Back to Nature: The Arcadian Myth in Urban America* (New York: Oxford University Press, 1969), p. 30.

3. Quoted in Paul Brooks, *Speaking for Nature* (Boston: Houghton Mifflin, 1980), p. 205.

4. See Worster, *Nature's Economy*, pp. 16–19.

5. Schmitt, *Back to Nature*, p. 6.

6. See Catherine L. Albanese, *Nature Religion in America: From the Algonkian Indians to the New Age* (Chicago: University of Chicago Press, 1990).

7. See especially Worster, *Nature's Economy*, pp. 16–21.

8. See, for example, Thoreau's essay "Huckleberries," in *The Natural History Essays*, pp. 211–62.

9. Thoreau, "The Natural History of Massachusetts," quoted in Worster, *Nature's Economy*, p. 96.

10. See Arthur Wrobel, ed., *Pseudo-Science and Society in Nineteenth-Century America* (Lexington: University Press of Kentucky, 1987); see also Robert C. Fuller, *Alternative Medicine and American Religious Life* (New York: Oxford University Press, 1989).

11. Gail Thain Parker, *Mind Cure in New England: From the Civil War to World War I* (Hanover, N.H.: University Press of New England,

1973), p. 20; quoted in Albanese, *Nature Religion in America*, pp. 106–07.

12. Ralph H. Lutts, *The Nature Fakers: Wildlife, Science, and Sentiment* (Denver: Fulcrum, 1990), p. 17. This most thorough account to date of the nature-faker controversy is the source of much of the information in this chapter.

13. Schmitt, *Back to Nature*, p. 96.

14. Ibid., p. 115.

15. See ibid., pp. 11–13.

16. When the first European settlers arrived, the forests of the continental United States covered at least 822 million acres and were considered inexhaustible. This opinion persisted well into the nineteenth century, even as Francis Parkman jokingly slaughtered buffalo and left their carcasses to rot on the plains in the 1840s. As late as 1891 there were still authorities such as Henry Gannett, head of the U.S. Geological Survey and president of the National Geographical Society, saying, "It's all bosh—this talk about the destruction of our forests. There is more wood growing in the United States now than there was one hundred years ago, more than we want and can use . . . And along the Pacific Coast the timber is simply inexhaustible." See Jenks Cameron, *The Development of Governmental Forest Control in the United States* (Baltimore: Johns Hopkins Press, 1928), pp. 5–8.

17. See Renehan, *John Burroughs*, p. 240.

18. See Hans Huth, *Nature and the American: Three Centuries of Changing Attitudes* (1957; reprint, Lincoln: University of Nebraska Press, 1990), p. 189.

19. Alfred Runte, *National Parks: The American Experience* (Lincoln: University of Nebraska Press, 1979), p. 158.

20. "Neighbors for a Night in Yellowstone Park," *Literary Digest* 82 (Aug. 30, 1924):45; quoted in Runte, *National Parks*, p. 157.

21. Jenks Cameron, *The National Park Service: Its History, Activities, and Organization*, Institute for Government Research, Service Monographs no. 11 (New York: Appleton, 1922), pp. 137–38; and see Schmitt, *Back to Nature*, 154–55. The creation of the national parks, threatened almost as soon as they were established, had been difficult and controversial. Abraham Lincoln designated Yellowstone country "a public park . . . for the benefit and enjoyment of the people" in 1864, but few people were able actually to visit its beau-

tiful and remote wilderness. Twenty-seven years later Congress quietly authorized for the first time the creation of national forests on
federal land. Initially, federal forests comprised 1.25 million acres.
Thirteen million acres were set aside in the next two years, and in
early 1897 President Grover Cleveland set aside another 21.4 million, over the strenuous objections of politicians and ranchers from
the Western states. (See Stephen Fox, *John Muir and His Legacy: The
American Conservation Movement* [Boston: Little, Brown, 1981], pp.
110–13.) Still, not until June 1897 did Congress pass provisions for
professional foresters actually to monitor the reserves, and a staff
was not organized in the Forest Service until 1905. (See Huth, *Nature and the American*, pp. 176–77.) The National Park Service was
established eleven years later.

22. Bliss Carman, *The Making of Personality* (Boston: Page, 1908), p.
315; quoted in Schmitt, *Back to Nature*, p. 13.

23. See H. Allen Anderson, *The Chief: Ernest Thompson Seton and the
Changing West* (College Station: Texas A & M University Press,
1986), p. 95.

24. Schmitt, *Back to Nature*, p. 125. The fifth best-selling novel was Har-
old Bell Wright's *The Winning of Barbara North*. The next two best
sellers of the period were Owen Siter's *The Virginian* and Jack London's *The Call of the Wild*.

25. See, for example, Richard Hofstadter, *Social Darwinism and American Thought* (New York: Braziller, 1959).

26. Liberty Hyde Bailey, *The Holy Earth* (New York: Scribner's, 1915);
quoted in Worster, *Nature's Economy*, p. 185.

27. Worster, *Nature's Economy*, p. 259.

28. John Burroughs, "Real and Sham Natural History," *Atlantic Monthly*,
March 1903, pp. 298–309.

29. See Lutts, *The Nature Fakers*, pp. 41–42; and Barrus, *Life and Letters
of Burroughs*, vol. 2, pp. 48–49.

30. Lutts, *The Nature Fakers*, p. 55.

31. William J. Long, "The Modern School of Nature-Study and Its Critics," *North American Review*, May 1903, pp. 687–98.

32. John Burroughs, "Current Misconceptions in Natural History," *Century Magazine*, Feb. 1904, p. 510. See also Lutts, *The Nature Fakers*,
p. 65.

33. William J. Long, "Animal Surgery," *Outlook*, Sept. 12, 1903, pp. 122–

27. See Lutts, *The Nature Fakers*, p. 73; and Renehan, *John Burroughs*, p. 235.

34. See also Lutts, *The Nature Fakers*, p. 77; and Renehan, *John Burroughs*, p. 235–36.

35. W. F. Ganong, "The Writings of William J. Long," *Science*, April 15, 1904, pp. 623–25.

36. Ellen Hayes, letter, *Science*, April 15, 1904, pp. 625–26; also quoted in Lutts, *The Nature Fakers*, p. 79.

37. See Lutts, *The Nature Fakers*, p. 82. Lutts (p. 221) also describes a similar specimen examined by William Brewster of the Harvard Museum of Comparative Zoology a few years before Long produced his specimen. Brewster's examination included x-rays, and he, along with other ornithologists and biologists, came to the conclusion that the casts of earth and feathers were formed by mud solidifying around an open wound. In 1988 the specimen, which still resides in the Harvard museum, was pronounced to be mud adhering to a blood clot. Lutts speculates that "Shorebirds often stand on one leg and the [specimen bird] certainly favored its good leg, drawing its injured leg against its body, where its feathers stuck to the bloody injury . . . The clot and bony calcification probably served as an effective cast and immobilized the injured joint. This cast, though, was the result of chance rather than design." Long may have seen a woodcock pecking at such a blood clot, muddied and with feathers adhering to it, and concluded that the bird was actually building up the cast.

38. Edward B. Clark, "Roosevelt on the Nature Fakirs," *Everybody's Magazine*, June 1907, pp. 770–74.

39. William J. Long, "I Propose to Smoke Roosevelt Out," *New York Times*, June 2, 1907. See also Renehan, *John Burroughs*, p. 238; and Lutts, *The Nature Fakers*, pp. 114–15.

40. "Dr. Long Tells More Animal Stories in an Effort to Confute the President," *New York Times*, July 7, 1907, pt. 5, p. 11. See also Lutts, *The Nature Fakers*, p. 115.

41. "Real Naturalists on Nature Faking," *Everybody's Magazine*, Sept. 1907, pp. 423–30.

42. Lutts, *The Nature Fakers*, p. 137.

43. John Burroughs, *Ways of Nature*, vol. 14 of *Writings of Burroughs*, p. vi.

44. Ibid., pp. 257–58.

45. Ibid., p. 256.

46. Donald R. Griffin, *Animal Minds* (Chicago: University of Chicago Press, 1992), p. 78.

47. Hiroyoshi Higuchi, "Bait-fishing by the Green-backed Heron *Ardeola striata* in Japan," *Ibis* 128 (1986):285–90; see also idem, "Cast Master," *Natural History* 96 (Aug. 1987):40–43.

48. G. Westergaard and D. Fragaszy, "Self-Treatment of Wounds by a Capuchin Monkey (*Cebus Apella*)," *Human Evolution* 1, no. 6 (1987):557–62; and Bill G. Ritchie and Dorothy M. Fragaszy, "Capuchin Monkey (*Cebus Apella*) Grooms Her Infant's Wound with Tools," *American Journal of Primatology* 16 (1988):345–48.

Notes to Chapter Six

1. Renehan, *John Burroughs*, p. 59.

2. See James W. Geary, *We Need Men: The Union Draft in the Civil War* (De Kalb: Northern Illinois University Press, 1991); and Eugene C. Murdock, *One Million Men: The Civil War Draft in the North* (Madison: State Historical Society of Wisconsin, 1971). See also Frederick Turner, *Rediscovering America: John Muir in His Time and Ours* (San Francisco: Sierra Club Books, 1985), pp. 109–11.

3. See Donald Worster, *The Wealth of Nature: Environmental History and the Ecological Imagination* (New York: Oxford University Press, 1993), pp. 192–93.

4. John Muir, *The Story of My Boyhood and Youth* (1913; reprint, Madison: University of Wisconsin Press, 1965), p. 33.

5. Ibid., p. 52.

6. Quoted in Michael P. Cohen, *The Pathless Way: John Muir and American Wilderness* (Madison: University of Wisconsin Press, 1984), p. 6.

7. William Frederick Badè, *The Life and Letters of John Muir*, 2 vols. (Boston: Houghton Mifflin, 1924), vol. 1, p. 111.

8. Muir, *Boyhood and Youth*, p. 228.

9. Badè, *Life and Letters of Muir*, vol. 1, p. 118.

10. Ibid., p. 121.

11. "The Calypso Borealis. Botanical Enthusiasm. From Prof. J. D. Butler," *Boston Recorder*, Dec. 21, 1866, p. 1; quoted in Badè, *Life and Letters of Muir*, vol. 1, p. 121; and in William F. Kimes and Maymie B. Kimes, *John Muir: A Reading Bibliography* (Fresno: Panorama West Books, 1986), p. 1.

12. Badè, *Life and Letters of Muir*, vol. 1, p. 148.
13. Quoted in Linnie Marsh Wolfe, *Son of the Wilderness: The Life of John Muir* (New York: Alfred A. Knopf, 1945), p. 110.
14. See Turner, *Rediscovering America*, p. 125.
15. Badè, *Life and Letters of Muir*, vol. 1, pp. 152, 155.
16. John Muir, *A Thousand-Mile Walk to the Gulf* (1916; reprint, New York: Penguin, 1992), p. 2.
17. Badè, *Life and Letters of Muir*, vol. 1, p. 158.
18. Muir, *A Thousand-Mile Walk*, p. 90.
19. Ibid., pp. 102–3.
20. See Turner, *Rediscovering America*, p. 154.
21. Muir, *A Thousand-Mile Walk*, pp. 136–39.
22. Cohen, *The Pathless Way*, p 19
23. Muir, *A Thousand-Mile Walk*, p. 99.
24. Ibid., pp. 92, 140.
25. Badè, *Life and Letters of Muir*, vol. 1, p. 177.
26. John Muir, *The Mountains of California* (1894; reprint, San Francisco: Sierra Club Books, 1988), p. 2; and idem, *My First Summer in the Sierra* (1911; reprint, San Francisco: Sierra Club Books, 1988), p. 183.
27. Badè, *Life and Letters of Muir*, vol. 1, p. 253.
28. Turner, *Rediscovering America*, p. 215.
29. Badè, *Life and Letters of Muir*, vol. 1, p. 261.
30. John Muir, "Explorations in the Great Tuolumne Cañon," *Overland Monthly* 11 (Aug. 1873):146.
31. Badè, *Life and Letters of Muir*, vol. 1, p. 297.
32. Lennie Marsh Wolfe, ed., *John of the Mountains: The Unpublished Journals of John Muir* (Boston: Houghton Mifflin, 1938), p. 34.
33. "Yosemite Glaciers. The Ice Streams of the Great Valley. Their Progress and Present Condition—Scenes among the Glacial Beds (From an Occasional Correspondent of the Tribune) Yosemite Valley, Cal., September 28, 1871," New York *Daily Tribune*, Dec. 5, 1871, p. 8.
34. Badè, *Life and Letters of Muir*, vol. 1, p. 377.
35. John Muir, "Twenty Hill Hollow," *Overland Monthly* 9 (July 1872): 80.
36. Robert Engberg and Donald Wesling, eds., *John Muir: To Yosemite and Beyond* (Madison: University of Wisconsin Press, 1980), p. 14.
37. Wolfe, *John of the Mountains*, p. 226.
38. Badè, *Life and Letters of Muir*, vol. 2, pp. 6–7.

39. Ibid., p. 28.

40. Wolfe, *John of the Mountains*, p. 86.

41. The effects of tourists—including hunters and fishermen—on Yosemite created a double bind for Muir and other preservationists, just as it does today. On the one hand, tourists were needed if the public was going to support the creation of a national park; on the other hand, tourists contributed to the degradation of the wild. Muir's views became more generous as he grew older, and he always maintained a basic optimism that once the visitor acquired "wilderness manners," he or she could not help but benefit from the wilderness experiences and the wilderness would not be hurt by such a visitor. See especially Fox, *John Muir and His Legacy*; and Cohen, *The Pathless Way*.

42. John Muir, *The Yosemite* (1912; reprint, San Francisco: Sierra Club Books, 1988), p. 52.

43. Muir, *The Mountains of California*, pp. 194–95.

44. Turner, *Rediscovering America*, p. 273.

45. See, among others, Alfred Runte, *National Parks: The American Experience* (Lincoln: University of Nebraska Press, 1979).

46. See, among others, Roderick Nash, *Wilderness and the American Mind*, rev. ed. (New Haven: Yale University Press, 1973), pp. 130–32.

47. California maintained jurisdiction over Yosemite until 1905, and even today the commitment to preservation of Yosemite's wilderness is in doubt. See Alfred Runte, "Planning Yosemite's Future: A Historical Retrospective," in Richard J. Orsi, Alfred Runte, and Marlene Smith-Baranzini, eds., *Yosemite and Sequoia: A Century of California National Parks* (Berkeley: University of California Press, 1993), pp. 121–30.

48. "The American Forests," *Atlantic Monthly* 80 (Aug. 1897), p. 157.

49. Barrus, *Life and Letters of Burroughs*, p. 59.

50. Turner, *Rediscovering America*, p. 320. Various versions of Muir's remarks have been reported. Among these, Muir is said to have chided, "Why, I am richer than Harriman. I have all the money I want and he hasn't." See Edwin Way Teale, *The Wilderness World of John Muir* (Boston: Houghton Mifflin, 1954), p. xvi.

51. Among the exaggerations and attacks on Muir were San Francisco Mayor John D. Phelan's charge that Muir "would sacrifice his own

family for the preservation of beauty. He considers human life very cheap, and he considers the works of God superior." See Fox, *John Muir and His Legacy*, p. 142.

52. Muir, *The Mountains of California*, p. 102.
53. Wolfe, *John of the Mountains*, p. 434.
54. Turner, *Rediscovering America*, p. 340.
55. Muir, *The Yosemite*, p. 19.
56. Wolfe, *John of the Mountains*, p. 438.

Notes to Chapter Seven

1. For a sympathetic account of the Boone and Crockett Club's contribution to conservation see John F. Reiger, *American Sportsmen and the Origins of Conservation* (New York: Winchester Press, 1975).

2. Quoted in Alfred Runte, *National Parks: The American Experience* (Lincoln: University of Nebraska Press, 1979), p. 70.

3. Quoted in Turner, *Rediscovering America*, p. 323.

4. Quoted in Fox, *John Muir and His Legacy*, p. 125.

5. Quoted in ibid.

6. Mary Austin, *Earth Horizon: An Autobiography* (Boston: Houghton Mifflin, 1932), p. 298.

7. Austin's collaboration with Ansel Adams on *Taos Pueblo*, published by Grabhorn Press in 1930, essentially launched Adams' career. Austin condescendingly referred to Adams as the "illustrator" for her book. See Esther Lanigan Stineman, *Mary Austin: Song of a Maverick* (New Haven: Yale University Press, 1989), p. 194.

8. Austin, *Earth Horizon*, p. 112.

9. Ibid.

10. Ibid., p. 195.

11. Augusta Fink, *Monterey* (San Francisco: Chronicle Books, 1972), p. 241; quoted in Stineman, *Mary Austin*, pp. 93–94.

12. Quoted in Stineman, *Mary Austin*, p. 106.

13. Ibid., p. 154.

14. John C. Van Dyke, *The Desert* (1903; reprint, Salt Lake City: Peregrine Smith, 1980), p. 193. Van Dyke's book was extremely successful when it appeared. At times rhapsodic, at other times stumbling, it is replete with what he called the aesthetic of "sensuous seeing." Van Dyke concluded that "the love of Nature is after all an acquired taste. One begins by admiring the Hudson-River landscape and ends

by loving the desolation of Sahara" (p. viii). But see also Peter Wild,
ed., *The Autobiography of John C. Van Dyke* (Salt Lake City: University of Utah Press, 1993).

15. Van Dyke, too, praised the beauty of rattlesnakes and lizards, as well
    as the coyote: "Even that desert tramp, the coyote, is entitled to ad-
    miration for the graceful way he can slip through patches of cactus.
    The fault is not in the subject. It is not vulgar or ugly. The trouble is
    that we perhaps have not the proper angle of vision. If we understood
    all, we should admire all"; *The Desert*, p. 173.

16. Austin, *Earth Horizon*, p. 368.

17. Curt Meine, *Aldo Leopold: His Life and Work* (Madison: University of
    Wisconsin Press, 1988), p. 90.

18. Aldo Leopold, *A Sand County Almanac and Sketches Here and There*
    (1949; reprint, New York: Oxford University Press, 1989), p. 129.

19. Curt Meine, "Aldo Leopold's Early Years," in J. Baird Callicott, ed.,
    *Companion to A Sand County Almanac: Interpretive and Critical Es-
    says* (Madison: University of Wisconsin Press, 1987), p. 27; see also
    Meine, *Leopold: Life and Work*, pp. 93–94.

20. Susan L. Flader, *Thinking like a Mountain: Aldo Leopold and the Evo-
    lution of an Ecological Attitude toward Deer, Wolves, and Forests* (Co-
    lumbia: University of Missouri Press, 1974), p. 10.

21. Meine, *Leopold: Life and Work*, p. 126.

22. Aldo Leopold, "Some Fundamentals of Conservation in the South-
    west," in Leopold, *The River of the Mother of God and Other Essays*, ed.
    Susan L. Flader and J. Baird Callicott (Madison: University of Wis-
    consin Press, 1991), pp. 86–97.

23. Max Oelschlaeger, *The Idea of Wilderness: From Prehistory to the Age
    of Ecology* (New Haven: Yale University Press, 1991), p. 213. See also
    J. Baird Callicott, "The Conceptual Foundations of the Land Ethic,"
    in Callicott, *Companion to A Sand County Almanac*, p. 200; and
    Meine, *Leopold: Life and Work*, p. 214.

24. Quoted in Roderick Nash, "Aldo Leopold's Intellectual Heritage," in
    Callicott, *Companion to A Sand County Almanac*, p. 77.

25. Worster, *Nature's Economy*, pp. 29–55.

26. See Oelschlaeger's assertion that Leopold was experiencing "cogni-
    tive dissonance" at this time; *The Idea of Wilderness*, pp. 214, 425 n.
    32.

27. Two years before, Leopold had made a philosophical break with
    those in the U.S. Forest Service and in the populace at large who ad-

vocated highest recreation use for all public lands—which meant automobile tourism, hotels, and concessions. In an article in the *Journal of Forestry*, Leopold suggested granting protected status to the Gila River area of New Mexico through a paradoxical argument that "highest use demands its preservation." As Leopold's biographer, Curt Meine, suggests, Leopold was showing that the line between utility and preservation was not so simple. Leopold was a complicated man—a hunter yet a conservationist, a believer in land use yet a believer in preservation, a defender of beauty for its own sake yet a disciplined scientist, a technician, and a pragmatist. And during this time he was attempting to reconcile the opposing parts of himself.

28. Muir, *Boyhood and Youth*, pp. 53, 56.
29. Meine, *Leopold: Life and Work*, pp. 329 30.
30. Ibid., p. 330.
31. Aldo Leopold, "The State of the Profession," in *The River of the Mother of God*, pp. 276–80.
32. See Dennis Ribbens, "The Making of *A Sand County Almanac*," in Callicott, *Companion to A Sand County Almanac*, pp. 91–109.
33. See John Tallmadge, "Anatomy of a Classic," in Callicott, *Companion to A Sand County Almanac*, pp. 110–27.
34. Worster, *The Wealth of Nature*, p. 182.
35. J. Baird Callicott, "The Land Aesthetic," in Callicott, *Companion to A Sand County Almanac*, p. 157.
36. See especially Nash, "Aldo Leopold's Intellectual Heritage," pp. 63–88.
37. Meine, *Leopold: Life and Work*, pp. 517–20.

Notes to Chapter Eight

1. Wallace Stegner, "Living on Our Principal," *Wilderness*, Spring 1985, p. 16.
2. John Burroughs, *Accepting the Universe* (Boston: Houghton Mifflin, 1920), pp. 32, 34.
3. Roderick Frazier Nash, *The Rights of Nature: A History of Environmental Ethics* (Madison: University of Wisconsin Press, 1989), p. 73.
4. The story of the attacks on *Silent Spring* is told in several books, including Frank Graham, Jr., *Since Silent Spring* (Boston: Houghton Mifflin, 1970), pp. 53–68.

5. *Time*, April 24, 1964, p. 73. See also Paul Brooks, *The House of Life: Rachel Carson at Work* (Boston: Houghton Mifflin, 1972), p. 298.

6. See, for example, Robert B. Downs, *Books That Changed America* (New York: Macmillan, 1970), p. 260. Many people recognized the landmark importance of *Silent Spring* from the moment it was written. In Senate hearings, for example, Ernest Gruening of Alaska compared it with *Uncle Tom's Cabin*.

7. See Fox, *John Muir and His Legacy*, p. 292; and Nash, *The Rights of Nature*, p. 78.

8. Worster, *The Wealth of Nature*, pp. 178–79.

9. Mary A. McCay, *Rachel Carson* (New York: Twayne, 1993), p. 3.

10. Brooks, *The House of Life*, p. 17.

11. McCay, *Rachel Carson*, p. 23; and Philip Sterling, *Sea and Earth: The Life of Rachel Carson* (New York: Crowell, 1970), pp. 39–40.

12. Brooks, *The House of Life*, pp. 20–21.

13. McCay, *Rachel Carson*, p. 25.

14. Rachel Carson, *The Sense of Wonder* (New York: Harper & Row, 1965), p. 34.

15. Brooks, *The House of Life*, p. 69.

16. Ibid., p. 110.

17. Leopold was deeply affected by the war, and its outcome may well have driven him more quickly toward his conclusions about a land ethic. In this regard he wrote, "science has so sharpened the fighter's sword that it is impossible for him to cut his enemy without cutting himself"; Meine, *Leopold: Life and Work*, p. 473.

18. Brooks, *The House of Life*, p. 122.

19. Rachel Carson, *The Sea Around Us* (New York: Oxford University Press, 1951; rev. ed., 1961), pp. 13–14.

20. Quoted in Sterling, *Sea and Earth*, pp. 132–33.

21. Quoted in Brooks, *The House of Life*, pp. 128–29.

22. Quoted in ibid., p. 132.

23. Quoted in ibid., p. 159.

24. Quoted in ibid., p. 160.

25. Rachel Carson, *The Edge of the Sea* (Boston: Houghton Mifflin, 1955).

26. Quoted in Brooks, *The House of Life*, p. 151.

27. Interview, *Washington Star Pictorial Magazine*, March 8, 1953; quoted in McCay, *Rachel Carson*, p. 59.

28. Quoted in Brooks, *The House of Life*, pp. 207–8.

29. Quoted in ibid., p. 228.

30. See, for example, James Whorton, *Before Silent Spring: Pesticides and Public Health in Pre-DDT America* (Princeton: Princeton University Press, 1974).

31. Brooks, *The House of Life*, p. 265.

32. Quoted in ibid., pp. 271–72.

33. Albert Schweitzer, *Out of My Life and Thought* (New York: Holt, 1933), pp. 185–86.

34. Quoted in Brooks, *The House of Life*, pp. 315–16.

35. Quoted in ibid., p. 314.

36. Quoted in ibid., pp. 326–27.

37. Speech to the Women's National Press Club, quoted in Graham, *Since Silent Spring*, p. 53.

Notes to Chapter Nine

1. See Edmund A. Schofield, "John Muir's Yankee Friends and Mentors: The New England Connection," *Pacific Historian* 29, no. 2–3 (1985):65–89.

2. Edward Abbey, *The Journey Home* (New York: Dutton, 1977), p. 88.

3. Edward Abbey, *Beyond the Wall* (New York: Holt, 1984), p. 195.

4. Abbey, *The Journey Home*, p. xii.

5. Edward Abbey, *Down the River* (New York: Dutton, 1982), p. 57.

6. Abbey, *The Journey Home*, pp. 1–2.

7. Ibid., p. 2.

8. James Hepworth and Gregory McNamee, eds., *Resist Much, Obey Little: Some Notes on Edward Abbey* (Tucson: Harbinger House, 1989), p. 97; Abbey, *The Journey Home*, p. 10.

9. Abbey, *The Journey Home*, p. 211.

10. Edward Abbey, *Abbey's Road* (New York: Dutton, 1979), pp. 149–50; Abbey, *The Journey Home*, p. 212.

11. Quoted in Jack Loeffler, "Edward Abbey, Anarchism, and the Environment," *Western American Literature* 28, no. 1 (Spring 1993):43–49.

12. Edward Abbey, *Desert Solitaire: A Season in the Wilderness* (New York: Simon & Schuster, 1968).

13. See Ann Ronald, *The New West of Edward Abbey* (Albuquerque: University of New Mexico Press, 1982), p. 66.

14. Abbey, *Abbey's Road*, p. xv.

15. This allusion to Robinson Jeffers' poem "Hurt Hawks" is an example

of the way Abbey invites other writers into his narratives. Jeffers says, "I'd sooner, except the penalties, kill a man than a hawk"; see *Cawdor and Other Poems* (New York: Liveright, 1928), pp. 153–54.

16. Interview with Judy Nolte Lensink in Stephen Trimble, ed., *Words from the Land: Encounters with Natural History Writing* (Salt Lake City: Peregrine Smith, 1988), p. 27.

17. For a discussion of the "presence" of one work in another—and how this offers a "critique" superior to conventional criticism—see George Steiner, *Real Presences* (Chicago: University of Chicago Press, 1989). Besides allusions to other nature writers, Abbey made many other figures "present" in his adventures, including Saint Francis, Saint Augustine, Rilke, Spinoza, Shakespeare, and Nietzsche.

18. See Ronald, *New West of Abbey*, pp. 66–67, for a discussion of Abbey's use of the continuous present and for many other insights. For a discussion of the voices in *Desert Solitaire* see David Copland Morris, "Celebration and Irony: The Polyphonic Voice of Edward Abbey's *Desert Solitaire*," *Western American Literature* 28, no. 1 (Spring 1993):21–32.

19. It is possible that Abbey was alluding to Thoreau in more ways than one with this parable. See Thoreau's lecture "Night and Moonlight," printed posthumously in *Excursions*, vol. 9 of *The Writings of Henry David Thoreau* (Boston: Houghton Mifflin, 1893); and William Howarth, "Successor to *Walden*? Thoreau's Moonlight—An Intended Course of Lectures," *Proof* 2 (1972):89–115. It is also hard to miss the fact that at one point the horse seems to be all "gleaming eyeball," much like Emerson's "transparent eyeball."

20. The definition of "parable" has filled many thick volumes of biblical and literary criticism. A definition with interesting implications for Abbey's work, and for much other nature writing, can be found in Bernard Harrison, "Parable and Transcendence," in *Ways of Reading the Bible*, ed. Michael Wadsworth (Sussex: Harvester Press, 1981), pp. 190–212.

21. See, for example, *Down the River*, where Abbey specifically returns to the story of Old Moon-Eye, p. 18; but the theme recurs in his novels as well as in his nonfiction. There are many other possible readings of this parable. One is simply that nature in its wild state can be ugly, stubborn, and indifferent to man; man can approach it with good intentions, but nature's laws are not compatible with man's desires.

They remain distinct, each unknowable to the other, each choosing its own way of dying.

22. Sharon Cameron, *Writing Nature: Henry Thoreau's Journal* (New York: Oxford University Press, 1985), p. 29.

23. Abbey, *The Journey Home*, p. 22.

24. Once again Abbey introduces a reference to Robinson Jeffers in the image of mankind's finitude seen through the eyes of the soaring bird, as in section XV of "Cawdor." For a discussion of Abbey's relationship to Jeffers see Morris, "Celebration and Irony"; see also James I. McClintock, "Edward Abbey's 'Antidote to Despair,'" *Critique* 31 (Fall 1989):41–54; and Paul T. Bryant, "The Structure and Unity of *Desert Solitaire*," *Western American Literature* 28, no. 1 (Spring 1993):3–19. See Abbey's deliberate linking of horse and bird through Thoreau in *Down the River*, p. 30.

25. Edward Abbey, *Slumgullion Stew* (New York: Dutton, 1984), p. x.

26. Edward Abbey, *Appalachian Wilderness* (New York: Dutton, 1970).

27. In *Cactus Country* he wrote, "I am not a naturalist; what I hope to evoke through words here is the way things *feel* on a stormy desert afternoon, the exact shade of color in shadows on the warm rock, the brightness of October, the rust and silence and echoes of human history along dusty desert roads, the fragrance of burning mesquite, and a few other simple, ordinary, inexplicable things like that"; p. 21.

28. Abbey, *The Journey Home*, p. xiv.

29. Abbey, *Down the River*, p. 29.

30. Abbey, *Abbey's Road*, pp. xxi, xxiii.

31. Abbey, *Beyond the Wall*, p. xvi.

32. Abbey, *The Journey Home*, p. 223.

33. See a fine discussion of *The Monkey Wrench Gang* in Ronald, *New West of Abbey*, pp. 181–209.

34. See, for example, Abbey's "Foreward!" to Dave Foreman and B. Haywood, eds., *Ecodefense: A Field Guide to Monkeywrenching*, 2d ed. (Tucson: Ned Ludd Books, 1987).

35. Edward Hoaglund, "Edward Abbey: Standing Tough in the Desert," *New York Times Book Review*, May 7, 1989, pp. 44–45.

36. Abbey, *Abbey's Road*, p. xxiii.

37. Hoagland, "Edward Abbey," p. 45.

38. Hepworth and McNamee, *Resist Much, Obey Little*, p. viii.

39. Abbey, *Beyond the Wall*, pp. xvi–xvii.

Notes to Chapter Ten

1. Bill McKibben, *The End of Nature* (New York: Random House, 1989).

2. See, for example, Lynn Margulis and Edwin Dobb, "Untimely Requiem," *The Sciences* 30, no. 1 (Jan./Feb. 1990): 44–49.

3. One of the greatest mass extinctions occurred when an early form of photosynthesizers "polluted" the atmosphere so completely with their respiration that all creatures incapable of adapting—creatures existing on the planet for perhaps a billion years—were finally wiped out. The exhalation of these early polluters who so transformed the Earth's atmosphere was the toxic element oxygen.

4. Laura Tangley, "Biological Diversity Goes Public," *BioScience* 36, no. 11 (Dec. 1985):708–9; and E. O. Wilson, "The Biological Diversity Crisis," ibid., pp. 700–706. One reason it is difficult to measure the extent of the current mass extinction of species is that no one knows the number of species on Earth. Although the figure of 30 million is often given, some scientists suggest there may be as many as 50 million species of insects alone. According to Wilson, through rainforest destruction the rate of extinction "is now about 400 times that recorded through recent geological time and is accelerating rapidly. Under the best conditions, the reduction of diversity seems destined to approach that of the great natural catastrophes at the end of the Paleozoic and Mesozoic eras, in other words, the most extreme for 65 million years." Moreover, the prevalent mass extinctions may have even worse consequences than did the catastrophes caused by large meteorite strikes because at that time "most of the plant diversity survived; now, for the first time, it is being mostly destroyed."

5. See, for example, Scott Russell Sanders, "Speaking a Word for Nature," *Michigan Quarterly Review* 26 (Fall 1987): 648–62.

6. In contrast, as Yi-fu Tuan points out, "in the Christian tradition sanctifying power is invested in man, God's vice-regent, rather than in nature. The church does not adapt to the spirit of the land; it imparts spirit to its environs." *Topophilia: A Study of Environmental Perception, Attitudes, and Values* (Englewood Cliffs, N.J.: Prentice-Hall, 1974; rev. ed., New York: Columbia University Press, 1990), p. 148.

7. Vincent Scully, *The Earth, the Temple, and the Gods* (New Haven: Yale University Press, 1962; rev. ed., New York: Praeger, 1969).

8. Henry David Thoreau, *The Natural History Essays* (Salt Lake City: Peregrine Smith, 1980), pp. 107, 113.

9. See Robert S. Root-Bernstein, "Setting the Stage for Discovery," *The Sciences* 28 (May/June 1988):33.

10. Thoreau, *Journal*, Sept. 2, 1851.

BIBLIOGRAPHY AND

FURTHER READINGS

Abbey, Edward. *Abbey's Road*. New York: Dutton, 1979.

———. *Beyond the Wall*. New York: Holt, 1984.

———. *Desert Solitaire. A Season in the Wilderness*. New York: Simon & Schuster, 1968.

———. *Down the River*. New York: Dutton, 1982.

———. *The Journey Home*. New York: Dutton, 1977.

———. *One Life at a Time, Please*. New York: Holt, 1988.

Allen, David Elliston. *The Naturalist in Britain: A Social History*. London: Allen Lane, 1976.

Anderson, H. Allen. *The Chief: Ernest Thompson Seton and the Changing West*. College Station: Texas A & M University Press, 1986.

Arthur, Elizabeth. *Island Sojourn*. New York: Harper & Row, 1980.

Austin, Mary. *Earth Horizon: An Autobiography*. Boston: Houghton Mifflin, 1932.

———. *The Flock*. Boston: Houghton Mifflin, 1906.

———. *The Land of Little Rain*. Boston: Houghton Mifflin, 1903.

Badè, William Frederick. *The Life and Letters of John Muir*. 2 vols. Boston: Houghton Mifflin, 1924.

Bailey, Liberty Hyde. *Wind and Weather*. New York: Scribner's, 1916.

Baker, John. *The Peregrine*. Moscow: University of Idaho Press, 1967.

Bakker, Elna. *An Island Called California*. Berkeley: University of California Press, 1971.

Barbier, Carl Paul. *William Gilpin: His Drawings, Teaching, and Theory of the Picturesque*. Oxford: Oxford University Press, 1963.

Barrette, Roy. *A Countryman's Journal.* New York: Rand, 1981.

Barrus, Clara. *John Burroughs, Boy and Man.* Boston: Houghton Mifflin, 1928.

―――. *Our Friend John Burroughs.* Boston: Houghton Mifflin, 1914.

―――. *Whitman and Burroughs: Comrades.* Boston: Houghton Mifflin, 1931.

―――. ed., *The Heart of Burroughs's Journals.* Boston: Houghton Mifflin, 1928.

―――. *The Life and Letters of John Burroughs.* 2 vols. Boston: Houghton Mifflin, 1925.

Bass, Rick. *Wild to the Heart.* Harrisburg, Pa.: Stackpole, 1987.

―――. *Winter: Notes from Montana.* Boston: Houghton Mifflin, 1991.

Bates, Marston. *The Forest and the Sea.* New York: Scribner's, 1950.

―――. *A Jungle in the House.* New York: Walker, 1970.

Bedichek, Roy. *Adventures with a Texas Naturalist.* Garden City, N.Y.: Doubleday, 1947.

―――. *Karankaway Country.* Garden City, N.Y.: Doubleday, 1950.

Beebe, William. *Half-Mile Down.* New York: Harcourt, 1934.

―――. *The Log of the Sun.* New York: Holt, 1906.

Berry, Wendell. *The Long-Legged House.* New York: Harcourt, Brace, 1965.

―――. *The Unsettling of America.* New York: Avon, 1978.

Beston, Henry. *The Outermost House.* Garden City, N.Y.: Doubleday, 1928.

Bodsworth, Fred. *The Last Curlew.* New York: Dodd, 1955.

Bohn, David. *Rambles through an Alaskan Wild.* Santa Barbara: Capra, 1979.

Bonner, John T. *The Evolution of Culture in Animals.* Princeton: Princeton University Press, 1980.

Borland, Hal. *Beyond Your Doorstep.* New York: Alfred A. Knopf, 1962.

―――. *Hal Borland's Book of Days.* New York: Alfred A. Knopf, 1978.

Boudreau, Gordon V. "Henry David Thoreau, William Gilpin, and the Metaphysical Ground of the Picturesque." *American Literature* 45 (1973):357–69.

Bowden, Charles. *Blue Desert.* Tucson: University of Arizona Press, 1986.

―――. *Desierto.* New York: W. W. Norton, 1991.

―――. *Red Line.* New York: W. W. Norton, 1989.

Brewster, William. *Concord River.* Cambridge, Mass.: Harvard University Press, 1937.

————. *October Farm*. Cambridge, Mass.: Harvard University Press, 1936.

Brooks, Paul. *The House of Life: Rachel Carson at Work*. Boston: Houghton Mifflin, 1972.

————. *The Pursuit of Wilderness*. Boston: Houghton Mifflin, 1971.

————. *Roadless Area*. New York: Alfred A. Knopf, 1964.

————. *The View from Lincoln Hill*. Boston: Houghton Mifflin, 1976.

Brower, Kenneth. *The Starship & the Canoe*. New York: Bantam, 1979.

————. *Wake of the Whale*. New York: Friends of the Earth, 1979.

Brown, Bruce. *Mountain in the Clouds*. New York: Simon & Schuster, 1982.

Burroughs, John. *The Writings of John Burroughs*. 23 vols. Boston: Houghton Mifflin, 1904–1923.

Callicott, J. Baird, ed. *Companion to A Sand County Almanac: Interpretive and Critical Essays*. Madison: University of Wisconsin Press, 1987.

Caras, Roger. *The Endless Migrations*. New York: Dutton, 1985.

Carr, Archie. *The Windward Road*. Gainesville: University Press of Florida, 1979.

Carrighar, Sally. *Icebound Summer*. New York: Alfred A. Knopf, 1953.

————. *One Day on Beetle Rock*. New York: Alfred A. Knopf, 1944.

————. *One Day at Teton Marsh*. New York: Alfred A. Knopf, 1947.

————. *Wild Heritage*. Boston: Houghton Mifflin, 1965.

Carson, Rachel. *The Edge of the Sea*. Boston: Houghton Mifflin, 1955.

————. *The Sea Around Us*. New York: Oxford University Press, 1951; rev. ed., 1961.

————. *The Sense of Wonder*. New York: Harper & Row, 1965.

————. *Silent Spring*. Boston: Houghton Mifflin, 1962.

————. *Under the Sea-Wind*. New York: Simon & Schuster, 1941.

Chadwick, Douglas. *A Beast the Color of Winter*. San Francisco: Sierra Club Books, 1983.

Cohen, Michael P. *The Pathless Way: John Muir and American Wilderness*. Madison: University of Wisconsin Press, 1984.

Cowles, Raymond. *Desert Journal*. Berkeley: University of California Press, 1978.

————. *Zulu Journal*. Berkeley: University of California Press, 1959.

Craighead, Frank. *Track of the Grizzly*. San Francisco: Sierra Club Books, 1979.

Crisler, Lois. *Arctic Wild*. New York: Harper, 1958.

Daniel, John. *The Trail Home*. New York: Pantheon, 1992.

Davis, H. L. *Kettle of Fire*. New York: Morrow, 1957.

Daws, Gavan. *Hawaii: Islands of Life*. Honolulu: Signature, 1988.

Dean, Barbara. *Wellspring*. Washington, D.C.: Island Press, 1979.

Dethier, Vincent G. *Crickets and Katydids, Concerts and Solos*. Cambridge, Mass.: Harvard University Press, 1992.

———. *The Ecology of a Summer House*. Amherst: University of Massachusetts Press, 1984.

DeVoto, Bernard, ed. *The Journals of Lewis and Clark*. Boston: Houghton Mifflin, 1953.

Dillard, Annie. *Pilgrim at Tinker Creek*. New York: Harper & Row, 1974.

———. *Teaching a Stone to Talk*. New York: Harper & Row, 1982.

Dobie, J. Frank. *The Mustangs*. Boston: Little, Brown, 1952.

———. *Rattlesnakes*. Boston: Little, Brown, 1965.

———. *The Voice of the Coyote*. Boston: Little, Brown, 1949.

Doig, Ivan. *Winter Brothers*. New York: Harcourt Brace, 1980.

Douglas, William O. *A Farewell to Texas*. New York: McGraw-Hill, 1967.

———. *My Wilderness: East to Katahdin*. Garden City, N.Y.: Doubleday, 1961.

———. *My Wilderness: The Pacific West*. Garden City, N.Y.: Doubleday, 1960.

Doyle, Helen MacKnight. *Mary Austin: Woman of Genius*. New York: Gotham House, 1939.

Dubos, René. *A God Within*. New York: Scribner's, 1973.

Eastman, Charles. *From the Deep Woods to Civilization*. Boston: Little, Brown, 1916.

Eckhart, Allan W. *Wild Season*. Boston: Little, Brown, 1967.

Ehrlich, Gretel. *The Solace of Open Spaces*. New York: Viking, 1985.

Eiseley, Loren. *The Immense Journey*. New York: Random House, 1953.

———. *The Night Country*. New York: Scribner's, 1971.

———. *Notes of an Alchemist*. New York: Scribner's, 1974.

———. *The Unexpected Universe*. New York: Harcourt Brace, 1972.

Enberg, Robert, and Donald Wesling, eds. *John Muir: To Yosemite and Beyond*. Madison: University of Wisconsin Press, 1980.

Errington, Paul. *Of Men and Marshes*. New York: Macmillan, 1957.

Fabre, Jean-Henri. *The Mason-Bees*. New York: Dodd, Mead, 1914.

Farber, Thomas. *On Water*. New York: Ecco, 1994.

Finch, Robert. *Common Ground*. Boston: Godine, 1981.

———. *Outlands: Journeys to the Outer Edges of Cape Cod*. Boston: Godine, 1986.

———. *The Primal Place*. New York: W. W. Norton, 1983.

Fink, Augusta. *I-Mary: A Biography of Mary Austin*. Tucson: University of Arizona Press, 1983.

Flader, Susan L. *Thinking like a Mountain: Aldo Leopold and the Evolution of an Ecological Attitude toward Deer, Wolves, and Forests*. Columbia: University of Missouri Press, 1974.

Fletcher, Colin. *The Man Who Walked through Time*. New York: Random House/Vintage, 1972.

———. *The Thousand-Mile Summer*. San Diego: Howell-North, 1964.

Fox, Stephen. *John Muir and His Legacy: The American Conservation Movement*. Boston: Little, Brown, 1981.

Galvin, James. *The Meadow*. New York: Holt, 1992.

Gartner, Carol B. *Rachel Carson*. New York: Ungar, 1983

Golemba, Henry. *Thoreau's Wild Rhetoric*. New York: New York University Press, 1990.

Graham, Frank, Jr. *Since Silent Spring*. Boston: Houghton Mifflin, 1970.

Graves, John. *From a Limestone Ledge*. New York: Alfred A. Knopf, 1980.

———. *Goodbye to a River*. New York: Alfred A. Knopf, 1960.

———. *Hardscrabble*. New York: Alfred A. Knopf, 1974.

Griffin, Donald R. *Animal Minds*. Chicago: University of Chicago Press, 1992.

———. *Animal Thinking*. Cambridge, Mass.: Harvard University Press, 1984.

Grinnell, George Bird. *American Big Game and Its Haunts*. New York: Forest and Stream, 1904.

Haines, John. *The Stars, the Snow, the Fire*. New York: Simon & Schuster/Washington Square Press, 1989.

Halle, Louis J. *Spring in Washington*. New York: Sloane, 1947.

Hansen, Gunnar. *Islands at the Edge of Time*. Washington, D.C.: Island Press, 1993.

Hay, John. *The Great Beach*. Garden City, N.Y.: Doubleday, 1964.

———. *In Defense of Nature*. Boston: Little, Brown, 1969.

———. *Nature's Year*. Garden City, N.Y.: Doubleday, 1961.

———. *The Run*. Garden City, N.Y.: Doubleday, 1959.

———. *Spirit of Survival*. New York: Dutton, 1974.

———. *The Undiscovered Country*. New York: W. W. Norton, 1981.

Hepworth, James, and Gregory McNamee, eds. *Resist Much, Obey Little: Some Notes on Edward Abbey*. Tucson: Harbinger House, 1989.

Hildebidle, John. *Thoreau: A Naturalist's Liberty*. Cambridge, Mass.: Harvard University Press, 1983.

Hildebrand, John. *Reading the River: A Journey Down the Yukon*. New York: Houghton Mifflin, 1989.

Hipple, John Walter, Jr. *The Beautiful, the Sublime, and the Picturesque in Eighteenth-Century British Aesthetic Theory*. Carbondale: Southern Illinois University Press, 1957.

Hoagland, Edward. *The Courage of Turtles*. New York: Random House, 1970.

———. *Heart's Desire*. New York: Simon & Schuster, 1988.

———. *Notes from the Century Before*. New York: Random House, 1969.

———. *Red Wolves and Black Bears*. New York: Random House, 1976.

———. *Walking the Dead Diamond River*. New York: Random House, 1973.

Hoover, Helen. *The Gift of the Deer*. New York: Alfred A. Knopf, 1966.

———. *The Long-Shadowed Forest*. New York: Crowell, 1963.

———. *A Place in the Woods*. New York: Alfred A. Knopf, 1969.

Hornaday, William Temple. *Our Vanishing Wildlife*. New York: Scribner's, 1913.

Hubbel, Sue. *A Country Year*. New York: Random House, 1983.

Jaeger, Edmund C. *Our Desert Neighbors*. Stanford: Stanford University Press, 1950.

Janovy, John, Jr. *Back in Keith County*. Lincoln: University of Nebraska Press, 1983.

———. *Keith County Journal*. New York: St. Martin's, 1978.

———. *Yellowlegs*. New York: St. Martin's, 1980.

Johnson, Josephine. *The Inland Island*. New York: Simon & Schuster, 1969.

Johnson, Walter. *Gilbert White: Pioneer, Poet, and Stylist*. London: John Murray, 1928.

Johnson, William C., Jr. *What Thoreau Said: Walden and the Unsayable*. Moscow: University of Idaho Press, 1991.

Kappel-Smith, Diana. *Wintering*. New York: McGraw-Hill, 1984.

Keith, W. J. *The Rural Tradition: A Study of the Non-fiction Prose Writers of the English Countryside*. Toronto: University of Toronto Press, 1974.

Keller, Betty. *Black Wolf: The Life of Ernest Thompson Seton*. Toronto: Douglas & McIntyre, 1984.

Kennedy, William Sloane. *The Real John Burroughs*. New York: Funk & Wagnalls, 1924.

Kohl, Judith, and Herbert Kohl. *The View from the Oak*. San Francisco: Sierra Club Books, 1977.

Krutch, Joseph Wood. *The Desert Year*. New York: Sloane, 1946.

———. *The Forgotten Peninsula*. New York: Sloane, 1961.

———. *Grand Canyon*. New York: Sloane, 1958.

———. *The Twelve Seasons*. New York: Sloane, 1949.

———. *The Voice of the Desert*. New York: Morrow, 1954.

La Bastille, Anne. *Woodswoman*. New York: Dutton, 1976.

Lehmberg, Paul. *In the Strong Woods*. New York: St. Martin's, 1980.

Leopold, Aldo. *The River of the Mother of God and Other Essays*. Edited by Susan L. Flader and J. Baird Callicott. Madison: University of Wisconsin Press, 1991.

———. *Round River*. Edited by Luna Leopold. New York: Oxford University Press, 1953.

———. *A Sand County Almanac and Sketches Here and There*. 1949; reprint. New York: Oxford University Press, 1989.

Lopez, Barry. *Arctic Dreams*. New York: Scribner's, 1986.

———. *Of Wolves and Men*. New York: Scribner's, 1978.

———. *Desert Notes*. Kansas City: Sheed, Andrews & McMeel, 1976.

———. *River Notes*. Kansas City: Sheed, Andrews & McMeel, 1979.

Lueders, Edward. *The Clam Lake Papers*. New York: Harper & Row, 1977.

Lutts, Ralph H. *The Nature Fakers: Wildlife, Science, and Sentiment*. Denver: Fulcrum, 1990.

Madson, John. *Where the Sky Begins*. Boston: Houghton Mifflin, 1982.

Marshall, Robert. *Alaska Wilderness*. Berkeley: University of California Press, 1970.

Matthiessen, F. O. *American Renaissance: Art and Expression in the Age of Emerson and Whitman*. New York: Oxford University Press, 1941.

Matthiessen, Peter. *Sand Rivers*. New York: Viking, 1981.

———. *The Snow Leopard*. New York: Viking, 1978.

———. *The Tree Where Man Was Born*. New York: Crescent, 1972.

Maxwell, Gavin. *Ring of Bright Water*. New York: Dutton, 1960.

McCann, Garth. *Edward Abbey*. Boise: Boise State University, 1977.

McCay, Mary A. *Rachel Carson*. New York: Twayne, 1993.

McPhee, John. *Basin and Range*. New York: Farrar, Straus & Giroux, 1981.

———. *Coming into the Country*. New York: Farrar, Straus & Giroux, 1977.

————. *Encounters with the Archdruid*. New York: Farrar, Straus & Giroux, 1971.

McNamee, Thomas. *The Grizzly Bear*. New York: Alfred A. Knopf, 1984.

Meine, Curt. *Aldo Leopold: His Life and Work*. Madison: University of Wisconsin Press, 1988.

Mills, Enos. *In Beaver World*. Boston: Houghton Mifflin, 1913; reprint, Lincoln: University of Nebraska Press, 1990.

Mitchell, John Hanson, *Ceremonial Time*. Garden City, N.Y.: Doubleday, 1984.

Momaday, N. Scott. *The Way to Rainy Mountain*. Albuquerque: University of New Mexico Press, 1976.

Muir, John. *The Mountains of California*. New York: Century, 1894; reprint, San Francisco: Sierra Club Books, 1988.

————. *My First Summer in the Sierra*. Boston: Houghton Mifflin, 1911; reprint, San Francisco: Sierra Club Books, 1988.

————. *Our National Parks*. Boston: Houghton Mifflin, 1901.

————. *The Story of My Boyhood and Youth*. Boston: Houghton Mifflin, 1913; reprint, Madison: University of Wisconsin Press, 1965.

————. *A Thousand-Mile Walk to the Gulf*. Boston: Houghton Mifflin, 1916; reprint, New York: Penguin, 1992.

————. *Travels in Alaska*. Boston: Houghton Mifflin, 1915; reprint, San Francisco: Sierra Club Books, 1988.

————. *The Yosemite*. New York: Century, 1912; reprint, San Francisco: Sierra Club Books, 1988.

Murie, Adolf. *A Naturalist in Alaska*. New York: Devin-Adair, 1961.

Murie, Margaret. *Island Between*. Fairbanks: University of Alaska Press, 1977.

————. *Two in the Far North*. New York: Alfred A. Knopf, 1962.

Murie, Olas, and Margaret Murie. *Wapiti Wilderness*. New York: Alfred A. Knopf, 1966.

Nabhan, Gary. *The Desert Smells like Rain*. San Francisco: North Point, 1982.

————. *Gathering the Desert*. Tucson: University of Arizona Press, 1985.

Nelson, Richard. *Make Prayers to the Raven*. Chicago: University of Chicago Press, 1983.

Nichols, John. *On the Mesa*. Salt Lake City: Peregrine Smith, 1986.

Novak, Barbara. *Nature and Culture: American Landscape Painting, 1825–1875*. New York: Oxford University Press, 1980.

Oelschlager, Max. *The Idea of Wilderness: From Prehistory to the Age of Ecology*. New Haven: Yale University Press, 1991.

Ogburn, Charlton. *The Winter Beach*. New York: Morrow, 1966.

Olson, Sigurd F. *Listening Point*. New York: Alfred A. Knopf, 1958.

———. *The Lonely Land*. New York: Alfred A. Knopf, 1961.

———. *Open Horizons*. New York: Alfred A. Knopf, 1969.

———. *Reflections from the North Country*. New York: Alfred A. Knopf, 1976.

———. *Runes of the North*. New York: Alfred A. Knopf, 1963.

———. *The Singing Wilderness*. New York: Alfred A. Knopf, 1956.

Peacock, Doug. *Grizzly Years*. New York: Holt, 1990.

Peattie, Donald Culross. *An Almanac for Moderns*. New York: Putnam's, 1935.

———. *A Prairie Grove*. New York: Simon & Schuster, 1938

———. *Singing in the Wilderness*. New York: Putnam's. 1935.

Peck, H. Daniel. *Thoreau's Morning Work: Memory and Perception in A Week on the Concord and Merrimack Rivers, the Journal, and Walden*. New Haven: Yale University Press, 1990.

Petite, Irving. *The Best Time of Year*. Garden City, N.Y.: Doubleday, 1966.

———. *The Elderberry Tree*. Garden City, N.Y.: Doubleday, 1964.

Porte, Joel. *Emerson and Thoreau: Transcendentalists in Conflict*. Middletown, Conn.: Wesleyan University Press, 1966.

Quammen, David. *Flight of the Iguana*. New York: Bantam, 1988.

———. *Natural Acts*. New York: Schocken, 1985.

Rand, Christopher. *The Changing Landscape*. New York: Oxford University Press, 1968.

Raymo, Chet. *The Soul of the Night*. Englewood Cliffs, N.J.: Prentice-Hall, 1985.

Reiger, George. *Wanderer on My Native Shore*. New York: Simon & Schuster, 1983.

Renehan, Edward J., Jr. *John Burroughs: An American Naturalist*. Post Mills, Vt.: Chelsea Green, 1992.

Richardson, Robert D., Jr. *Henry Thoreau: A Life of the Mind*. Berkeley: University of California Press, 1986.

Ronald, Ann. *The New West of Edward Abbey*. Albuquerque: University of New Mexico Press, 1982.

Ruess, Everett. *On Desert Trails*. El Centro, Calif.: Desert Magazine Press, 1940.

Russell, Franklin, *Secret Islands*. New York: W. W. Norton, 1966.

Samson, John G. *The Pond*. New York: Alfred A. Knopf, 1979.

Scheffer, Victor. *The Year of the Whale*. New York: Scribner's, 1969.

Schmitt, Peter J. *Back to Nature: The Arcadian Myth in Urban America*. New York: Oxford University Press, 1969.

Schneider, Richard J. "Thoreau and Nineteenth-Century American Landscape Painting." *ESQ* 31, no. 2 (1985):67–88.

Schultheis, Rob. *The Hidden West*. New York: Random House, 1982.

Scott, Walter S. *White of Selborne and His Times*. London: John Westhouse, 1946.

Skutch, Alexander. *A Naturalist on a Tropical Farm*. Berkeley: University of California Press, 1980.

Slovic, Scott. *Seeking Awareness in American Nature Writing*. Salt Lake City: University of Utah Press, 1992.

Smith, Dwight. *Above Timberline*. New York: Alfred A. Knopf, 1981.

Stegner, Wallace. *The Sound of Mountain Water*. Garden City, N.Y.: Doubleday, 1969.

———. *Wolf Willow*. Garden City, N.Y.: Doubleday, 1962; reprint, Lincoln: University of Nebraska Press, 1980.

Sterling, Philip. *Sea and Earth: The Life of Rachel Carson*. New York: Crowell, 1970.

Stineman, Esther Lanigan. *Mary Austin: Song of a Maverick*. New Haven: Yale University Press, 1989.

Tanner, Thomas, ed. *Aldo Leopold: The Man and His Legacy*. Ankeny, Iowa: Soil Conservation Society of America, 1987.

Teal, John, and Mildred Teal. *Life and Death of the Salt Marsh*. New York: Ballantine, 1969.

Teale, Edwin Way. *Autumn across America*. New York: Dodd, Mead, 1956.

———. *Circle of the Seasons*. New York: Dodd, Mead, 1953.

———. *Journey into Summer*. New York: Dodd, Mead, 1960.

———. *The Lost Woods*. New York: Dodd, Mead, 1945.

———. *North with the Spring*. New York: Dodd, Mead, 1951.

———. *Wandering through Winter*. New York: Dodd, Mead, 1965.

———. *The Wilderness World of John Muir*. Boston: Houghton Mifflin, 1954.

Templeman, William D. "The Life and Work of William Gilpin." *Studies in Language and Literature* 24 (1939):9–336.

———. "Thoreau, Moralist of the Picturesque." *PMLA* 47 (1932): 864–89.

Thomas, Lewis. *Lives of a Cell*. New York: Viking, 1974.

———. *The Medusa and the Snail*. New York: Viking, 1979.

Thoreau, Henry David. *The Correspondence of Henry David Thoreau*. Edited by Walter Harding and Carl Bode. New York: New York University Press, 1985.

———. *The Journal of Henry D. Thoreau*. Edited by Bradford Torrey and Francis H. Allen. 14 vols. Boston: Houghton Mifflin, 1906; reprint, Salt Lake City: Peregrine Smith, 1984.

———. *Walden*. Edited by J. Lyndon Shanley. Princeton: Princeton University Press, 1971.

———. *The Writings of Henry David Thoreau*. 6 vols. Princeton: Princeton University Press, 1971–.

Torrey, Bradford. *Birds in the Bush*. Boston: Houghton Mifflin, 1895

———. *A Rambler's Lease*. Boston: Houghton Mifflin, 1899.

Turner, Frederick. *Rediscovering America: John Muir in His Time and Ours*. San Francisco: Sierra Club Books, 1985.

Van Dyke, John C. *The Desert*. New York: Scribner's, 1903; reprint, Salt Lake City: Peregrine Smith, 1980.

Wagenknecht, Edward. *Henry David Thoreau: What Manner of Man?* Amherst: University of Massachusetts Press, 1981.

Wallace, David Rains. *Dark Range*. San Francisco: Sierra Club Books, 1978

———. *Idle Weeds*. San Francisco: Sierra Club Books, 1980.

———. *The Klamath Knot*. San Francisco: Sierra Club Books, 1983.

White, Gilbert. *Gilbert White's Journals*. Edited by Walter Johnson. London: Routledge and Sons, 1931.

———. *The Natural History of Selborne*. Edited by Richard Mabey. New York: Penguin, 1987.

Williams, Terry Tempest. *Coyote's Canyon*. Salt Lake City: Peregrine Smith, 1989.

———. *Pieces of White Shell*. New York: Scribner's, 1984.

Wilson, E. O. *Biophilia*. Cambridge, Mass.: Harvard University Press, 1984.

———. *The Diversity of Life*. Cambridge, Mass.: Harvard University Press, 1992.

———. *On Human Nature*. Cambridge, Mass.: Harvard University Press, 1978.

———. *Sociobiology: The New Synthesis*. Cambridge, Mass.: Harvard University Press, 1975.

Wolfe, Linnie Marsh. *Son of the Wilderness: The Life of John Muir.* New York: Alfred A. Knopf, 1945.

————, ed. *John of the Mountains: The Unpublished Journals of John Muir.* Boston: Houghton Mifflin, 1938.

Woodin, Ann. *Home Is the Desert.* Tucson: University of Arizona Press, 1984.

Worster, Donald. *Nature's Economy: A History of Ecological Ideas.* Cambridge: Cambridge University Press, 1985.

————. *The Wealth of Nature: Environmental History and the Ecological Imagination.* New York: Oxford University Press, 1993.

Wright, Mabel Osgood. *Citizen Bird.* New York: Macmillan, 1897.

————. *The Friendship of Nature.* 1895; reprint, New York: Macmillan, 1906.

Zwinger, Ann. *Beyond the Aspen Grove.* New York: Random House, 1970.

————. *A Desert Country near the Sea.* New York: Harper & Row, 1983.

————. *Run, River, Run.* New York: Harper & Row, 1975..

————. *Wind in the Rock.* New York: Harper & Row, 1978.

INDEX